BLACK CONGRESSIONAL
RECONSTRUCTION ORATORS
AND THEIR ORATIONS
1869-1879

by
Annjennette Sophie McFarlin

The Scarecrow Press, Inc.
Metuchen, N.J.   1976

Library of Congress Cataloging in Publication Data
Main entry under title:

Black congressional Reconstruction orators and their ora-
    tions, 1869-1879.

    Includes bibliographies.
    1.   Negroes--Civil rights--Addresses, essays, lectures.
2.   Negroes--History--1863-1877--Sources.   3.   Negroes--
Biography.   4.   United States.   Congress--Biography.
I.   McFarlin, Annjennette Sophie, 1935-
E185. 2. B52   320. 9'73'082   75-45194
ISBN 0-8108-0902-8

Dedicated to

Thecimar, Cynthia, Annjennette, Jr.
Clifford, Christopher & Michael.
The contents of this book will help
you understand your past.

PREFACE

This volume is a survey of Black Reconstruction Congressional politicians and their orations. It is limited to those sixteen Congressmen who served in the 41st through the 45th Congresses, covering a time period from 1869 to 1879.

I am well aware that historically Reconstruction continued up to 1901. But I have limited this study to that period which was considered, by some historians, to be the period of Radical Reconstruction or, as one historian characterized it, "The Tragic Era."

From the 41st Congress, 1869, to the 45th Congress, 1879, there were sixteen Black Congressmen who were elected and allowed to take their seats. Two others, Menard and Pinchback, both of Louisiana, were elected but were denied their seats. Pinchback is not included in this volume because he never was admitted to the House. Although Menard was ejected from his seat, he was allowed to make a speech in the House; in fact, he made the first speech ever given in the House by a Black man. Menard's speech, therefore, is included in this book.

In researching other anthologies on Black speakers I did not find an anthology which specifically contained the texts of speeches of Black Reconstruction Congressmen. Alice Dunbar, in Masterpieces of Negro Eloquence, included orations given by two Black Reconstruction politicians, John R. Lynch on Civil Rights and Social Equality, and Robert Brown Elliot on the Civil Rights Bill. Carter G. Woodson, in Negro Orators and their Orations, included representative speeches given by ten of the 16 Black Reconstruction Congressmen, but because of the length of the entire texts many of the congressional speeches in the Woodson text have been edited. [1]

There is a definite need for this kind of an anthology. It is warranted if for no other reason than to establish that the Black Congressmen, during Reconstruction, did positively contribute to and were directly involved in the political structure of the United States during the "Tragic Era."

Secondly, Black Reconstruction Congressmen did propose and support meaningful bills for passage through the House, even though they may have been defeated. Many of the bills the Black Congressmen introduced were deemed unworthy; others died a natural death on the road from one house to the other to the President's desk. Taylor (1922) stated that there were "two preeminent causes for the failure of some of these bills. The Negro membership in any Congress, in the first place, was always an exceedingly small minority, was never a determining factor in the passage of a measure proposed by one of this particular group. Secondly, the objects of the suspicion of their party colleagues, and regarded by them as an experiment in the legislative program of the nation, these men were not generally able to secure for their measures sufficient white Republican votes. Considered from this point of view, the failure of those measures is in no wise an evidence of the lack of ability and statesmanship." (23:171)*

My thanks to Gloria Melton and Howard Jones for their valuable assistance in a field in which I have the interest but lack their expertise. To my mentor, Dr. David Strother, Speech professor, whose general negativism kept me going. Lastly, not the least, to my family, especially, my mother and father; without their sacrifices I would not have been able to take up such a needed chore.

NOTE

1. For a complete list and the titles of these speeches, see the section titled, "Deliberative Oratory, Speeches of Negro Congressmen," 262-410.

---

*These references in parentheses throughout refer to numbered items in the Bibliography, with page references following the colon.

CONTENTS

INTRODUCTION

Historians paint the pictures of the past and, in effect, help to establish the beliefs, values and attitudes of future generations. Some historical writings have been so negatively skewed that it takes years to undo their effect on attitudes and beliefs. In some instances, even after centuries, the sting of this negative type of historical reporting has not yet been eliminated.

A very poignant example is that period called "Radical Reconstruction"--1865 to 1877. Many noted historians re-created this particular era either from their own regional biases or according to their political affiliations. This kind of history was usually very negative and in many instances stretched or distorted the truth.

The Radical Reconstruction period was called by many names, at the caprice of the historian. Most of these titles were negatively oriented, "The Tragic Era," "The Dreadful Decade," "The Age of Hate," and "The Black-out of Honest Government." To many historians, Reconstruction represented the "ultimate shame of the American People.... It was that period that most Americans wanted to forget."

In their haste to forget this period historians, through their negative recording of history, aided and abetted in the historical destruction of millions of Blacks. This was a-chieved through the negative picture historians painted of Blacks throughout this period. Blacks, according to the historians, were the reason for the failure of Reconstruction.

Opposite: The first Black Senator and Representatives in the 41st and 42nd Congress of the United States. Standing: Robert C. DeLarge (S. Carolina) and Jefferson H. Long (Georgia). Seated, l. to r., Senator H. R. Revels (Mississippi); Benjamin S. Turner (Alabama); Josiah T. Walls (Florida); Joseph H. Rainey (S. Carolina); R. Brown Elliot (S. Carolina).

1

Blacks made Reconstruction fail because of their innate inferiority.

If Reconstruction, as painted by historians, was a
twelve-year period of national disgrace for white Americans,
for Black Americans it was and continues to be an eternal
disgrace. "... the legend of reconstruction ... has had
serious consequences, because it has exerted a powerful influence upon the political behaviors of many white men, north
and south. " (22:23)

John R. Lynch, a Black Reconstruction Congressmen
from Mississippi (1873-1883), after reading John Ford
Rhodes's History of the United States from 1850-1877, stated,
"I regret to say that, so far as the Reconstruction period is
concerned, it is not only inaccurrate [sic] and unreliable but
it is the most biased, partisan and prejudiced historial work
I have ever read. " (13:345)

Lynch continues with an indictment of Rhodes's re-
search techniques. "But the reader of Rhodes's history will
look in vain for anything that will give him accurrate [sic]
information along these lines. His history, therefore, is remarkable, not only for what it says, but for what it leaves
unsaid. In fact, it is plain to the intelligent reader that he
started out with preconceived notions as to what the facts
were or should have been, and that he took particular pains
to select such data and so to color the same as to make
them harmonize his opinions. He thus passed over in silence
all facts which could not be so distorted as to make them thus
harmonize. " (13:357)

Lynch's indictment of a particular history text is applicable to many history texts written prior to the 1930s,
when revisionist historians started to take a fresh look at
Reconstruction. Stampp stated that the view of "Reconstruction History as held [by Rhodes] was rarely challenged until
the 1930s when a small group of revisionist historians began
to give life and a new direction to the study of reconstruction. " (22:8)

In taking a critical look at the Rhodes text it becomes
obvious that he ascribes the failure of Reconstruction to the
presence of Black Americans in the political arena, either
through vote or direct representation. Rhodes stated that "No
large policy in our country has ever been so conspicuous a
failure as that of forcing universal negro suffrage upon the
South. " (20:168)

In speaking of "universal Negro" suffrage Rhodes
stated that "Negroes were innately inferior to whites. [Ne-
groes were] one of the most inferior races of mankind ...
[that they] had through agency of their superiors been trans-
formed from slavery to freedom." (18:556) Rhodes felt that
the children of the freed slaves might "show an intellectual
development equal to white children up to the age of thirteen
or fourteen; but then there comes a diminution, often a cessa-
tion, of their mental development. The physical overslaughs
the psychical and they turn away from the pursuit of culture."
(18:556)

To support his belief in Black inferiority, Rhodes in-
dicts Sumner for not asking scientists about the innate inferiority of Blacks before advocating to the Senate the immediate
enfranchisement of this

> Ignorant mass of an alien race.... We should be-
> ware how we give to the blacks rights, by virtue
> of which they may endanger the progress of the
> whites before temper has been tested by a prolonged
> experience. Social equality I deem at all times im-
> practicable,--a natural impossibility, from the very
> character of the negro race.... negroes are ...
> indolent, playful, sensual, imitative, subservient,
> good-natured, versatile, unsteady in their purpose,
> devoted and affectionate.... I am not prepared to
> state what political privileges they are fit to enjoy
> now; though I have no hesitation in saying that they
> should be equal to other men before the law. The
> right of owning property, of bearing witness, of
> entering into contracts, of buying and selling, of
> choosing their own domicile, would give them ample
> opportunity of showing in a comparatively short
> time what political rights might properly and safely
> be granted to them in successive installments. No
> man has a right to what he is unfit to use....
> [this information was available] before we ventured
> on the policy of trying to make negroes intelligent
> by legislative acts. (19:37-38)

In referring to the Black American political astuteness,
which he said was "thrust" upon them by the Republicans,
Rhodes said that the Republicans had performed a great dis-
service to the Blacks. "From the Republican policy came no
real good to the negroes. Most of them developed no political
capacity, and the few who raised themselves above the mass

did not reach a high order of intelligence. At different periods two served in the United States Senate, thirteen in the
House; they left no mark on the legislation of their time;
none of them, in comparison with their white associates, at-
tained the least distinction. In a word he [the Black] has
been politically a failure and he could not have been otherwise. In spite of all the warnings of science and political
experience, he has started at the top, as is the fate of most
such unfortunates he fell to the bottom. " (20:169-170)

Lynch responds to Rhodes's statement about the political capabilities of Black Reconstruction politicians: "He
[Rhodes] could find nothing that was creditable or meritorious in the career of any colored member of either house of
Congress, notwithstanding the favorable impression made and
the important and dignified service rendered by Revels and
Bruce in the Senate and by Rainey, Rapier, Elliot, Smalls,
Cain, Langston, Miller, O'Hara, Cheathem, White and others
in the House. " (13:358)

In addition to Rhodes, three other Reconstruction historians have had a lasting affect on attitudes about Reconstruction. D. W. Dixon's book The Clansman, was made into the
nation's first major motion picture. The film was "Birth of
a Nation. " In it Black politicians were portrayed as thieves,
cheats and chicken-loving demogogues who couldn't tell a
piece of legislation or a ballot from a label off a bottle of
rat poison.

The showing of "Birth of a Nation" had such a damning
effect on Black Americans that in 1955, when a Hollywood
producer wanted to make the film available for public showing to other than academic institutions, ethnic civil rights
groups promptly banded together and got a court injunction
against the firm which wished to sell the film.

The other two Reconstruction historians who have left
their mark are Claude Bowers in his book, The Tragic Era,
possibly the greatest perpetrator of all Reconstruction negativism, and William Dunning, author of The Political and
Economic History of the United States.

Bowers pictures the Reconstruction period as a "trav-
esty on honest and on good government. " Dunning's book is
called by some historians "the definitive statement of the most
influential of the early historians of the period. "

While Dunning was still writing and researching his
book, Rhodes's book came off the press.   In the preface to
his book Dunning noted that "the appearance of Dr. John Ford
Rhodes's last two volumes, covering the years 1866-1877, in
time to be used in the final revisions of my manuscript, is
a mercy the greatness of which cannot in a preface be ade-
quately expressed" (6:xvi).   This note of thanks makes it
evident that Dunning's book was influenced by Rhodes.

Dunning stated that "... blacks whose ignorance and
inexperience in respect to political methods were equalled
only by the crudeness and distortion of their ideas as to political and social ends" (6:112).   He continues, "The negro
had no pride of race and no aspiration or ideals save to be
like whites.   With civil rights and political power, not won,
but almost forced upon him, he came gradually to understand
and crave those more elusive privileges that constitute social
equality.   A more intimate association with the other race
than that which business and politics involved was the end
towards which the ambition of the blacks tended consciously
or unconsciously to direct itself." (6:213)

Dunning's basic belief was that the coexistence in one
society of two races so distinctly different was impossible;
they could not both function within the same environment.

Dunning's influence was much broader than the reader-
ship of his book.   He was a history professor at Columbia
University, and he established what later became the Dunning
School of History.   Most of the States' Reconstruction his-
tories were written by Dunning scholars.   "Most of the studies
of reconstruction," Stampp stated, "were written by scholars
influenced by Dunning.   Most of them have not yet been super-
seded." (22:224)

Stampp summarizes the emphasis of most of the historical writings on Reconstruction: "... from Rhodes ... and
Dunning ... the central emphasis of most historical writings
about reconstruction has been upon sordid motives and human
depravity" (22:6).   Lynd feels that his concept of Reconstruction was largely accepted by historians: "well into the New
Deal, the historian's view of Reconstruction largely accepted
the long-standing Southern contention that the Negro himself
was the essential reason that Reconstruction failed." (14:3)

The basic expressions of opinion by Reconstruction

historians about the qualities and characteristic of Blacks
can be summarized in seven categories: "The contented
slave, the wretched Freedman, the Comic Negro, the Brute
Negro, the Tragic Mulatto, the Local Color Negro, and the
Exotic Primitive" (22:225). Stampp states that a "good general study of the roles of the Negro in reconstruction remains
to be written. " (22: 225)

In this anthology, I hope to contribute toward correct-
ing some of the errors that have been recorded by historians
concerning the role of the Black Reconstruction politician at
the federal level. This anthology contains a collection of all
speeches made by Black Reconstruction Congressmen and
Senators. The primary purpose is to reveal the types of
legislation in which they were involved, and the kind of bills
and petitions that they brought before their respective houses
--Senate or House. Secondly, the collection shows the kind
and the magnitude of the issues in which Black Congressional
Reconstruction politicians were involved.

Among the issues that were before the public were
questions of reconstruction, economic, social and political;
the plea for sound money; the economic regeneration of the
south; and the proper adjustment of the social relations between the two races living in the former Confederate States.
These were the great issues upon which the first Black Reconstruction politician entered Congress, and they continued
throughout the twelve-year period of what were called the
Radical Reconstruction Congresses.

In addition to these general problems that plagued all
Reconstruction politicians, the Black politicians had three
other problems for which they had to seek solutions: first,
to secure for themselves civil rights; second, to obtain national funds to aid education; and third, to determine whether
their former masters should be relieved of their political
disabilities.

The bills of the Black Congressmen did not meet with
success, but the reasons for failure were beyond their control. "Most of the measures, regardless of merit, met in
general one of three fates; they were either side-tracked in
committee, reported adversely, or defeated after debate in
open session. " (23:168)

II. BLANCHE KELSO BRUCE

Bruce, Blanche Kelso, a Senator from Mississippi; born near Farmville, Prince Edward county, Va., March 1, 1841; was of the Negro race and raised as a slave; was tutored by his Master's son; left his master at the beginning of the Civil War; taught school for a time in Hannibal, Mo., and later in Mississippi; member of the Mississsippi Levee Board; sheriff and tax collector of Bolivar County, 1872-1875; elected as a Republican to the United States Senate and served from March 4, 1875 to March 3, 1881; delegate to several Republican National Conventions; appointed Register of the Treasury by President Garfield, May 19, 1881; recorder of deeds for the District of Columbia, 1891-1893; again Register of the Treasury from 1897 until his death in Washington, D. C. on March 17, 1898 (1:655).

Senator Blanche K. Bruce, who had been a tax collector in Natchez, a sheriff and a superintendent of schools before being elected to the Senate at the age of thirty-three.

ADMISSION OF P. B. S. PINCHBACK AS SENATOR

... Mr. Pinchback is the representative of a majority of the legal voters of Louisiana, and entitled to a seat in the senate ... holding this question in abeyance, is, in my judgment, an unconstitutional deprivation of the right of a State, and a provocation to popular disquiet; and, in the interest of good-will and good government, the most judicious and consistent course is to admit to the claimant to his seat. (2:1444)

Mr. BRUCE. Mr. President, I desire briefly to lay before the Senate my views upon the question under consideration.

When I entered upon my duties here as a Senator from Mississippi, the question had ceased to be novel, and had already been elaborately and exhaustively discussed. So far as opportunity has permitted me to do so, I have dispassionately examined the question in the light of this discussion, and I venture my views now with the diffidence inspired by my limited experience in the consideration of such questions and by a just appreciation of the learning and ability of the gentlemen who have already attempted to elucidate and determine this case.

I believe, Mr. President, whatever seeming informalities may attach to the manner in which the will of the people was ascertained, that Mr. Pinchback is the representative of a majority of the legal voters of Louisiana, and entitled to a seat in the Senate. In the election of 1872, the white population of the State exceeded, by the census of 1872, the colored population by about two thousand, including in the white estimate 63,000 foreigners, only half of whom were naturalized. This estimate, at the same ratio in each race, would give a large majority of colored voters. The census and registration up to 1872 substantially agree, and both sustain this conclusion. The census of 1875, taken in pursuance of an article of the State constitution, gives, after including the foreign population (naturalized and unnaturalized) in the white aggregate, a majority of 45, 695 colored population.

This view of the question is submitted, not as determining the contest, but as an offset to the allegation that Mr. Pinchback does not fairly represent the popular will of the State, and as a presumption in favor of the legal title of the assembly that elected him.

The State government elected in 1872, and permanently inaugurated in January, 1873, in the face of contest and opposition, obtained for its authority the recognition of the inferior and supreme courts of the State. When organized violence threatened its existence and the United States Government was appealed to for troops to sustain it, the national Executive, in pursuance of his constitutional authority and duty, responded to the demand made for help, prefacing said action by an authoritative declaration, made through the Attorney-General, addressed to Lieutenant-Governor Pinchback, then acting governor, of date of December 12, 1872, that said Pinchback was "recognized as the lawful executive of Louisiana, and the body assembled at Mechanics' Institute as the lawful Legislature of the State"; and similar recognition of his successor was subsequently given. When, in September, 1874, an attempt was made to overthrow this government, the President again interposed with the Army and Navy for its protection and the maintenance of its authority.

This government has proceeded to enact and enforce laws for more than three years which not only affect life, liberty, and property, but which have received the general obedience of the citizens of the State. The present government also has frequently been brought in official contact with the United States Congress--through its Legislatures of 1873 and 1875, by memorials and joint resolutions addressed to the respective Houses; and through its executive, by credentials, borne by Congressmen and by Senators--and in no case has the legitimate authority of the Legislature been excepted to save in its action of electing a United States Senator; and in no instance has the sufficiency of the executive's credentials been questioned, in either House, except in the matter of the senatorial claimant.

Now, sir, shall we admit by our action on this case that for three years the State of Louisiana has not had a lawful Legislature; that its laws have been made by an unauthorized mob; that the President of the United States, actively,

and Congress, by non-action at least, have sustained and perpetuated this abnormal, illegal, wrongful condition of things,
thereby justifying and provoking the indignant and violent pro-
tests of one portion of the people of that State, and inviting
them to renewed and continued agitation and violence? Such
action by us would be unjust to the claimant, a great wrong
to the people who sent him here, and cruel even to that class
who have awaited an opportunity to bring to their support the
overwhelming moral power of the nation in the pursuit of
their illusion--which has so nearly ruined the future of that
fair State--a government based upon the prejudices of caste.

I respectfully ask the attention of Senators to another
view of this subject, which is not without weight in determining the obligations of this body to the State of Louisiana and
in ascertaining the title of the claimant. If the assumption
that the present government, inaugurated in 1873, is without
legal authority and a usurpation is true, the remedy for this
state of things was to be found in the exercise by Congress
through the joint action of the two Houses of the powers conferred under the guaranteeing clause of the Constitution relative to republican forms of government in the several States.

Failing to exercise her power and perform her duty
in this direction, and thus practically perpetuating the present
government, I submit that, in my judgment, we cannot now
ignore our obligation to give the State her full representation
on the score of the alleged irregularity of the government
through which she has expressed her will; and there does
seem to me, in this connection, something incongruous in the
proposition that we may impose upon the people a government without legal sanction and demand their obedience to
and support thereof, said government meanwhile determining
the character of its successors and thus perpetuating its taint,
and yet are powerless to admit a Senator elected thereby.

In my judgment, this question should at this juncture
be considered and decided not on abstract but practical
grounds. Whatever wrongs may have been done or mistakes
made in Louisiana by either party, the present order of
things is accepted by the people of the State and by the nation, and will be maintained as a final settlement of the political issues that have divided the people there; and no
changes in the administration of public affairs can or will be
made, except by the people, through the ballot, under the
existing government and laws of the Commonwealth.

Under these circumstances, holding this question in abeyance, is, in my judgment, an unconstitutional deprivation of the right of a State, and a provocation to popular disquiet; and, in the interest of good-will and good government, the most judicious and consistent course is to admit the claimant to his seat.

I desire, Mr. President, to make a personal reference to the claimant. I would not attempt one nor deem one proper were it not that his personal character has been assailed.

As a father, I know him to be affectionate and worthy; as a husband, the idol of a pleasant home and cheerful fireside; as a citizen, loyal, brave, and true. And in his character and success we behold an admirable illustration of the excellence of our republican institutions.

VOTING PRACTICES IN THE STATE OF MISSISSIPPI

The conduct of the late election in Mississippi affected not merely the fortunes or partisans--as the same were necessarily involved in the defeat or success of the respective parties to the contest; but put in question and jeopardy the sacred rights of the citizens; and the investigation contemplated in the pending resolution has for its object not the determination of the question whether the offices shall be held and the public affairs of that State be administered by democrats or republicans but the higher and more important end, the protection in all their purity and significance of the political rights of the people and the free institutions of the country. (3:2101)

Mr. BRUCE. Mr. President, I had hoped that no occasion would arise to make it necessary for me again to claim the attention of the Senate until at least I had acquired a larger acquaintance with its methods of business and a fuller experience in public affairs; but silence at this time would be infidelity to my senatorial trust and unjust to both the people and the State I have the honor in part to represent.

The conduct of the late election in Mississippi affected not merely the fortunes of partisans--as the same were necessarily involved in the defeat or success of the respective parties to the contest--but put in question and jeopardy the sacred rights of the citizen; and the investigation contemplated in the pending resolution has for its object not the determination of the question whether the offices shall be held and the public affairs of the State be administered by the democrats or republicans, but the higher and more important end, the protection in all their purity and significance of the political rights of the people and the free institutions of the country. I believe the action sought is within the legitimate province of the Senate; but I shall waive a discussion of that phase of the question, and address myself to the consideration of the importance of the proposed investigation.

The demand of the substitute of the Senator from
Michigan proceeds upon the allegation that fraud and intimidation were practiced by the opposition in the late State
election, so as not only to deprive many citizens of their
political rights, but so far as practically to have defeated a
fair expression of the will of a majority of the legal voters
of the State of Mississippi, resulting in placing in power
many men who do not represent the popular will.

The truth of the allegations relative to fraud and violence is strongly suggested by the very success claimed by
the democracy. In 1873 the republicans carried the State by
20, 000 majority; in November last the opposition claimed to
have carried it by 30, 000; thus a democratic gain of more
than 50, 000. Now, by what miraculous or extraordinary interposition was this brought about? I can conceive that a
large State like New York, where free speech and free press
operate upon intelligent masses--a State full of railroads,
telegraphs, and newspapers--on the occasion of a great national contest, might furnish an illustration of such a thorough
and general change in the political views of the people; but
such a change of front is unnatural and highly improbable in
a State like my own, with few railroads, and a widely scattered and sparse population. Under the most active and
friendly canvass the voting masses could not have been so
rapidly and thoroughly reached as to have rendered this result probable.

There was nothing in the character of the issues nor
in the method of the canvass that would produce such an
overwhelming revolution in the sentiments of the colored
voters of the State as is implied in this pretended democratic success. The republicans--nineteen-twentieths of
whom are colored--were not brought, through the press or
public discussions, in contact with democratic influences to
such an extent as would operate a change in their political
convictions, and there was nothing in democratic sentiments
nor in the proscriptive and violent temper of their leaders to
justify such a change of political relations.

The evil practices so naturally suggested by this view
of the question as probable will be found in many instances
by the proposed investigation to have been actual. Not desiring to anticipate the work of the committee nor to weary
Senators with details, I instance the single county of Yazoo
as illustrative of the effects of the outrages of which we
complain. This county gave in 1873 a republican majority

of nearly two thousand.   It was cursed with riot and bloodshed prior to the late election, and gave but seven votes for
the republican ticket, and some of these, I am credibly informed, were cast in derision by the democrats, who declared that republicans must have some votes in the county.

To illustrate the spirit that prevailed in that section,
I read from the Yazoo Democrat, an influential paper published at its county seat:

> Let unanimity of sentiment pervade the minds of
> men.   Let invincible determination be depicted on
> every countenance.   Send forth from our delibera-
> tive assembly of the eighteenth the soul-stirring
> announcement that Mississippians shall rule Missis-
> sippi though the heavens fall.   Then will woe, ir-
> retrievable woe, betide the radical tatterdemalions.
> Hit them hip and thigh, everywhere and at all
> times.
> Carry the election peaceably if we can, forcibly if
> we must.

Again:

> There is no radical ticket in the field, and it is
> more than likely there will be some; for the lead-
> ers are not in this city, and dare not press their
> claims in this county.

Speaking of the troubles in Madison County, the Yazoo
Democrat for the 26th of October says:

> Try the rope on such characters.   It acts finely on
> such characters here.

The evidence in hand and accessible will show beyond
peradventure that in many parts of the State corrupt and violent influences were brought to bear upon the registrars of
voters, thus materially affecting the character of the voting
or poll lists; upon the inspectors of election, prejudicially
and unfairly thereby changing the number of votes cast; and,
finally, threats and violence were practiced directly upon the
masses of voters in such measure and strength as to produce
grave apprehensions for their personal safety, and as to de-
ter them from the exercise of their political franchises.

Lawless outbreaks have not been confined to any particular section of the country, but have prevailed in nearly every State at some period in its history. But the violence complained of and exhibited in Mississippi and other Southern States, pending a political canvass, is exceptional and peculiar. It is not the blow that the beggared miner strikes that he may give bread to his children, nor the stroke of the bondsman that he may win liberty for himself, nor the mad turbulence of the ignorant masses when their passions have been stirred by the appeals of the demagogue; but, it is an attack by an aggressive, intelligent, white political organization upon inoffensive, law-abiding fellow-citizens; a violent method for political supremacy, that seeks not the protection of the rights of the aggressors, but the destruction of the rights of the party assailed. Violence so unprovoked, inspired by such motives, and looking to such ends, is a spectacle not only discreditable to the country, but dangerous to the integrity of our free institutions.

I beg Senators to believe that I refer to this painful and reproachful condition of affairs in my own State not in resentment, but with sentiments of profound regret and humiliation.

If honorable Senators ask why such flagrant wrongs were allowed to go unpunished by a republican State government, and unresented by a race claiming 20,000 majority of the voters, the answer is at hand. The civil officers of the State were unequal to meet and suppress the murderous violence that frequently broke out in different parts of the State, and the State executive found himself thrown for support upon a militia partially organized and poorly armed. When he attempted to perfect and call out this force and to use the very small appropriation that had been made for their equipment, he was met by the courts with an injunction against the use of the money, and by the proscriptive element of the opposition with such fierce outcry and show of counter-force, that he became convinced a civil strife, a war of races, would be precipitated unless he staid his hand. As a last resort, the protection provided in the national Constitution for a State threatened with domestic violence was sought; but the national Executive--from perhaps a scrupulous desire to avoid the appearance of interference by the Federal authority with the internal affairs of that State-- declined to accede to the request made for Federal troops.

It will not accord with the laws of nature or history to brand the colored people as a race of cowards. On more

than one historic field, beginning in 1776 and coming down to
this centennial year of the Republic, they have attested in
blood their courage as well as love of liberty. I ask Senators to believe that no consideration of fear or personal
danger has kept us quiet and forbearing under the provoca-
tions and wrongs that have so sorely tried our souls. But
feeling kindly toward our white fellow-citizens, appreciating
the good purposes and offices of the better classes, and,
above all, abhorring a war of races, we determined to wait
until such time as an appeal to the good sense and justice of
the American people could be made.

A notable feature of the outrages alleged is that they
have referred almost exclusively to the colored citizens of
the State. Why is the colored voter to be proscribed? Why
direct the attack upon him? While the methods of violence,
resorted to for political purposes in the South, are foreign
to the genius of our institutions as applied to citizens gen-
erally--and so much is conceded by even the opposition--yet
they seem to think we are an exceptional class and citizens,
rather by sufferance than right; and when pressed to account
for their bitterness and proscription toward us they, with
more or less boldness, allege incompetent and bad government as their justification before the public opinion of the
country. Now, I declare that neither political incapacity
nor venality are qualities of the masses of colored citizens.
The emancipation of the colored race during the late civil
strife was an expression alike of the magnanimity and needs
of the nation; and the subsequent and early subtraction of
millions of industrial values from the resources of the insurrectionary States and the presence of many thousand additional brave hearts and strong hands around the flag of the
country vindicated the justice and wisdom of the measure.

The close of the war found four millions of freedmen,
without homes or property, charged with the duty of self-
support and with the oversight of their personal freedom,
yet without civil and political rights! The problem presented
by this condition of things was one of the gravest that has
ever been submitted to the American people. Shall these
liberated millions of a separate race, while retaining personal liberty, be derprived of political rights? The practical sense of the American people definitely settled this
delicate and difficult question, and the demand for a more
pronounced loyal element in the work of reconstruction in the
lately rebellious States furnished an opportunity for the recognition of the political rights of the race, both in the in-

The history of my race since enfranchisement, considered in connection with the difficulties that have environed us, will exhibit hopeful progress and attest that we have been neither ungrateful for the civil and political privileges received nor wanting in appreciation of the correspondingly weighty obligations imposed upon us.

As evidence, not only of our aptitude for improvement but of our actual progress since 1865, I submit a partial but nevertheless illustrative statistical statement gathered from the census of 1860 and 1870 and from data obtained by the State authorities in the interval between these periods. The statistics cover the questions of marriage, churches, and industrial pursuits. I avail myself of exhibits and comments on these points found in the annual message of my colleague, an ex-slaveholder, to the Legislature of Mississippi, session of 1871:

Marriage Statistics

Class	Population in 1860	Marriage Licenses Issued					
		1865	1866	1867	1868	1869	1870
White	189, 645	2, 708	3, 129	2, 829	2, 546	2, 655	2, 204
Colored	239, 930	564	3, 679	3, 524	2, 802	3, 584	3, 427

The percentages of those white marriages to the total number of the whites, and of those colored marriages to the total number of colored, are as follows, namely:

Class	1865	1866	1867	1868	1869	1870
White	1. 43	1. 64	1. 49	1. 34	1. 40	1. 16
Colored	0. 23	1. 53	1. 47	1. 17	1. 49	1. 43

Governor Alcorn, in commenting on the marriage statistics that represent fully thirty-one counties of the State says:

A people trained under circumstances precluding the marriage contract stood exposed, when released from restraints of force, to the danger of

running into extreme sexual license.   Our constitution anticipated such a social evil, and therefore
dignified all who had been living together in the intercourse of the sexes under slavery by giving
them in law the status of husband and wife....
     These figures are full of encouragement to men
who doubted the practicability of educating the great
body of our labor to the moral level of freedom.
They will be read with surprise, when taken in
connection with the fact that up to the close of the
war the negro was incapable of making a contract
of marriage. They prove conclusively that the
colored people are striving to rise to the moral
level of their new standing before the law, to the
extent of a strict adherence to, at all events, the
formularies of sexual propriety.
     But the marriage contracts of the negroes are not
mere formularies. Taking the production of
children as an evidence of marital fidelity--which
it is held to be--the census of the six counties
selected as a basis of my inquiries bears the following evidence to the general good faith of the
colored people in contracts of marriage:

Population by Ages

Class	Total	Under 1 year	1 to 5 years	5 to 10 years	10 to 60 years	Over 60 years
White	33, 092	6. 02	10. 52	13. 13	66. 92	3. 38
Colored	43, 748	7. 31	11. 16	14. 57	62. 25	3. 70

     The table of population embraces six counties, and is
submitted to show the purity of the marriage relations among
the colored people.   The governor in commenting thereon
adds:

     The fact remains on the face of the national in-
ventory that the colored people show in the proportion of their infants a rate of production which
constitutes an incontestable proof that negro marriages are, as a rule, observed with encouraging
fidelity.

Number of Churches

Class	Population in 1860	Years					
		1865	1866	1867	1868	1869	1870
White	138, 991	510	505	528	531	548	563
Colored	179, 677	105	125	165	201	235	283

Number of Preachers Employed

Class	Population in 1860	Years					
		1865	1866	1867	1868	1869	1870
White	125, 629	328	339	343	349	373	354
Colored	163, 733	73	102	134	177	194	262

These tables embrace returns from twenty-two counties, and the governor commenting says:

> The religious progress among the negroes shown in this table, in corroboration of that shown in the table next preceding, is full of good omen for the perfection of the work you, gentlemen, have inaugurated for crowning the State of Mississippi with the peace and prosperity of a well-ordered society of free labor.

Number of Shoemaker's Shops

Class	Population in 1860	Years					
		1865	1866	1867	1868	1869	1870
White	105, 023	99	104	101	94	93	99
Colored	165, 169	21	28	24	49	54	63

Number of Smith's Shops

Class	Population in 1860	Years					
		1865	1866	1867	1868	1869	1870
White	105, 896	128	128	145	152	157	182
Colored	156, 556	40	63	74	83	98	113

The exhibit shows not only the enterprise of the colored man under great embarrassment, but his aptitude for skilled and diversified labor, and is so far favorable, not only to his diligence, but intelligent capacity.

Tenant-farming

Class	Bales Produced	
	1869	1870
White	27, 075	20, 893
Colored	40, 561	50, 978

The governor very appropriately selects this form of agricultural endeavor as illustrative of the thrift of the negro, and in connection therewith adds:

Tenant-farming has expanded among the whites since 1860 about 100 percent. In that year it was, of course, unknown among the negroes.

The improvidence of the negro is another subject of popular apprehension as to his future under freedom. The laws of 1865 had excluded him from putting that accusation to trial by having made him a pariah.

A military government is certainly not a very favorable school for the development of industry and thrift. And yet the inauguration of that rule was the first moment at which the negro had, in fact, had the opportunity of realizing wealth. Four years have passed since that time, and but one of four years has been blessed with civil government; and now, at the expiration of that brief period, what evidence do we find on which to found

an opinion as to the future identity of the negro
with the direct interests of property?
Negro property owners in the seven counties:

69 colored people own real estate to a gross value of $30, 680
3, 798 colored people own real estate to a gross value of   630, 860
178 colored people own real estate to a gross value of   229, 700

The governor adds:

> Among the forty-three thousand negroes of Wash-
> ington, Madison, Holmes, Rankin, Neshoba, Jones,
> and Lauderdale, who had been plucked pennyless
> four short years ago from the clutches of the un-
> wise legislation of 1865, three thousand four hun-
> dred and forty-one accumulated wealth--what the
> economists hold to represent the political virtue of
> 'denial'--to the enormous amount of $882, 240! And
> here again is undoubted proof that the industry and
> thrift of the negro are developing with extraordinary
> rapidity the production of a mass of property-own-
> ers who constitute an unimpeachable guarantee that
> reconstruction goes forward to the consolidation of
> a society in which the reward of labor goes hand
> in hand with the safety of property.

The data here adduced, though not exhaustive, is sufficiently full to indicate and illustrate the capacity and progress of this people in the directions specified, and the fuller
statistics, derived from subsequent and later investigations,
and exhibiting the operation of the more liberal and judicious
legislation and administration introduced since 1870, will
amply sustain the conclusion authorized by the facts I have
adduced.   I submit that the showing made, relative to the
social, moral, and industrial condition of the negro, is favorable, and proves that he is making commendable and hopeful
advances in the qualities and acquisitions desirable as a
citizen and member of society; and, in these directions,
attest there is nothing to provoke or justify the suspicion
and proscription with which he has been not infrequently met
by some of his more highly favored white fellow-citizens.

Again, we began our political career under the disadvantages of the inexperience in public affairs that generations
of enforced bondage had entailed upon our race.   We suffered
also from the vicious leadership of some of the men whom
our necessities forced us temporarily to accept.   Consider

further that the States of the South, where we are supposed
to control by our majorities, were in an impoverished and
semi-revolutionary condition--society demoralized, the industries of the country prostrated, the people sore, morbid,
and sometimes turbulent, and no healthy controlling public
opinion either existent or possible--consider all these conditions, and it will be seen that we began our political novitiate
and formed the organic and statutory laws under great embarrassments.

Despite the difficulties and drawbacks suggested, the
constitutions formed under colored majorities, whatever their
defects may be, were improvements on the instruments they
were designed to supersede; and the statutes framed, though
necessarily defective because of the crude and varying social
and industrial conditions upon which they were based, were
more in harmony with the spirit of the age and the genius of
our free institutions than the obsolete laws that they sup-
planted.   Nor is there just or any sufficient grounds upon
which to charge an oppressive administration of the laws.

The State debt proper is less than a half million dollars, and the State taxes are light.   Nor can complaint be
reasonably made of the judiciary.   The records of the supreme judicial tribunal of the State will show, in 1859-'60,
266 decisions in cases of appeal from the lower courts, of
which 169 were affirmed and 97 reversed.   In 1872-'73 the
records show 328 decisions rendered in cases of appeal
from below, of which 221 were affirmed and 107 reversed;
and in 1876, of appeals from chancellors, appointed by Governor Ames, up to date, 41 decisions have been rendered,
of which 33 were affirmed and 8 reversed.   This exhibit,
whether of legislation or administration, shows there has
been no adequate provocation to revolution and no justification
for violence in Mississippi.   That we should have made mistakes, under the circumstances, in measures of both legislation and administration, was natural, and that we have had
any success is both creditable and hopeful.

But if it can be shown that we have used the ballot
either to abridge the rights of our fellow-citizens or to oppress them; if it shall appear that we have ever used our
newly acquired power as a sword of attack and not as a
shield of defense, then we may with some show of propriety
be charged with incapacity, dishonesty, or tyranny.   But,
even then, I submit that the corrective is in the hands of
the people, and not of a favored class, and the remedy is in

the honest exercise of the ballot, and not in fraud and violence.

Mr. President, do not misunderstand me; I do not
hold that all the white people of the State of Mississippi
aided and abetted the white-league organizations. There is
in Mississippi a large and respectable element among the
opposition who are not only honest in their recognition of the
political rights of the colored citizen and deprecate the fraud
and violence through which those rights have been assailed,
but who would be glad to see the color line in politics aban-
doned and good-will obtain and govern among all classes of
her people. But the fact is to be regretted that this better
class of citizens in many parts of the State is dominated by
a turbulent and violent element of the opposition, known as
the White League--a ferocious minority--and has thus far
proved powerless to prevent the recurrence of the outrages
it deprecates and deplores.

The uses of this investigation are various. It will be
important in suggesting such action as may be found necessary not only to correct and repair the wrongs perpetrated,
but to prevent their recurrence. But I will venture to assert that the investigation will be most beneficial in this,
that it will largely contribute to the formation of a public
sentiment that, while it restrains the vicious in their attacks
upon the rights of the loyal, law-abiding voters of the South,
will so energize the laws as to secure condign punishment to
wrongdoers, and give a security to all classes, which will
effectively and abundantly produce the mutual good-will and
confidence that constitute the foundations of the public prosperity.

We want peace and good order at the South; but it can
only come by the fullest recognition of the rights of all
classes. The opposition must concede the necessity of
change, not only in the temper but in the philosophy of their
party organization and management. The sober American
judgment must obtain in the South as elsewhere in the Republic, that the only distinctions upon which parties can be
safely organized and in harmony with our institutions are
differences of opinions relative to principles and policy of
government, and that differences of religion, nationality, or
race can neither with safety nor propriety be permitted for
a moment to enter into the party contests of the day. The
unanimity with which the colored voters act with a party is
not referable to any race prejudice on their part. On the

contrary, they invite the political co-operation of their white
brethren, and vote as a unit because proscribed as such.
They deprecate the establishment of the color line by the opposition, not only because the act is unwise and wrong in
principle, but because it isolates them from the white men
of the South, and forces them, in sheer self-protection and
against their inclination, to act seemingly upon the basis of
a race prejudice that they neither respect nor entertain. As
a class they are free from prejudices, and have no uncharitable suspicions against their white fellow-citizens, whether
native born or settlers from the Northern States. They not
only recognize the equality of citizenship and the right of
every man to hold, without proscription, any position of
honor and trust to which the confidence of the people may
elevate him; but owing nothing to race, birth, or surroundings, they, above all other classes in the community, are
interested to see prejudices drop out of both politics and the
business of the country, and success in life proceed only
upon the integrity and merit of the man who seeks it. They
are also appreciative--feeling and exhibiting the liveliest
gratitude for counsel and help in their new career, whether
they come from the men of the North or of the South. But
withal, as they progress in intelligence and appreciation of
the dignity of their prerogatives as citizens, they, as an
evidence of growth, begin to realize the significance of the
proverb, "When thou doest well for thyself, men shall praise
thee"; and are disposed to exact the same protection and
concession of rights that are conferred upon other citizens
by the Constitution, and that, too, without the humiliation involved in the enforced abandonment of their political convictions.

We simply demand the practical recognition of the
rights given us in the Constitution and laws, and ask from
our white fellow-citizens only the consideration and fairness
that we so willingly extend to them. Let them generally
realize and concede that citizenship imports to us what it
does to them, no more and no less, and impress the colored
people that a party defeat does not imperil their political
franchise. Let them cease their attempts to coerce our political cooperation, and invite and secure it by a policy so
fair and just as to commend itself to our judgment, and resort to no motive or measure to control us that self-respect
would preclude their applying to themselves. When we can
entertain opinions and select party affiliations without proscription, and cast our ballots as other citizens and without
jeopardy to person or privilege, we can safely afford to be

governed by the considerations that ordinarily determine the political action of American citizens. But we must be guaranteed in the unproscribed exercise of our honest convictions and be absolutely, from within or without, protected in the use of our ballot before we can either wisely or safely divide our vote. In union, not division, is strength, so long as White League proscription renders division of our vote impracticable by making a difference of opinion opprobrious and an antagonism in politics a crime. On the other hand, if we should, from considerations of fear, yield to the shot-gun policy of our opponents, the White League might win a temporary success, but the ultimate result would be disastrous to both races, for they would first become aggressively turbulent, and we, as a class, would become servile, unreliable, and worthless.

It has been suggested, as the popular sentiment of the country, that the colored citizens must no longer expect special legislation for their benefit, nor exceptional interference by the National Government for their protection. If this is true, if such is the judgment relative to our demands and needs, I venture to offset the suggestion, so far as it may be used as reason for a denial of the protection we seek, by the statement of another and more prevalent popular conviction. Back of this, and underlying the foundations of the Republic itself, there lies deep in the breasts of the patriotic millions of the country the conviction that the laws must be enforced, and life, liberty, and property must, alike to all and for all, be protected. But I allege that we do not seek special action in our behalf, except to meet special danger, and only then such as all classes of citizens are entitled to receive under the Constitution. We do not ask the enactment of new laws, but only the enforcement of those that already exist.

The vicious and exceptional political action had by the White League in Mississippi has been repeated in other contests and in other States of the South, and the colored voters have been subjected therein to outrages upon their rights similar to those perpetrated in my own State at the recent election. Because violence has become so general a quality in the political canvasses of the South and my people the common sufferers in each instance, I have considered this subject more in detail than would, under other circumstances, have been either appropriate or necessary. As the proscription and violence toward the colored voters are special and almost exclusive, and seem to proceed upon the assump-

tion that there is something exceptionally offensive and unworthy in them, I have felt, as the only representative of my
race in the Senate of the United States, that I was placed, in
some sort, upon the defensive, and I have consequently endeavored to show how aggravated and inexcusable were the
wrongs worked upon us, and have sought to vindicate our title
to both the respect and good-will of the just people of the
nation.   The gravity of the issues involved has demanded
great plainness of speech from me.   But I have endeavored
to present my views to the Senate with the moderation and
deference inspired by the recollection that both my race and
myself were once bondsmen, and are to-day debtors largely
to the love and justice of a great people for the enjoyment of
our personal and political liberty.   While my antecedents and
surroundings suggest modesty, there are some considerations
that justify frankness, and even boldness of speech.

Mr. President, I represent, in an important sense,
the interest of nearly a million of voters, constituting a new,
hopeful, permanent, and influential political element, and
large enough to affect in critical periods the fortunes of this
great Republic; and the public safety and common weal alike
demand that the integrity of this element should be preserved
and its character improved.   They number more than a million of producers, who, since their emancipation and outside
of their contributions to the production of sugar, rice, tobacco, cereals, and the mechanical industries of the country,
have furnished nearly forty million bales of cotton, which, at
the ruling prices of the world's market, have yielded
$2, 000, 000, 000, a sum nearly equal to the national debt;
producers who, at the accepted ratio that an able-bodied
laborer earns, on an average $800 per year, annually bring
to the aggregate of the nation's great bulk of values more
than $800, 000, 000.

I have confidence, not only in my country and her institutions, but in the endurance, capacity, and destiny of my
people.   We will, as opportunity offers and ability serves,
seek our places, sometimes in the field of letters, arts,
sciences, and the professions.   More frequently mechanical
pursuits will attract and elicit our efforts; more still of my
people will find employment and livelihood as the cultivators
of the soil.   The bulk of this people--by surroundings,
habits, adaptation, and choice--will continue to find their
homes in the South, and constitute the masses of its yeo-
manry.   We will there probably, of our own volition and
more abundantly than in the past, produce the great staples

that will contribute to the basis of foreign exchange, aid in
giving the nation a balance of trade, and minister to the
wants and comfort and build up the prosperity of the whole
land. Whatever our ultimate position in the composite civilization of the Republic and whatever varying fortunes attend
our career, we will not forget our instincts for freedom nor
our love of country. Guided and guarded by a beneficent
Providence, and living under the genial influence of liberal
institutions, we have no apprehensions that we shall fail from
the land from attrition with other races, or ignobly disappear
from either the politics or industries of the country.

Mr. President, allow me here to say that, although
many of us are uneducated in the schools, we are informed
and advised as to our duties to the Government, our State,
and ourselves. Without class prejudice or animosities, with
obedience to authority as the lesson and love of peace and
order as the passion of our lives, with scrupulous respect
for the rights of others, and with the hopefulness of political
youth, we are determined that the great Government that gave
us liberty, and rendered its gift valuable by giving us the
ballot, shall not find us wanting in a sufficient response to
any demand that humanity or patriotism may make upon us;
and we ask such action as will not only protect us in the enjoyment of our constitutional rights, but will preserve the integrity of our republican institutions.

SEPARATE BLACK REGIMENTS IN THE ARMY

> We believe we are competent for military service
> and are entitled to enlist in any arm thereof, and
> I assert that we are willing to stand upon our own
> merits and rest our fortunes upon the same forces
> that give success to other citizens.   (4:2441)

Mr. BRUCE. Mr. President, I was necessarily ab-
sent from the Senate pending the discussion of this bill a few
days ago, and have only by a hurried reference to the
RECORD been able to ascertain the views of Senators touching it.   I heartily indorse the bill as reported by the Senator
from Rhode Island, with the amendment of the Senator from
Maine.   I think I comprehend the scope and effect of the
measure.   I do not see that the passage of this bill will confer any additional rights and privileges upon the colored citizen.   Under existing laws, exclusive of sections 1104 and
1108 of the Revised Statutes, they have a right to enlist in
any arm of the service, whether artillery, cavalry, infantry,
or engineers, subject to the same conditions that are applied
to other citizens, but sections 1104 and 1108, which the
pending bill proposes to repeal, are supplemental in their
character, making mandatory provisions for the creation of
four regiments that should be constituted exclusively of
colored soldiers.   These sections doubtless were enacted
after careful consideration and from just and honorable motives and with the belief not only that the efficiency of the
public service would be increased, but that protection of this
class of citizens from the dangers to which their rights were
supposed to be exposed from the prejudice of the recruiting
and distributing officers of the service would be secured.

It was evidently apprehended that these officers would
not be willing to enlist colored soldiers in the absence of
these positive provisions of law, but would rather use their
power to prevent such enlistment.

I am inclined to believe that this danger of unfriendly
discrimination existed and that for a year or two or more

these gentlemen will relax their efforts in some instances to secure colored enlistments.

But admit the grounds for this apprehension and suppose further that the passage of the bill reported by the Senator from Rhode Island should result temporarily in the elimination to some extent of the colored soldier from the Army, still I am in favor of the bill.

I believe that under the influence of a healthy public sentiment this discouraging prejudice against this class of our citizens will pass away, and that the day is not far distant when all men, without regard to complexion or previous condition, will be received into the Army as they are to-day admitted into the Navy. So far as I am informed, there are no such discriminating provisions of law existing relative to enlistments in the Navy; yet we find the naval crews are mixed, and that, too, without impairment of their efficiency.

There is an additional reason why I am in favor of repealing these sections. If they are stricken from the statutes I believe that a better class of colored men will apply for enlistment. Whatever the purposes of this legislation, we have looked upon them as creating an opprobrious distinction. I think I may say safely that there are hundreds of our people who are unwilling to enlist in the Army because these special provisions of law are supposed to limit their enlistment and distribution exclusively to these four regiments.

We are American citizens, and are beginning to appreciate the value and dignity of the rights of our citizenship. We believe we are competent for military service and are entitled to enlist in any arm thereof, and I assert that we are willing to stand upon our own merits and rest our fortunes upon the same forces that give success to other citizens.

Mr. President, I am anxious to see the color line drop out of the business and politics of this country. Its introduction thereto is contrary to the genius of our institutions, and when it is obliterated from the legislation of the country every interest of every class will be greatly subserved. The time has been when it was necessary for the protection of the rights of this class that a peculiar sort of legislation should be provided, but is it to be presumed that this necessity must last always? Is there no time in our history as citizens when we--

Mr. BRUCE. Mr. President, I do not know that I
have anything more to say at present, but I may, perhaps,
add that we do not ask special legislation now. We believe
that, clothed with all the powers and privileges of citizens,
we are able, if I may use the expression, "to paddle our
own canoe'; and, indeed, if we fail to do so successfully
under just and proper laws, I do not know but that it is
about time for us to sink. We do not ask particular favors.
We believe we have passed that period. We believe now
that we must rest our claim upon our manhood, and that our
integrity, industry, capacity, and all those virtues that go to
make up good men and citizens are to measure our success
before the American people. I repeat now, the sooner we
can get rid of class legislation the sooner the necessity
therefor will cease.

We are amenable to the same laws that you are, and
we are to be held amenable; and now let every man who
wants to go into the Army present himself to the recruiting
officer, and let him be accepted or refused, not because he
is white or black, but because he fills the requirements of
the branch of the military service into which he wants to enlist. Just so long, however, as it is deemed proper and
necessary to keep up these distinctions in the Army, just so
long will there be found a large class in this country ready
to assault the rights of these people. I hope we have passed
the critical period in our history in which race distinctions
even for protection are to be considered necessary, and that
we will in this and all other matters of public concern forget
the question of complexion or previous condition and go forward hand in hand as American citizens.

BIBLIOGRAPHY

1.   Biographical Directory of the American Congress, 1774-
     1971. Washington, D. C.: United States Government
     Printing Office, 1971.

2.   U. S Congress. Senate. A Resolution to Admit Pinch-
     back from Louisiana. 44th Congress, 1st session,
     1876.

3.   U. S. Congress. Senate. Voting Practices in the State
     of Mississippi. 44th Congress, 1st session, 1876.

4. U. S. Congress. Senate. <u>A Speech Against Separate
    Black Regiments in the Army.</u> 45th Congress, 2nd
    session, 1877.

III. RICHARD H. CAIN

Cain, Richard Harvey, a Representative from South Carolina; born in Greenbrier County, Va., April 12, 1825; was
of the Negro race; moved with his father to Gallipolis, Ohio
in 1831 and attended school; entered the ministry, and was
a pastor in Brooklyn, N. Y. from 1861 to 1865; moved to
South Carolina in 1865 and settled in Charleston: delegate
to the constitutional convention of South Carolina in 1868;
member of the State senate, 1868-1872; manager of a newspaper in Charleston in 1868; elected as a Republican to the
43rd Congress (March 4, 1873-March 3, 1875); was not a
candidate for renomination in 1874; elected to the 45th
Congress (March 4, 1877-March 3, 1879); was not a candidate for renomination in 1878; appointed a bishop of the AME
Church in 1880 and served until his death in Washington,
D.C., January 18, 1887 (1:689).

RICHARD H. CAIN

CIVIL RIGHTS (January 10, 1874)

My conception of the effect of this bill, if it be
passed into a law, will be simply to place colored
men of this country upon the same footing with
every other citizen under the law, and would not
at all enforce social relationship with any other
class of persons in the Country whatsoever. It is
merely a matter of law. What we desire is that
our civil rights shall be guaranteed by law as they
are guaranteed to every other class of persons;
and when that is done all other things come in as
a necessary sequence, the enforcement of the
rights following the enactment of the law. (2:565)

Mr. CAIN. Mr. Speaker, I feel called upon more
particularly by the remarks of the gentleman from North
Carolina (Mr. VANCE) on civil rights to express my views.
For a number of days this question has been discussed, and
various have been the opinions expressed as to whether or
not the pending bill should be passed in its present form or
whether it should be modified to meet the objections entertained by a number of gentlemen whose duty it will be to
give their votes for or against its passage. It has been
assumed that to pass this bill in its present form Congress
would manifest a tendency to override the Constitution of the
country and violate the rights of the States.

Whether it be true or false is yet to be seen. I take
it, so far as the constitutional question is concerned, if the
colored people under the law, under the amendments to the
Constitution, have become invested with all the rights of citizenship, then they carry with them all rights and immunities
accruing to and belonging to a citizen of the United States.
If four, or nearly five, million people have been lifted from
the thralldom of slavery and made free; if the Government by
its amendments to the Constitution has guaranteed to them
all rights and immunities, as to other citizens, they must
necessarily therefore carry along with them all the privileges
enjoyed by all other citizens of the Republic.

Sir, the gentleman from North Carolina (Mr. VANCE) who spoke on the question stated some objections, to which I desire to address a few words of reply. He said it would enforce social rights, and therefore would be detrimental to the interests of both the whites and the blacks of the country. My conception of the effect of this bill, if it be passed into a law, will be simply to place the colored men of this country upon the same footing with every other citizen under the law, and will not at all enforce social relationship with any other class of persons in the country whatsoever. It is merely a matter of law. What we desire is that our civil rights shall be guaranteed by law as they are guaranteed to every other class of persons; and when that is done all other things will come in as a necessary sequence, the enforcement of the rights following the enactment of the law.

Sir, social equality is a right which every man, every woman, and every class of persons have within their own control. They have a right to form their own acquaintances, to establish their own social relationships. Its establishment and regulation is not within the province of legislation. No laws enacted by legislators can compel social equality. Now, what is it we desire? What we desire is this: inasmuch as we have been raised to the dignity, to the honor, to the position of our manhood, we ask that the laws of this country should guarantee all the rights and immunities belonging to that proud position, to be enforced all over this broad land.

Sir, the gentleman states that in the State of North Carolina the colored people enjoy all their rights as far as the highways are concerned; that in the hotels, and in the railroad cars, and in the various public places of resort, they have all the rights and all the immunities accorded to any other class of citizens of the United States. Now, it may not have come under his observation, but it has under mine, that such really is not the case; and the reason why I know and feel it more than he does is because my face is painted black and his is painted white. We who have the color--I may say the objectionable color--know and feel all this. A few days ago, in passing from South Carolina to this city, I entered a place of public resort where hungry men are fed, but I did not dare--I could not without trouble--sit down to the table. I could not sit down at Wilmington or at Weldon without entering into a contest, which I did not desire to do. My colleague, the gentleman who so eloquently spoke on this subject the other day (Mr. ELLIOTT), a few months ago entered a restaurant at Wilmington and sat down to be served, and while there a gentlemen stepped up to him and said, "You cannot eat here." All the other gentlemen upon the railroad as passengers were eating there; he had only twenty minutes, and was compelled to leave the restaurant or have a fight for it. He showed fight, however, and got his dinner; but he has never been back there since. Coming here last week I felt we did not desire to draw revolvers and present the bold front of warriors, and therefore we ordered our dinners to be brought into the cars, but even there we found the existence of this feeling; for, although we had paid a dollar apiece for our meals, to be brought by the servants into the cars, still there was objection on the part of the railroad people to our eating our meals in the cars, because they said we were putting on airs. They refused us in the restaurant, and then did not desire that we should eat our meals in the cars, although we paid for them. Yet this was in the noble State of North Carolina.

Mr. Speaker, the colored men of the South do not want the adoption of any force measure. No; they do not want anything by force. All they ask is that you will give them, by statutory enactment under the fundamental law, the right to enjoy precisely the same privileges accorded to every other class of citizens.

The gentleman, moreover, has told us that if we pass this civil-rights bill we will thereby rob the colored men of the South of the friendship of the whites. Now, I am at a loss to see how the friendship of our white friends can be lost to us by simply saying we should be permitted to enjoy the rights enjoyed by other citizens. I have a higher opinion of the friendship of the southern men than to suppose any such thing. I know them too well. I know their friendship will not be lost by the passage of this bill. For eight years I have been in South Carolina, and I have found this to be the fact, that the higher class, comprising gentlemen of learning and refinement, are less opposed to this measure than are those who do not occupy so high a position in the social scale.

Sir, I think that there will be no difficulty. But I do think this, that there will be more trouble if we do not have those rights. I regard it important, therefore, that we should make the law so strong that no man can infringe those rights.

But, says the gentleman from North Carolina, some

ambitious colored man will, when this law is passed, enter
a hotel or railroad car, and thus create disturbance. If it
be his right, then there is no vaulting ambition in his enjoying that right. And if he can pay for his seat in a first-
class car or his room in a hotel, I see no objection to his
enjoying it. But the gentleman says more. He cited, on
the school question, the evidence of South Carolina, and says
the South Carolina University has been destroyed by virtue of
bringing into contact the white students with the colored. I
think not. It is true that a small number of students left
the institution, but the institution still remains. The buildings are there as erect as ever; the faculty are there as
attentive to their duties as ever they were; the students are
coming in as they did before. It is true, sir, that there is
a mixture of students now; that there are colored and white
students of law and medicine sitting side by side; it is true,
sir, that the prejudice of some of the professors was so
strong that it drove them out of the institution; but the philanthropy and good sense of others were such that they remained; and thus we have still the institution going on, and
because some students have left, it cannot be reasonably
argued that the usefulness of the institution has been destroyed. The University of South Carolina has not been
destroyed.

But the gentleman says more. The colored man can
not stand, he says where this antagonism exists, and he deprecates the idea of antagonizing the races. The gentleman
says there is no antagonism on his part. I think there is
no antagonism so far as the country is concerned. So far
as my observation extends, it goes to prove this: that there
is a general acceptance upon the part of the larger and
better class of the whites of the South of the situation, and
that they regard the education and the development of the
colored people as essential to their welfare, and the peace,
happiness, and prosperity of the whole country. Many of
them, including the best minds of the South, are earnestly
engaged in seeking to make this great system of education
permanent in all the States. I do not believe, therefore,
that it is possible there can be such an antagonism. Why,
sir, in Massachusetts there is no such antagonism. There
the colored and the white children go to school side by side.
In Rhode Island there is not that antagonism. There they
are educated side by side in the high schools. In New York,
in the highest schools, are to be found, of late, colored men
and colored women. Even old democratic New York does
not refuse to give the colored people their rights, and there

is no antagonism. A few days ago, when in New York, I
made it my business to find out what was the position of
matters there in this respect. I ascertained that there are,
I think, seven colored ladies in the highest school in New
York, and I believe they stand No. 1 in their class, side by
side with members of the best and most refined families of
the citizens of New York, and without any objection to their
presence.

I cannot understand how it is that our southern friends,
or a certain class of them, always bring back this old ghost
of prejudice and of antagonism. There was a time, not very
far distant in the past, when this antagonism was not recognized, when a feeling of fraternization between the white and
the colored races existed, that made them kindred to each
other. But since our emancipation, since liberty has come,
and only since--only since we have stood up clothed in our
manhood, only since we have proceeded to take hold and help
advance the civilization of this nation--it is only since then
that this bugbear is brought up against us again. Sir, the
progress of the age demands that the colored man of this
country shall be lifted by law into the enjoyment of every
right, and that every appliance which is accorded to the
German, to the Irishman, to the Englishman, and every
foreigner, shall be given to him; and I shall give some reasons why I demand this in the name of justice.

For two hundred years the colored men of this nation
have assisted in building up its commercial interests. There
are in this country nearly five millions of us, and for a
space of two hundred and forty-seven years we have been
hewers of wood and drawers of water; but we have been with
you in promoting all the interests of the country. My distinguished colleague, who defended the civil rights of our
race the other day on this floor, set this forth so clearly
that I need not dwell upon it at this time.

I propose to state just this: that we have been identified with the interests of this country from its very foundation. The cotton crop of this country has been raised and
its rice-fields have been tilled by the hands of our race.
All along as the march of progress, as the march of commerce, as the development of your resources has been wid-
ening and expanding and spreading, as your vessels have
gone on every sea, with the stars and stripes waving over
them, and carried your commerce everywhere, there the
black man's labor has gone to enrich your country and to

augment the grandeur of your nationality. This was done in
the time of slavery. And if, for the space of time I have
noted, we have been hewers of wood and drawers of water;
if we have made your cotton-fields blossom as the rose; if
we have made your rice-fields wave with luxuriant harvests;
if we have made your corn-fields rejoice; if we have sweated
and toiled to build up the prosperity of the whole country by
the productions of our labor, I submit, now that the war has
made a change, now that we are free--I submit to the nation
whether it is not fair and right that we should come in and
enjoy to the fullest extent our freedom and liberty.

A word now as to the question of education. Sir, I
know that, indeed, some of our republican friends are even
a little weak on the school clause of this bill; but, sir, the
education of the race, the education of the nation, is paramount to all other considerations. I regard it important,
therefore, that the colored people should take place in the
educational march of this nation, and I would suggest that
there should be no discrimination. It is against discrimination in this particular that we complain.

Sir, if you look over the reports of superintendents
of schools in the several States, you will find, I think, evi-
dences sufficient to warrant Congress in passing the civil-
rights bill as it now stands. The report of the commissioner of education of California shows that, under the operation of law and of prejudice, the colored children of that
State are practically excluded from schooling. Here is a
case where a large class of children are growing up in our
midst in a state of ignorance and semi-barbarism. Take the
report of the superintendent of education of Indiana, and you
will find that while efforts have been made in some places to
educate the colored children, yet the prejudice is so great
that it debars the colored children from enjoying all the
rights which they ought to enjoy under the law. In Illinois,
too, the superintendent of education makes this statement:
that, while the law guarantees education to every child, yet
such are the operations among the school trustees that they
almost ignore, in some places, the education of colored
children.

All we ask is that you, the legislators of the nation,
shall pass a law so strong and so powerful that no one shall
be able to elude it and destroy our rights under the Constitution and laws of our country. That is all we ask.

But, Mr. Speaker, the gentleman from North Carolina
(Mr. VANCE) asks that the colored man shall place himself
in an attitude to receive his rights. I ask, what attitude can
we assume? We have tilled your soil, and during the rude
shock of war, until our hour came, we were docile during
that long, dark night, waiting patiently the coming day. In
the Southern States during that war our men and women stood
behind their masters; they tilled the soil, and there were no
insurrections in all the broad lands of the South; the wives
and daughters of the slaveholders were as sacred then as
they were before; and the history of the war does not record
a single event, a single instance, in which the colored people
were unfaithful, even in slavery; nor does the history of the
war record the fact that on the other side, on the side of the
Union, there were any colored men who were not willing at
all times to give their lives for their country. Sir, upon
both sides we waited patiently. I was a student at Wilberforce University, in Ohio, when the tocsin of war was
sounded, when Fort Sumter was fired upon, and I never forget the thrill that ran through my soul when I thought of the
coming consequences of that shot. There were one hundred
and fifteen of us, students at that university, who, anxious
to vindicate the stars and stripes, made up a company, and
offered our services to the governor of Ohio; and, sir, we
were told that this was a white man's war and that the negro
had nothing to do with it. Sir, we returned--docile, patient,
waiting, casting our eyes to the heavens whence help always
comes. We knew that there would come a period in the history of this nation when our strong black arms would be
needed. We waited patiently; we waited until Massachusetts,
through her noble governor, sounded the alarm, and we
hastened then to hear the summons and obey it.

Sir, as I before remarked, we were peaceful on both
sides. When the call was made on the side of the Union we
were ready; when the call was made for us to obey orders
on the other side, in the confederacy, we humbly performed
our tasks, and waited patiently. But, sir, the time came
when we were called for; and, , I ask, who can say that when
that call was made, the colored men did not respond as
readily and as rapidly as did any other class of your citizens? Sir, I need not speak of the history of this bloody
war. It will carry down to coming generations the valor of
our soldiers on the battle-field. Fort Wagner will stand forever as a monument of that valor, and until Vicksburgh
shall be wiped from the galaxy of battles in the great contest
for human liberty that valor will be recognized.

And for what, Mr. Speaker and gentlemen, was the
great war made? The gentleman from North Carolina (Mr.
VANCE) announced before he sat down, in answer to an in-
terrogatory by a gentleman on this side of the House, that
they went into the war conscientiously before God. So be it.
Then we simply come and plead conscientiously before God
that these are our rights, and we want them. We plead
conscientiously before God, believing that these are our rights
by inheritance, and by the inexorable decree of Almighty God.

We believe in the Declaration of Independence, that
all men are born free and equal, and are endowed by their
Creator with certain inalienable rights, among which are life,
liberty, and the pursuit of happiness. And we further believe
that to secure these rights governments are instituted. And
we further believe that when governments cease to subserve
those ends the people should change them.

I have been astonished at the course which gentlemen
on the other side have taken in discussing this bill. They
plant themselves right behind the Constitution, and declare
that the rights of the State ought not to be invaded. Now, if
you will take the history of the war of the rebellion, as published by the Clerk of this House, you will see that in 1860
the whole country, each side, was earnest in seeking to
make such amendments to the Constitution as would forever
secure slavery and keep the Union together under the circumstances. The resolutions passed, and the sentiments expressed in speeches at that time, if examined by gentlemen,
will be found to bear out all that I have indicated. It was
felt in 1860 that anything that would keep the "wayward sisters" from going astray was desirable. They were then
ready and willing to make any amendments.

And now, when the civil rights of our race are hanging upon the issue, they on the other side are not willing to
concede to us such amendments as will guarantee them; indeed, they seek to impair the force of existing amendments
to the Constitution of the United States, which would carry
out the purpose.

I think it is proper and just that the civil-rights bill
should be passed. Some think it would be better to modify
it, to strike out the school clause, or to so modify it that
some of the State constitutions should not be infringed. I
regard it essential to us and the people of this country that
we should be secured in this if in nothing else. I cannot

regard that our rights will be secured until the jury-box and
the school-room, those great palladiums of our liberty, shall
have been opened to us.   Then we will be willing to take our
chances with other men.

                We do not want any discriminations to be made.   If
discriminations are made in regard to schools, then there
will be accomplished just what we are fighting against.   If
you say that the schools in the State of Georgia, for instance,
shall be allowed to discriminate against colored people, then
you will have discriminations made against us.   We do not
want any discriminations.   I do not ask any legislation for
the colored people of this country that is not applied to the
white people.   All that we ask is equal laws, equal legislation, and equal rights throughout the length and breadth of
this land.

                The gentleman from North Carolina (Mr. VANCE) also
says that the colored men should not come here begging at
the doors of Congress for their rights.   I agree with him. I
want to say that we do not come here begging for our rights.
We come here clothed in the garb of American citizenship.
We come demanding our rights in the name of justice.   We
come, with no arrogance on our part, asking that this great
nation, which laid the foundation of civilization and progress
more deeply and more securely than any other nation on the
face of the earth, guarantee us protection from outrage.   We
come here, five millions of people--more than composed this
whole nation when it had its great tea-party in Boston Harbor,
and demanded its rights at the point of the bayonet--asking
that unjust discriminations against us be forbidden.   We come
here in the name of justice, equity, and law, in the name of
our children, in the name of our country, petitioning for our
rights.

                Our rights will yet be accorded to us, I believe, from
the feeling that has been exhibited on this floor of the growing sentiment of the country.   Rapid as the weaver's shuttle,
swift as the lightning's flash, such progress is being made
that our rights will be accorded to us ere long.   I believe
the nation is perfectly willing to accord this measure of justice, if only those who represent the people here would say
the word.   Let it be proclaimed that henceforth all the
children of this land shall be free; that the stars and stripes,
waving over all, shall secure to every one equal rights, and
the nation will say "amen."

Let the civil-rights bill be passed this day, and five
million black men, women, and children, all over the land,
will begin a new song of rejoicing, and the thirty-five millions of noble-hearted Anglo-Saxons will join in the shout of
joy. Thus will the great mission be fulfilled of giving to all
the people equal rights.

Inasmuch as we have toiled with you in building up
this nation; inasmuch as we have suffered side by side with
you in the war; inasmuch as we have together passed through
affliction and pestilence, let there be now a fulfillment of the
sublime thought of our fathers--let all men enjoy equal liberty
and equal rights.

In this hour, when you are about to put the cap-stone
on the mighty structure of government, I ask you to grant us
this measure, because it is right. Grant this, and we shall
go home with our hearts filled with gladness. I want to
"shake hands over the bloody chasm." The gentleman from
North Carolina has said he desires to have forever buried
the memory of the recent war. I agree with him. Representing a South Carolina constituency, I desire to bury forever the tomahawk. I have voted in this House with a free
heart to declare universal amnesty. Inasmuch as general
amnesty has been proclaimed, I would hardly have expected
there would be any objection on this floor to the civil-rights
bill, giving to all men the equal rights of citizens. There
should be no more contest. Amnesty and civil rights should
go together. Gentlemen on the other side will admit that we
have been faithful; and now, when we propose to bury the
hatchet, let us shake hands upon this measure of justice; and
if heretofore we have been enemies, let us be friends now
and forever.

Our wives and our children have high hopes and aspirations; their longings for manhood and womanhood are
equal to those of any other race. The same sentiment of
patriotism and of gratitude, the same spirit of national pride
that animates the hearts of other citizens, animates theirs.
In the name of the dead soldiers of our race, whose bodies
lie at Petersburgh and on other battlefields of the South; in
the name of the widows and orphans they have left behind; in
the name of the widows of the confederate soldiers who fell
upon the same fields, I conjure you let this righteous act be
done. I appeal to you in the name of God and humanity to
give us our rights, for we ask nothing more.

CIVIL RIGHTS (January 24, 1874)

I believe the time is coming when the Congress of
the United States, when the whole nation, will
recognize the importance of the passage of this bill
in order to settle this question once and for ever.
I regard the interests of the black man in this
country as identical with the interests of the white
man. I would have that set forth so clearly and
unmistakably that there should be no antagonism
between the races, no friction that should destroy
their peace and prosperity. I believe Almighty
God has placed both races on this broad theater of
activity, where thoughts and opinions are freely
expressed, where we may grasp every idea of manhood, where we may take hold of every truth and
develop every art and science that can advance the
prosperity of the nation. I believe God designed
us to live here together in this continent, and in
no other place, to develop this great idea that all
men are the children of one Father. We are here
to work out the grand experiment of the homogeneity of nations, the grand outburst of the greatness
of humanity, by the development in us of the rights
that belong to us, and the performances of the
duties that we owe each other. (3:901-903)

Mr. CAIN. Mr. Speaker, I had supposed "this cruel
war was over, " and that we had entered upon an era of
peace, prosperity and future success as a nation. I had
supposed that after the sad experience of more than five
years, after we had sought to heal the wounds the war had
made, after we had passed amnesty bills, and, as we thought,
had entered upon the smooth, quiet road of future prosperity,
we would meet on a common level in the halls of Congress,
and that no longer would we brood over the past; that we
would strike out a new line of policy, a new national course,
and thus succeed in laying broad and deep the foundations of
the future welfare of this country; that every man, of every

45

race, of every section of this country, might strike hands
and go forward in national progress.

I regret, however, that it again becomes my lot to
answer a member from a neighboring State--North Carolina.
It was my misfortune a few Saturdays ago to have to answer
a gentleman from the same state (Mr. VANCE) in relation
to strictures upon my race. I regret that it becomes my
duty again, simply in defense of what I regard as a right--
in defense of the race to which I belong--to meet the arguments of another gentleman from North Carolina (Mr. ROB-
BINS), to show, if I can, their fallacy and to prove they are
not correct.

The gentleman starts out by saying that if we pass
the pending civil-rights bill it may indeed seem pleasant to
the northern people, but to his section, and to the South, it
will be death. I do not think he is correct, for the reason
that they have in the South suffered a great many more terrible things than civil rights, and still live. I think if so
harmless a measure as the civil-rights bill, guaranteeing to
every man of the African race equal rights with other men,
would bring death to the South, then certainly that noble
march of Sherman to the sea would have fixed them long ago.

I desire to answer a few of the strictures which the
gentleman has been pleased to place upon us. He states that
the civil-rights bill will be death to that section. I cannot
see it in that light. We lived together before the war--four
millions of colored men, women, and children, with the
whites of the South--and there was no special antagonism
then. There might have been some friction in some places
and in some cases, but no special antagonism between the
two races in the South. I fail, therefore, to see the force
of the gentleman's argument. I would like to ask why, in
all conscience, after the measures of education, these noble
efforts to educate these "barbarians, " as he terms us, for
two hundred years or more--after all the earnest efforts on
their part, with their superior civilization, and all the ap-
pliances which the gentleman from North Carolina (Mr. ROB-
BINS) claims were brought to bear on these "barbarians"--
I ask why there was no such antagonism then, but just at
this time? Why, sir, if it be true, as the gentleman says,
that such philanthropic efforts have been put forth for the
education and improvement of the black race, there would be
no occasion for antagonism. It is, I believe, a law of education to assimilate, to bring together, to harmonize dis-

cordant elements, to bring about oneness of feeling and sentiment, to develop similarity of thought, similarity of action,
and thus tend to carry forward the people harmoniously.
That does not seem to have been the case, if the argument
of the gentleman from North Carolina is correct.   Now, look
at the fallacy of the gentleman's argument.   This race of
barbarians, in spite of all their disadvantages, had been educated to such an extent that the white community of the
South were not afraid of them after their emancipation.   Is
not that singular?

The gentleman further states that the negro race is
the world's stage actor--the comic dancer all over the land;
that he laughs and he dances.   Sir, well he may; there are
more reasons for his laughing and dancing now than ever before.   There are more substantial reasons why he should be
happy now than during all the two hundred years prior to this
time.   Now he dances as an African; then he crouched as a
slave.

The gentleman further states that not more than
eighteen hundred negroes were killed during the four years
of the war.   The gentleman forgets some battles; he forgets
Vicksburgh; I presume he does not remember Petersburgh;
he does not know anything of Fort Pillow   He knows nothing
about all the great achievements of the black men while
Sherman's army was moving on to victory.   He forgets who
entered Charleston first; he forgets who entered Richmond
first; he forgets all this in the blindness of his prejudice
against a race of men who have vindicated themselves so
nobly on the battle-field.   But I will grant the gentleman the
charity of dwelling no longer on that point.

Mr. Speaker, the gentleman states that during the
struggle for freedom four millions of negroes lifted no hand
to liberate themselves; that no stroke was made by them to
deliver themselves from their thralldom; yet a few moments
afterward he makes the statement that their kind-heartedness
prevented them from riding up and destroying the wives and
children of the rebel soldiers who were at the front.   I accept the admission.   Sir, there dwells in the black man's
heart too much nobleness and too much charity to strike
down helpless women and children when he has a chance to
do so.   No; though the liberty of our race was dear to us,
we would not purchase it at such a dastard price as the
slaying of helpless women and children, while their husbands
and fathers were away.   I would scorn the men of my race

forever if they had lifted their hands at such a period as that against helpless women and children, who were waiting in silent anxiety the return of their natural and lawful protectors. Our strong black arms might have destroyed every vestige of their homes; our torches might have kindled a fire that would have lighted up the whole South, so that every southern man fighting in the army would have hastened back to find his home in ashes. But our race had such nobleness of heart as to forbear in an hour of such extremity, and leave those men their wives and children.

Sir, I mean no disrespect to the gentleman, but I think the facts will bear me out in the statement that on every occasion on the battle-field where the black man met the white man of the South there was no flinching, no turning back, on the part of the black man. He bravely accepted his part in the struggle for liberty or death.

The gentleman says he still looks upon the whites as the superior race. That may be the case in some respects; but, sir, if they educated us they certainly should not find fault with us if we follow out what they have taught, and show ourselves obedient servants.

But, Mr. Speaker, there is another point. The gentleman states that we would make no movement to achieve our liberty. Why, sir, the education which those gentleman gave the southern slaves was of a peculiar kind. What school-house in all the South was open to the colored race? Point to one. Name the academy where you educated black men and black women as lawyers or doctors, or in any other department of science or art. Point out the county. Give us the name of the district. Tell the name of the school commissioner. Name the teacher. I will name one. Her name was Missa Douglas. And for the attempt to educate those of our race she was incarcerated in prison, and remained there for five years. That is the only instance, so far as I remember, of the education of the colored people of the South.

Examine the laws of the South, and you will find that it was a penal offense for any one to educate the colored people there. Yet these gentleman come here and upbraid us with our ignorance and our stupidity. Yet you robbed us for two hundred years. During all that time we toiled for you. We have raised your cotton, your rice, your corn. We have attended your wives and your children. We have made wealth for your support and your education, while we

were slaves, toiling without pay, without the means of education, and hardly of sustenance.   And yet you upbraid us
for being ignorant; call us a horde of barbarians! Why, sir,
it is ill-becoming in the gentleman to tell us of our barbarism, after he and his have been educating us for two hundred
years. If New England charity and benevolence had not accomplished more than your education has done we would still
be in that condition. I thank the North for the charity and
nobleness with which it has come to our relief. The North
has sent forth those leading ideas, which have spread like
lightning over the land; and the negro was not so dumb and
not so obtuse that he could not catch the light, and embrace
its blessings and enjoy them.   Sir, I hurl back with contempt all the aspersions of the gentleman on the other side
against my race.   There is but very little difference, even
now, between the condition of the whites of the South and the
condition of the blacks of the South.   I have given some attention to the statistics of education in the Southern States.
I find this pregnant fact, that there is about 12 percent more
ignorance existing among the whites in the South than there
is among the colored people in the South, notwithstanding the
slavery of the colored race.   I wish I had the reports here,
that I might show the gentleman how the facts stand in reference to his own State especially, because, if I remember
correctly, his State shows there is a preponderating aggregate of ignorance in the State of North Carolina, amounting
to 60 percent, and upward, compared with the entire number
of the inhabitants in that State.

     Tell us of our ignorance--the ignorance of the colored
race! Why, Mr. Speaker, it appears to me to be presumption on the part of the gentleman to state that we--we whom
they have wronged, whom they have outraged, whom they
have robbed, whose sweat and toil they have had the benefit
of for two hundred years; whose labor, whose wives, whose
children, have been at their beck and call--I say it ill-be-
comes them to taunt us now with our barbarism and our
ignorance.   Sir, if he will open to us the schoolhouse, give
us some chance, we would not have to measure arms with
him now.   But even now, Mr. Speaker, although there is
such disparity between us and him so far as relates to education and resources, even now we fear not a comparison in
the condition of education in the last eight years between the
whites and the blacks of North Carolina.

     The gentleman, moreover, states that the reason why
they did not educate the colored race was that the colored

man was not ready. Not ready, Mr. Speaker; if I had that
gentleman upon the floor, with my foot upon his neck, and
holding a lash over him, with his hands tied, with him bound
hand and foot, would he expect that I should boast over him
and tell him, "You are a coward, you are a traitor, because
you do not resist me?" Would he expect me to tell him that
when I had him down under my foot, with his hands tied and
the lash in my hand lashing his back? Would he tell me
that, in conscience, I would be doing justice to him? Oh,
no, no! And yet such was the condition in which he had my
race. Why, sir, the whipping-post, the thumb-screw, and
the lash, were the great means of education in the South.
These were the school-houses, these were the academies,
these were the great instruments of education, of which the
gentleman boasts, for the purpose of bringing these barbarians into civilization. When men boast, they ought to have
something to boast of. When I boast, Mr. Speaker, I shall
boast of some noble deed. I will boast not of the wrongs inflicted upon the weak; I will boast not of the outrages inflicted upon the indigent; I will not boast, Mr. Speaker, of
lashing the weak and trampling under foot any class of people
who ought to have my sympathy, nor will I reproach them
for being ignorant, when they have been kept away from every
means to educate them.

He says we are not ready for it. How long would it
have taken us to get ready under their kind of teaching? How
long, O Lord, how long! How long would it have taken to
educate us under the thumb-screw, to educate us with the
whip, to educate us with the lash, with instruments of tor-
ture, to educate us without a home? How long would it have
taken to educate us under their system? We had no wives;
we had no children; they belonged to the gentleman and his
class. We were homeless, we were friendless, although
those stars and stripes hanging over your head, Mr. Speaker,
ought to have been our protection. That emblem of the Declaration of Independence, initiated by the fathers of the Republic, that all men are born free and equal, ought to have
been our protection. Yet they were to us no stars of hope,
and the stripes were only stripes of our condemnation.

The gentleman talked something, I believe, about buz-
zards or crows taking the place of our brave eagle. Sir,
the crow would, I think, more beautifully represent the condition of the South now--the croaking bird, you know. They
have been croaking ever since the rebellion came on, and
they have been croaking against emancipation and the Consti-

tution ever since.   They are a nation of croakers, so to
speak.   Like the crow they are cawing, cawing, cawing,
eternally cawing.   Mr. Speaker, you will pardon me, for I
did not expect to speak this morning.

The gentleman says the negro has done less for himself than any other race of men on earth; and he instances
the German, the Irishman, the Scotchman, the Englishman,
and the Frenchman, as having done something.   But he forgets the men of those nationalities come from stations which
are the proud, educated, refined, noble, advancing nations of
the earth.   He forgets that those nations of which he speaks,
from which those men have sprung, have given, and are still
giving, to the world some of the brightest minds that ever
adorned the galaxy of human intellect.

But he tells us that the negroes never produced anything.   Well, sir, it may be that in the gentleman's opinion
negroes have never produced anything.   I wonder if the
gentleman ever read history.   Did he ever hear tell of any
persons of the name of Hannibal, of Hanno, of Hamilear, of
Euclid--all great men of ancient times--of Aesop, and
others?   No, sir; no; for that kind of literature does not
come to North Carolina.   It grows, it flourishes, on the
free mountain peaks and in the academies of the North.   That
kind of literature comes to such men as Wendell Phillips, as
Lloyd Garrison, as Charles Sumner, as Benjamin Butler,
and other distinguished men, men of the North, men that are
thinkers, men that do not croak, but let the eagle ever soar
high in the conception of high ideas.   They are ideas that
belong to a free people; they are not consistent with or con-
sonant with slavery.   No, sir; they do not tell the negro of
Euclid, the man that in his joy cried out "Eureka, I have
found it"; no, that is not the language for the slave.   No;
that is not the language they teach by the whip and the
thumb-screw; no, sir, it is not that.

But I must pass on.   The gentleman says that the
black men in the South, since emancipation and enfranchisement, have put bad men into office.   Well, sir, that may be
true, and I regret that we have put so many bad men in
office.   No one regrets it more than I do, but they were not
colored men after all.   They were not black men, those bad
men in office, who have done so much to deteriorate the
value of the country.   Not at all.   Why, sir, they did not
elect our distinguished friend (Mr. VANCE) from North
Carolina by black votes.   They did not elect Mr. Holman,

or a gentleman of some such name, in North Carolina. They
did not run the State in debt.   They were not the men who
took the cash; they were simply mudsills who did the voting,
while another class of individuals did the stealing.   That is
the difference.

Well, Mr. Speaker, I beg to say that we did the best
we could; and one of the results of our education was that
we had been taught to trust white men in the South.   We
trusted them, and if they did wrong it was no fault of ours;
not at all.   I presume the gentleman who addressed the
House to-day had some colored constituents who voted for
him and sent him here.   I will not dare to say, however,
that he is a bad man.   He may be one of the very best of
men; but I think he has some very bad ideas, so far as my
race is concerned.

The gentleman says that this is a white man's land
and government.   He says it has been committed to them in
a sacred relationship.   I ask in all conscience what becomes
of our black men and women and children, to the number of
five millions; have we no rights?   Ought we to have no
privileges; ought we not to have the protection of the law?
We did not ask any more.   The gentleman harps upon the
idea of social equality.   Well, sir, he has not had so much
experience of that as I have had, or as my race have had.
We have some objections to social equality ourselves, very
grave ones.   For even now, though freedom has come, it is
a hard matter, a very hard matter, to keep sacredly guarded
the precincts of our sacred homes.   But I will not dwell
upon that.   The gentleman knows more about that than I do.

The gentleman wishes that we should prepare ourselves
to go to Africa, or to the West Indies, or somewhere else.
I want to enunciate this doctrine upon this floor--you have
brought us here, and here we are going to stay.   We are
not going one foot or one inch from this land.   Our mothers
and our fathers and our grandfathers and great-grandfathers
have died here.   Here we have sweated.   Here we have
toiled.   Here we have made this country great and rich by
our labor and toil.   It is mean in you now to want to drive
us away, after having taken all our toil for two hundred
years.   Just think of the magnitude of these gentlemen's
hearts.   After having taken all our toil for two hundred
years; after having sold our wives and children like so many
cattle in the shambles; after having reared the throne of
great king cotton on our labors; after we have made their

rice-fields wave with luxuriant harvests while they were fighting against the Government and keeping us in bondage--now
we are free they want us to go away. Shame on you!

Now, Mr. Speaker, we are not going away. We are
going to stay here. We propose to stay here and work out
this problem. We believe that God Almighty has made of
one blood all the nations upon the face of the earth. We believe we are made just like white men are. Look; I stretch
out my arms. See; I have two of them, as you have. Look
at your ears; I have two of them. I have two eyes, two
nostrils, one mouth, two feet. I stand erect like you. I
am clothed with humanity like you. I think, I reason, I
talk, I express my views, as you do. Is there any difference between us? Not so far as our manhood is concerned,
unless it be in this: that our opinions differ, and mine are
a little higher up than yours.

The gentleman states that this idea of all men being
created equal is a fallacy, announced some years ago by
Thomas Jefferson, that old fool-hardy man, who announced
so many ideas that have been woven into the woof of the nation, who announced so many foolish things that have made
this nation strong and great, and powerful. Sir, if he was
in error, I accept the error with pleasure. If he was a
foolish man, I would to God that North Carolina had been
baptized in that foolishness about two hundred years ago.

The gentleman also states that if you pass this bill
your power over the South will pass away; that the power of
the republican party in the South will pass away. Sir, let
me tell the gentleman that behind this bill are nine hundred
thousand voters; that, like the warriors of the tribe of Benjamin, every one of them is left-handed and can "sling a
stone at a hair's breadth"; that each will come up stronger
and mightier and more infused with power than ever before
when you pass this bill giving them their rights, as other
men have them. They will come up as never before to the
support of the republican party, and they will make the South
a source of joy and gladness.

The gentleman also talks about the colored people de-
teriorating. Sir, who tills your lands now? Who plants
your corn? Who raises your cotton? I have been in the
South during the last ten years. I have traveled over the
Southern States, and have seen who did this work. Going
along I saw the white men do the smoking, chewing, tobacco,

riding horses, playing cards, spending money, while the
colored men are tilling the soil, and bringing the cotton,
rice, and other products to market.

Sir, I do not believe the gentleman from North Carolina wants us to go to Africa; I do not believe it. It was a
slip of the tongue; he does not mean that the black people
should leave North Carolina; not a bit of it. If they did you
would see such an exodus of white people from that State as
you never saw before, for they would follow them wherever
they might go.

Sir, we feel that we are part and parcel of this great
nation; and as such, as I said before, we propose to stay
here and solve this problem of whether the black race and
the white race can live together in this country. I made the
statement that I regard it as essential to their welfare and
interests that they should live together in this country. Why
not? I can see no reason why not, if they contribute their
quota to the advancement of progress and civilization. Sir,
the mechanics of the South are almost altogether colored
people. The carpenters, the machinists, the engineers--
nearly all the mechanics in the Southern States are colored
people. Why can we not stay here and work out this problem?

I ask Congress to pass this bill for the reason that it
would settle this question, once and forever. The gentleman
says that he does not desire that the colored people shall be
crowded into the schools of the white people. Well, I do not
think that they would be harmed by it; some few of them
might be. But experience has taught us that it is not true
that great harm will come from any such measure. I think,
therefore, that if we pass this bill we will be doing a great
act of justice, we will settle for all time the question of the
rights of all people. And until that question is settled there
cannot be that peace and harmony in the country that is necessary to its success.

The gentleman says the colored people and the white
people are living together now in North Carolina in amicable
relations. I am glad for that admission, for he rounded off
all that he had said before by that last sentence. He said
that the two races could not live together, and yet at the
close of his speech he says that the whites and blacks are
now living in North Carolina in amicable relations. Sir, if
they are so living now, why not hereafter? Will peace and

good order be destroyed because all are to have their rights?
Sir, I do not think so.

I close with this thought: I believe the time is coming
when the Congress of the United States, when the whole nation, will recognize the importance of the passage of this bill
in order to settle this question once and forever. I regard
the interests of the black man in this country as identical
with the interests of the white man. I would have that set
forth so clearly and unmistakably that there should be no antagonism between the races, no friction that should destroy
their peace and prosperity. I believe Almighty God has
placed both races on this broad theater of activity, where
thoughts and opinions are freely expressed, where we may
grasp every idea of manhood, where we may take hold of
every truth and develop every art and science that can advance the prosperity of the nation. I believe God designed
us to live here together on this continent, and in no other
place, to develop this great idea that all men are the children
of one Father. We are here to work out the grand experiment of the homogeneity of nations, the grand outburst of the
greatness of humanity, by the development in us of the
rights that belong to us, and the performance of the duties
that we owe each other.

Our interests are bound up in this country. Here we
intend to stay and work out the problem of progress and education and civilization. I say to the gentleman from North
Carolina (Mr. ROBBINS) and to the gentleman from Virginia
(Mr. HARRIS) and to the gentleman from New York (Mr.
COX), who discussed civil rights the other day, and to gentlemen from the other States, that we are going to remain in
this country side by side with the white race. We desire to
share in your prosperity and to stand by you in adversity.
In advancing the progress of the nation we will take our
part; and if the country should again be involved in the devastation of war, we will do our part in the struggle. We
propose to identify ourselves with this nation, which had done
more than any other on earth to illustrate the great idea that
all races of men may dwell together in harmony, working
out together the problem of advancement and civilization and
liberty.

Mr. Speaker, we will drive the buzzard away; we will
scare the crow back to North Carolina. We will take the
eagle as the emblem of liberty; we will take that honored
flag which has been borne through the heat of a thousand

battles.   Under its folds Anglo-Saxon and Africo-American
can together work out a common destiny, until universal
liberty, as announced by this nation, shall be known throughout the world.

CIVIL RIGHTS (February 3, 1875)

Why not pass the civil-rights bill? Are there not
five millions of men, women, and children in this
country, a larger number than inhabited this
country when the fathers made the tea party in
Boston harbor, five millions whose rights are as
dear and sacred to them, humble though they be,
as are rights of the thirty-odd millions of white
people in this land? I am at a loss to understand
the philosophy which these gentlemen have learned;
how they can arrogate to themselves all rights, all
liberty, all laws, all government, all programs,
all science, all arts, all literature, and deny them
to other men formed of God equally as they are
formed, clothed with the same humanity, and endowed with the same intellectual powers, but robbed
by their connivance of the means of development.
I say I am at a loss to understand how they can
deny to us these privileges and claim them for
themselves. The civil-rights bill simply declares
this: that there shall be no discriminations between citizens of this land so far as the laws of
the land are concerned. I can find no fault with
that. The great living principle of the American
Government is that all men are free. (4:956-57)

Mr. CAIN. Mr. Speaker, there are periods in the
history of nations and of peoples when it is necessary that
men belonging to a race or races whose rights and interests
are at stake should lay aside all feelings of delicacy and
hesitation and vindicate their rights, their character, and
their nationality. I have listened with some surprise to the
speech of the gentleman who has just taken his seat (Mr.
WHITEHEAD). I have been surprised at his attempt to
ridicule and cast a slur upon a race of men whose labor has
enabled him and his for two hundred years to feed, and
drink, and thrive, and fatten.

I have sat in this House nearly nine months, and I

have listened to gentlemen recognized as the leaders on the
other side attempting to demonstrate as they supposed the inferiority of a race of men whom they have so long outraged,
and to cast a slur upon them because they have been helpless. But revolutions never go backward. The mills of the
gods grind slowly, but surely and exceeding fine. The times
have changed. The wheels have rolled up different circumstances from those that were rolled up in the days of the old
regime.

The gentleman from Virginia calls in question the
propriety of passing the civil-rights bill. I cannot agree
with him, and for this reason; my understanding of human
rights, of democracy if you please, is all rights to all men,
the government of the people by the people, and for the
people's interest, without regard to sections, complexions,
or anything else.

Why not pass the civil-rights bill? Are there not five
millions of men, women, and children in this country, a
larger number than inhabited this country when the fathers
made the tea party in Boston harbor, five millions whose
rights are as dear and sacred to them, humble though they
be, as are the rights of the thirty-odd millions of white
people in this land? I am at a loss to understand the philosophy which these gentlemen have learned; how they can
arrogate to themselves all rights, all liberty, all law, all
government, all progress, all science, all arts, all literature,
and deny them to other men formed of God equally as they
are formed, clothed with the same humanity, and endowed
with the same intellectual powers, but robbed by their connivance of the means of development. I say I am at a loss
to understand how they can deny to us these privileges and
claim them for themselves.

The civil-rights bill simply declares this: that there
shall be no discriminations between citizens of this land so
far as the laws of the land are concerned. I can find no
fault with that. The great living principle of the American
Government is that all men are free. We admit from every
land and every nationality men to come here and under the
folds of that noble flag repose in peace and protection. We
assume that, whatever education his mind may have received,
each man may aspire to and acquire all the rights of citizenship. Yet because, forsooth, God Almighty made the face of
the negro black, these gentlemen would deny him that right
though he be a man. Born on your soil, reared here amid

the toils and sorrows and griefs of the land, producing by his
long years of toil the products which have made your country
great, earnestly laboring to develop the resources of this
land, docile though outraged, yet when the gentlemen who
held them in bondage--sir, I will not repeat the dark scenes
that transpired under the benign influence and direction of
that class of men.

He tells you that since the liberation of the negro the
people of the North want to stir up strife.   Why, sir, you of
the South stir up the strife.   When the Government of the
United States had made the black man free; when Congress,
in the greatness of its magnanimity prepared to give to every
class of men their rights, and in reconstructing the Southern
States guaranteed to all the people their liberties, you refused to acquiesce in the laws enacted by Congress; you refused to "accept the situation, " to recognize the rights of that
class of men in the land.   You sought to make the reconstruction acts a nullity, if possible.   You sought to re-en-
slave the black man by every means in your power.   You
denied the validity of those reconstruction acts which undertook to protect him in his liberty.   It is because you thus
refused to accept the situation as it ought to have been accepted that there is now strife in the land.   And I will tell
you further that there will be strife all over this land as long
as five millions of black men, women, and children are deprived of their rights.   There will be no real and enduring
peace so long as the rights of any class of men are trampled
under foot, North or South, East or West.

Gentlemen say that the republican party is keeping up
a continual strife among classes.   Why, sir, it is not the
republican party that is keeping up strife.   The republican
party is seeking to maintain peace.   It is the southern men
that make the strife, because they will not let us have our
liberties, because they seek to thwart the designs of the
Government.   No man can read the tales of horror now being
brought out by the investigating committees in the South,
without realizing the fact that it is not the northern people
or the republican party that makes this strife in the country.

I regard it as essential to the peace of the country
that there shall be no discrimination between citizens; and
the civil-rights bill I regard as a just and righteous measure
which this Government must adopt in order to guarantee to
all citizens equal rights.

And, Mr. Speaker, I am astonished that there is an apparent disposition in some quarters to give this question the go-by. "O, " gentlemen say, "you will stir up strife in the country"--"bad blood, " the gentleman from Virginia said. Well, I think there has been a good deal of "bad blood" in the South already. It seems to me that a few years ago they had some "bad blood" in the South--very bad blood. And if any one will read the transactions in the South during the last few months, he will find that the "bad blood" has not all got out of the South--bad blood stirred up, not by the northern people, but by the southern people themselves.

Now, I do not think there is so much bad blood between the blacks and whites. The gentleman tells us in the next breath that they have the best laborers in the country. Well, if the labor is so good why do you not treat your laborers well? If they are the best class of laborers, if they do so much, why not guarantee to them their rights? If they are good laborers, if they produce your corn and your rice, if they give you such grand products, is it not proper and just that you should accord to them the rights that belong to them in common with other men?

The gentleman said that the slaves lived better than their masters. That is susceptible of grave doubt. I think there is a great difference between hog and hominy in the log cabin and all the luxuries of life in the richly-carpeted mansion. It seems to me there is a great difference when one class bear all the labor and produce all the crops, while the other class ride in their carriages, do all the buying and selling, and pocket all the money.

The gentleman says he wishes to defend "old Virginny. " Now I do not think that Virginia is any better than the rest of the States in this respect. My colleague has already stated that they do not allow colored people to ride in the cars except in cars labeled "Colored people allowed in this car. " "Old Virginny never tires!" In this connection let me bring another fact to the gentleman's notice. Eight or ten months ago a lady acquaintance of mine was traveling from South Carolina to Washington; she had ridden in a first-class car through North Carolina, having paid a first-class fare; but when she got to the gentleman's noble State of "old Virginny, " she was rudely taken and pushed out of the first-class car into the smoking-car, where she was obliged to remain until she passed out of "old Virginny. " It is in this way that they give colored people all their rights and privi-

leges in "old Virginny." It seems to me that such things as
this must make "bad blood for somebody.

But, Mr. Speaker, the gentleman says that this measure is merely an attempt on the part of the people at the
North to continue agitation and strife. Sir, I believe that if
Congress had boldly passed the civil-rights bill a year ago;
if it had let the nation know that the mandates of the highest
authority of the land must be obeyed, there would be no
trouble to-day about the civil-rights bill, nor about "mixed
schools, " etc. The laws of the country would be obeyed.
The trouble is merely that there has been a disposition to
some extent on the part of some republicans to minister to
the prejudices of southern men. Why is it that southern men
make all this ado about schools? I think, Mr. Speaker, you
will find that of all the men who have voted against the civil-
rights bill in the contest that has been going on, there have
been more men from the South than from the North on the
republican side. The trouble arises in that direction.

But gentlemen speak about "bad blood." Sir, the
statistics show--I want to illustrate the manner in which
some of the southern people feel about the "bad blood"--the
statistics show that there are 1, 728, 000 mulattoes in the
South. One would naturally think there was a good deal of
"bad blood" between the two classes--a great deal of unkind
feeling!

Mr. Speaker, I regard the civil-rights bill as among
the best measures that ever came before Congress. Why,
sir, it is at the very foundation of good government. I take
a higher view of the question than that of prejudice between
the two classes. I regard this five million of men, women
and children in the country as an integral part of the country,
interwoven with all its interests. The laboring class of the
South are as much a part of the population of this country as
any other laboring class. The gentleman says that the South
has its laborers. So they have. Very well; why should you
not keep those laborers there? Why are the gentleman's
friends desirous of killing them off? Why do you drive them
from the fields? Why do you drive them from their homes?
A committee of this House tells us the testimony taken before
them shows there are two or three thousand men, women,
and children who have been driven from plantations simply
because the men voted the republican ticket. That is all.
The bad blood of the South comes because the negroes are
republicans. If they would only cease to be republicans, and

vote the straight-out democratic ticket there would be no
trouble.   Then the bad blood would sink entirely out of sight.

Mr. WHITEHEAD.   Will the gentleman permit me to
ask him a single question?

Mr. CAIN.   Certainly.

Mr. WHITEHEAD.   You were speaking of street cars
just now and I should like to say just this in regard to the
street cars in Richmond.   More than four years ago the
street cars of Richmond were thrown open to all classes.
Let me read the authority I have for that statement.

> More than four years ago the street cars of Rich-
> mond were thrown open to all classes.
> JOHN W. WOLTZ.

Mr. RAINEY.   I desire to say to the gentleman
from Virginia I am prepared to give my affidavit that I was
in the State of Virginia less than two years ago, and in the
city of Richmond.   They have cars set apart for the colored
people running in the streets of that city.   I was prohibited
from riding in any other cars than the ones designated for
colored people.

Mr. WHITEHEAD.   I have this to say.   I do not know
what was the cause of the gentleman's being put out of the
ordinary street cars of that city.   The statement I have given
is the statement of Mr. Woltz, a leading republican of the
State of Virginia and the city of Richmond, who is in full
favor now with his party.

Mr. RAINEY.   I do not know whether the gentleman
who representes [sic] the district gives that information or
not, but I state to the gentleman from Virginia exactly what
occurred to myself.

Mr. CAIN.   In less time than that spoken of, the
gentleman from South Carolina, a personal friend of mine,
was thrust from the street cars in Richmond.   He entered a
suit in the courts to recover damages for being thrust out of
those cars, but was afterward prevailed upon to withdraw his
suit.

But, Mr. Speaker, I was about to say this question
of civil-rights is one which ought to be met plainly and fully.

It ought to be made clear and plain to the whole country.
What are you going to do with these people? They are here
and here they are going to stay. We are going to fight it
out on this line if it takes the whole summer. Here we are,
part and parcel of this Union, born here and here we expect
to die.

But, sir, I have no fear for the future. I believe the
time will come when the sense of justice of this nation, when
the enlightenment of this country, when the wisdom of our
legislators, when the good feeling of the whole people will
complete this grand work by lifting up out of degradation a
race of men which has served long and faithfully by placing
it, so far as the laws are concerned, upon an equal footing
with all other classes. I have faith in this country. My
ideas are progressive. I recognize the fact that there has
been a constant progress in the development of ideas in this
country. The great principle which underlies our Government, of liberty, of justice, of right, will eventually prevail
in this land and we shall enjoy equal rights under the laws.
I regret exceedingly, gentlemen, talk of social equality. That
seems to be their great bugaboo. O, if you put colored men
upon an equality before the law they will want social equality! I do not believe a word of it. Do you suppose I would
introduce into my family a class of white men I see in this
country? Do you suppose for one moment I would do it?
No, sir; for there are men even who have positions upon this
floor, and for whom I have respect, but of whom I should be
careful how I introduced them into my family. I should be
afraid indeed their old habits acquired beyond Mason and
Dixon's line might return. No, Mr. Speaker, it is a damn-
able prejudice, the result of the old cursed system of slavery.
It is that which brought about this prejudice and has caused
it to overshadow the whole land. Slavery has left the poison
still in their minds. Slavery and its effects have nearly ex-
pired. It is, to be sure, in its last dying throes. The rude
hand of war opened a cavern into which ran much of the bad
blood spoken of. The stamp of Phil Sheridan's gallant troop-
ers let much more of it out. Before this Congress closes
it will pass the civil-rights bill, giving equal rights and protection to all classes throughout the country. Then indeed,
thank God, the last vestige of that old barbarism will have
disappeared, and peace shall spread her wings over a united,
prosperous, and happy people.

Mr. Speaker, I possibly owe an apology to the House
for these remarks, because I entered the House only twenty

minutes before the gentleman from Virginia (Mr. WHITE-
HEAD) stopped speaking; but I felt it was a duty I owed to
myself and to the race to which I belong to hurl back his
aspersions against the people with whom I am identified, and
whom I have endeavored to vindicate here tonight.

There has been a great cry, Mr. Speaker, about
schools.   Let me give you some statistics bearing upon that
part of the case.   I have been at some pains to look over
the statistics of education in the South, the East, the West,
and the North.   And in the returns of the last census I find
these figures: The number of whites who read throughout the
Union was 6, 412, 246.   The number of colored who read was
172, 779; the difference being 6, 239, 467.   Number of whites
who cannot write, 2, 842, 062.   Colored who cannot write,
2, 778, 515.   I think, so far as the educational clause of the
civil-rights bill is concerned, we shall not lose anything if
it is struck out.   There is more ignorance in proportion in
this country among the whites than there is among the colored.
The prejudice, therefore, against the clause, so far as that
is concerned, will not injure us a great deal after all.   We
could afford for the sake of peace in the republican ranks, if
for nothing else--not as a matter of principle--to except the
school clause.

So far as the grave-yards are concerned, why, we
are not much troubled where we shall be buried.   We know
very well we shall be buried somewhere if we die.   We are
certain of that; somebody will get us out of the way.

Mr. Speaker, I regard it as essential, therefore, that
this bill should pass.   These five millions of people for whom
I speak are waiting for its passage.   Their hopes, their
prospects, their lives to a certain extent depend upon it.
And I think this country owes it to them.   Having lifted them
out of slavery, having emancipated them, having given them
manhood in a sense, I regard it as essential to the interests
of this country that they shall make them citizens of this
country, with all that that word imports, and that they shall
guarantee to them the protection necessary for their lives
and for their property.

It is also necessary, Mr. Speaker, that this bill
should pass that we may go through the length and breadth
of this country without let or hindrance.   I know there are
prejudices; but we must expect that these will exist.   Let
the laws of the country be just; let the laws of the country

be equitable; that is all we ask, and we will take our chances under the laws in this land.   We do not want the laws of this country to make discriminations between us.   Place all citizens upon one broad platform; and if the negro is not qualified to hoe his row in this contest of life, then let him go down.   All we ask of this country is to put no barriers between us, to lay no stumbling blocks in our way, to give us freedom to accomplish our destiny, that we may thus acquire all that is necessary to our interest and welfare in this country.   Do this, sir, and we shall ask nothing more.

CIVIL RIGHTS (February 10, 1875)

We are bound up together in this country--the two
races--no legerdemain can separate us. I do not
care what efforts may be made, we are going to
stick right here. Here we began the work, and
here we are going to stay and finish it. ... You
cannot rub out our manhood by any constitutional
enactment or legislation or by any edict of the governor of a State. We will be men still. ... If it
be decreed that while the Stars and Stripes wave
an American citizen shall be protected on every
soil, we shall claim the same protection as you do.
We are American citizens, with all the rights and
privileges of American citizens, and hence our destiny will be linked with yours in the future.
I hope that the time is not distant ... when liberty
in its true sense will prevail in this country; when
equal and exact justice shall be meted out to all;
when the American people shall have forgotten their
prejudices; when the lapse of ages shall have
washed out forever the virus of slavery from our
hearts; when the genius of liberty with all its glowing beauty shall extend its sway over all this nation; when there shall be no white, no black, no
East, no West, no North, no South, but one common brotherhood and one united people, going forward forever in the progress of nations. (5:1151-
1153)

Mr. CAIN. Mr. Speaker, I presume that every man
sent to the Congress of the United States, from whatever
State or community, ought to have some views upon the great
questions that are now agitating the nation. I confess I have
mine, however humble they may be, and I wish to express
those views in regard to the affairs of this Government. I
had, however, marked out for myself a different line of argument from that to which other gentlemen have addressed
themselves. But so much has been said on the other side
against the policy of the Government, so much against the

66

usurpation of the Executive of the United States, that I am
constrained to say, altering somewhat the language of the
song:

> Woodman, spare the tree,
> Touch not a single bough;
> In slavery it protected me,
> And I'll defend it now.

Sir, it is strange that gentlemen cannot see the true
idea of freedom and liberty. I do not know whether they are
most blinded by their passions or their prejudices. I regret, however, that on these occasions my friend from North
Carolina (Mr. ROBBINS) and myself so often come in contact.
I will, however, pass by his remarks without any special
answer, because his frank expressions of good-will certainly
should extort from me a recognition. Therefore I will say,
so far as his remarks apply to the State of South Carolina
and to myself, that we are in peace and good-will down there.
The only class of persons who are not in peace are those who
are dissatisfied with the Government. Perfect peace reigns
in South Carolina outside of Edgefield County. When gentlemen speak of the ill-feeling existing in the South between the
two classes, I wish to say that I do not know any State in
this Union where there exists a better feeling between the
two classes than in the State of South Carolina. So far as
regards our government, I think it is shown by our last elections, by the inaugural address, and the messages of our
governor, as well as the other reports upon the condition of
affairs there, that to-day South Carolina stands as fair as
any State in the South reconstructed under the laws of Congress. While it is true that much has been done which we
ourselves have regretted, I do not think this is so much our
fault as the fault of others.

But I am happy to say that a great change has come
over us; that within eight years we have learned something;
and our democratic friends in South Carolina have learned
something also. They have learned that, being in a minority, it is a good thing to accept the situation and to recognize
the fact that there is a majority on the other side. This
having been done, we have shaken hands to a certain extent,
and have inaugurated a new era of affairs. A large number
of the best citizens of South Carolina are now members of
the "negro Legislature" (as it is called) of that State. Things
are now going on harmoniously. Hence I do not think there
is much complaint to be made in regard to the condition of
our state.

But, Mr. Speaker, there is another consideration to
which I wish to refer. I regard it as the duty of the nation
to look after the education and development of the masses of
the people who have been thrown upon their own resources by
the great change that has taken place in the country. No
gentleman on this floor fails to recognize the fact that the
more intelligent any class of people are the more easily they
are governed. Hence I desire tonight to express my thoughts
on the importance of education in this country.

I regard it as essential to the welfare of the nation
that there shall be inaugurated a system of education which
shall meet the needs of the vast number of illiterate in this
land. Sir, there is more danger to this country from illit-
eracy than there is from the five million negroes who have
been made free. Possibly the prejudices existing in the
South are the result of the vast mass of ignorance prevailing
not only among the blacks but among the whites as well.
Ignorance and superstition are the parents of almost all the
evils which nations suffer. Hence I desire to dwell upon
this subject of education.

Now, suppose that our friends and our opponents as
well--those who deprecate our emancipation, those who dis-
card the measures of reconstruction as applied to the colored
race--should throw aside their prejudices and say that with
heart and hand and purse they would strive to educate this
great mass of ignorant people, to lift them up by every
means of development, to open the school-house and the
academy, to establish and maintain all the means of educational development; would there not be a great change in the
South and in the country generally?

The complaint of many southern white people and of
some gentlemen on this floor is our ignorance.

I will not tarry, Mr. Speaker, to say anything that
might offend gentlemen on the other side. I will not answer
the remark of the gentleman from North Carolina (Mr. ROB-
BINS) that when the war closed there was not another four
millions of people so well educated as we were. I answered
that last winter, and I now pass it by. It is a sorry picture,
however; a sad commentary on the system of education which
obtained before the war. Why, in the name of Heaven, if
you gave us such a good system of education before the war,
if you gave us such high development of moral worth, as the
gentleman has said, do you now find fault with us for seek-

ing still greater development? Your instructions have not
done us any harm, but then why not continue them? If we
were so well qualified under the system the gentleman speaks
of, why complain now? We have only accepted what you gave
us, and if there is any fault in our education it lies at your
door. Shake not thy gory locks at us; thou canst not say we
did it. Our debasement, whatever it is, and all the evils
which the negro suffers from throughout the land to-day lie
at the doors of those who held us in bondage and withheld us
from the enjoyment of the same rights and privileges which
they themselves enjoyed.

But I wish to speak, Mr. Speaker, of another matter,
and this is in reference to the agricultural interests of the
Southern States. Here we are, and here, as I have said, we
are going to stay. Then what is the best policy to adopt in
order to make us an integral portion of this Union? It is to
seek by every means to lift us up to the level of manhood
and womanhood; to develop our intellects, to develop our resources; to bring out of us that which is within us, to enable
us to accomplish our destiny in this land and add largely to
the welfare of the whole nation.

We are the agriculturists of the South. All the agricultural States of the South are in the hands of the black man.
All acknowledge this. Your rice, your cotton, your tobacco,
all the agricultural productions of the South, are in the main
the fruit of the labor of the colored man. Is it not a fact the
more intelligent operators are, the greater is the relative
production? In other words, intelligent laborers produce
more than those who are not intelligent. This I think is a
truth which everybody will admit. Take the northern mechanics, the northern farmers, the northern machinists; they have
had vast development. They have been wonderfully developed
in science and art; and what has been the result in the North?
The adoption of these measures in the North have developed
the people and have lifted them up to a higher standard of
science and art. Apply the same standard to the negroes of
the South, and in less than two years you will have no reason
to complain of their ignorance or of anarchy, but on the contrary you will be proud of the black man as a citizen of the
United States of America.

No, sir, the system of slavery was antagonistic to
this grand idea of legislation and the development of man.
The more besotted, the more bestial the slave was, the better he was controlled, and vice versa; the more enlightened

the slave, the less he was under control in slavery. It is
just so with the white man. My distinguished friend from
Kentucky (Mr. MILLIKEN) said that human nature was the
same all over the world. That is true; and black human
nature is the same the world over under the same circumstances. Why, five hundred years ago the Norman made the
Saxon his slave, and the latter around his neck wore his
master's collar with his master's name inscribed upon it.
But what is the proud Saxon to-day? What has the Saxon
done in that time? The distinguished statesman, Mr. Pitt,
on one occasion made a notable remark in the House of Par-
liament while discussing the question of the abolition of
slavery in the West Indies. His opponent spoke contemptuously of the negro race, and Pitt then said that--

> It ill becomes an Englishman to talk of the African
> as being a slave, for only three hundred years ago
> your ancestors wore their masters' collars.

But what has the Anglo-Saxon race done since then?
Under the circumstances, gentlemen, under the same influences, enjoying the same privileges, possessed of the same
rights, elevated by the same means, this country will have
no reason to regret the existence of the black men in this
country.

I regard it as essential that the black race should be
encouraged in their progress. What we ask in the South
now, what is our right, is that the white people of the North
should encourage us. I have felt that we were between the
upper and nether millstones to be ground to powder. It is
not an enviable position for any man, white or black, to be
in; but, sir, I see a brighter future. As I have said before,
I have hopes in the future of this nation. We need the same
encouragement the white man needs under the same circumstances. We have human nature, too; we are Americans in
feeling and in sentiment.

The colored people accept the proposition of the gentleman from North Carolina. We need peace. We have no ill-
will toward you. God knows we have reason enough. We
have no disposition other than one of kindness, and we are
disposed to accept what you give us. We only ask you to
give us a chance in the race of life.

My friend from North Carolina (Mr. ROBBINS) said
in the course of his remarks that he was astonished to find

colored men on this floor asking for their liberties now that
they have been made free. The only reason is that they do
not want down in North Carolina to accept the fact that we
are free. We regret that it is necessary for us to come to
the Congress of the United States and to ask them to give us
protection in our liberties. If the kindly feeling in the South
of which we have heard would throw itself around us; if the
law of kindness was exercised toward us; if they guaranteed
to us the free operation of the reconstruction laws; if they
would let us enjoy the privileges guaranteed us by the Constitution of this country, we would have no reason to come
to Congress or anywhere else and ask protection from midnight riders who would shoot us down and burn our cabins.
No; we would have no reason for that.

There are two classes of whites in the South, and I
make a discrimination between them; for I want to say here
that there is a class of white men and women, too, in the
South, noble-hearted, generous-hearted people, for whom I
have now and always will have the greatest respect. Take
the highest classes, the refined classes, and we have no
trouble with them. It is the class of men thrown up by the
war, that rude class depicted by Helper--you who have read
his book know the class of men I mean, the "tar-heels" and
the "sand-hillers, " and the "dirt eaters" of the South--it is
with that class we have all our trouble, and it is from them
we have to get protection. It is that class who ride at night,
who burn school-houses, who drive us from place to place.
It is against that class we have to get some protection.

I regard it, therefore, of importance that we should
have a change in the South. I will say in a word that all the
South wants is peace and good-will, and no class of people
can give us that so readily as the southern people themselves.

I believe that to-day the southern people have in their
own hands the key to unlock all the doors through which will
come peace to this country; and that is by acknowledging the
laws of the country, and obeying the laws of the country, and
letting all men enjoy their God-given rights according to the
dictates of their consciences and the laws of their country.
It is the violation of the laws of the country that makes the
trouble in the South. They do not have it in New York or in
any of the other States where the people accept and obey the
laws. There is no trouble there at all. It is only where
men are in defiance of the laws, and where men are deter-

mined that all classes of people shall not enjoy their rights--
it is there only that we have trouble in the country.

Gentlemen have spoken of Louisiana. Why, sir, just
think of it. Since 1866, for political reasons, there have
been twenty-one hundred and forty-four murders outright,
says General Sheridan, who is good authority; and there have
been twenty-one hundred and fifteen people wounded because
of their political opinions; making forty-two hundred and fifty-
six maimed and murdered on account of their opinions, because they supported the republican party in Louisiana.

The gentleman from North Carolina says they have
accepted the situation. Yes, sir, they have done so; they
have accepted it in a way of their own. They now propose
a change of the constitution of their State, as in the State of
Arkansas they have changed theirs, overturning the government, without regard to any principle of honor, and putting
in their own men to govern according to their own desires.
It is because the revolutionary spirit is abroad that there is
trouble in the South.

I say, then, Mr. Speaker, we want a change of policy
in the South; and I say it would be for the advantage of the
whole country the more readily the southern people accepted
this great fact, that the Government must maintain the rights
of all classes of its people. The more thoroughly they do
this the better it will be for us all. I do not regard this as
a fight against the black man especially. I regard it rather
as a fight against the genius of our institutions. I regard it
as a fight against the reconstruction acts of Congress. I regard it as a fight against the republican party, simply because the republican party has guaranteed to these people
their rights and privileges. The fight is waged against principles and against the party now in power. But the South
needs something else. It wants peace. It wants good-will.
The great need of the South is good-will among its people,
all classes of them. The rights and the value of the working
classes must be recognized. Why, sir, every raid in the
South drives away commerce. Every outrage down there
keeps away capital from the South.

Give the South peace. I wonder the southern people
cannot see that it is for their own advantage to give them
peace, and it will give to their country and to those citizens
all the means of development, all the means of advancement,
all the great measures for the advancement of agriculture,

all the great measures for the refinement of manufactures,
and then the country will be blessed and benefitted by this
change. Without it we cannot have prosperity. Every outrage, every commotion, takes us further away from development and from the measures for our prosperity which right-
fully belong to us.

Why, sir, the Southern States, as has been asserted
here very truly, possess a climate unsurpassed and resources not yet developed; with broad rivers sweeping down
from the mountains to the sea-board; with its vast savannas
all pouring into the breast of the ocean; its resources, which
with God's blessing might be used to make that country
blossom like the rose. Instead of shipping our produce to
New England, we might have factories established where we
could put our raw material and have it manufactured there
into goods which we could ship ourselves to other portions of
the country. To accomplish this we must have capital and
labor. But so long as this constant howl is kept up capital
will not come to the South, and the southern people will
never have an opportunity to develop their resources and to
send forth their commerce to whiten the sea.

This is the trouble with the Southern States. It is that
the spirit of rebellion still reigns there, and as long as that
spirit reigns the Southern States will never be enabled to establish their commerce to advance in commercial prosperity,
or to develop that commerce which is their due. We have
iron ore, we have coal-beds in our Southern States; we have
a vast system of mines which need development. What the
South needs is peace and good-will only. We need some system adopted in the Southern States to bring about these results, and until we attain that we cannot be prosperous, because capital and labor will not come and northern men will
not come within our borders. Capital has no partialities;
and where there is peace then assistance in the shape of capital and labor will come from other States, because it keeps
away from those States those men that would give her success
and prosperity.

Sir, the South must have a change in its sentiments as
relates to this race with a view to its future prosperity; a
rigid and earnest effort by all classes of its population, as
far as possible with any people, to re-establish peace and
thus lay the foundations for a new civilization among that
class against whom this prejudice exists, and on the part of
all classes of men there. The future prosperity, therefore,

of this nation would be advanced by the education and development of this race.

Sir, I have no feeling of unkindness to any class of
men in this country. I look at this subject, I trust, from a
higher stand-point than mere prejudice of race. I have
learned to sink out of sight a race prejudice and to look
higher. Sir, the highest conception of the great duties of
the national character and statesmanship recognize the importance of the unification of these races and classes of
people, and the opening of the doors to them for national
progress and development. I regard the future of our State
and country as important to us, as I said before, as an integral part of the nation.

Sir, I feel a pride that in the Halls of the National
Legislature of the nation I may present my views as a Representative from one of the States, in part, and of five millions of the people of this country. It is an honor to my
conscience to vindicate the rights of the whole people of the
country. In the language of the lamented and martyred Lincoln, "with malice toward none and charity toward all," we
are ready to bury forever out of sight all the asperity and
ill-feeling which have resulted from the recent contest.

Mr. Speaker, I will conclude with this thought: We
are bound up together in this country--the two races--no
legerdemain can separate us. I do not care what efforts
may be made, we are going to stick right here. Here we
began the work, and here we are going to stay and finish it.
I rejoice to-day in this fact, that our democratic friends
cannot succeed without us in the South or our republican
friends either, because we are a part of this nation and you
cannot get rid of us. The same principle that gives the
democrat his liberty gives the black man his liberty also;
the same principle that guarantees the republican in his liberties guarantees the black man also in his rights because
he is a man. You cannot rub out our manhood by any constitutional enactment or legislation or by any edict of the
governnor [sic] of a State. We will be men still.

I want to say in closing that whatever the heated
imagination of men may invent, in whatever movements you
may make for the improvement and development of this
country, the colored race must move with you step by step.
If your commerce, bearing the products of your industry,
whiten the ocean, we shall have our share in those products.

If it be decreed that while the Stars and Stripes wave an
American citizen shall be protected on every soil, we shall
claim the same protection as you do. We are American citizens, with all the rights and privileges of American citizens,
and hence our destiny will be linked with yours in the future.

I hope that the time is not distant when our friends
upon the other side will see as we see; when our friends
upon this side will see as we see; when liberty in its true
sense will prevail in this country; when equal and exact justice shall be meted out to all; when the American people
shall have forgotten their prejudices; when the lapse of ages
shall have washed out forever the virus of slavery from our
hearts; when the genius of liberty with all its glowing beauty
shall extend its sway over all this nation; when there shall
be no white, no black, no East, no West, no North, no
South, but one common brotherhood and one united people,
going forward forever in the progress of nations.

BIBLIOGRAPHY

1. Biographical Directory of the American Congress 1774-
    1971. Washington, D. C. : United States Government
    Printing Office, 1971.

2. U. S. Congress. House. Civil Rights Bill. 43rd Con-
    gress, 1st session, 1874.

3. U. S Congress. House. Civil Rights Bill. 43rd Con-
    gress, 1st session, 1874.

4. U. S. Congress. House. Civil Rights Bill. 43rd Con-
    gress, 2nd session, 1875.

5. U. S. Congress. House. Civil Rights Bill. 43rd Con-
    gress, 2nd session, 1875.

Robert Carlos DeLarge

IV. ROBERT CARLOS DeLARGE

DeLarge, Robert Carlos, a Representative from South Carolina; born in Aiken, S. C. March 15, 1842; was of the Negro race; received such education as was then attainable and was graduated from Wood High School; engaged in agricultural pursuits; delegate to the State constitutional convention in 1868; member of the State house of representatives, 1868-1870; was one of the State commissioners of the sinking fund; elected State land commissioner; presented credentials as a Republican member-elect to the Forty-Second Congress and served from March 4, 1871 until January 24, 1873, when the seat was declared vacant, the election having been contested by Christopher C. Bowen; local Magistrate until his death in Charleston, S. C., February 14, 1874 (1:845).

ENFORCEMENT OF FOURTEENTH AMENDMENT

... allow me to make a suggestion.... while
legislation is necessary, yet unless they are ready
to concede along with this legislation for the protection of the loyal people of the South some accompanying measure to go hand in hand with this
and remove as far as in our power rests some of
the evils that have brought about the existing condition of things, neither this legislation nor any
other that you may pass from now until the hour
of doom will be of any benefit.   (2:appendix)

Mr. DeLARGE.   Mr. Speaker, I had supposed that in
the consideration of this matter of legislation for the South,
party lines would not have been so distinctly drawn, but that
we would have at least first endeavored to ascertain whether
or not there was any necessity for the legislation, and then
decide what kind of legislation would be best.   I say I did
not expect that party lines would be drawn so distinctly while
considering a matter of such grave import.

I believe that if there was a single gentleman upon
the floor of this House who, before the commencement of
this debate, doubted that lawlessness, confusion, and anarchy
existed in some portions of the South, he is at least cured
of that doubt by this time.   Gentlemen upon both sides of the
House have in their speeches acknowledged, and, by the evidence produced, proven to my satisfaction, and I believe, to
the satisfaction of a majority of the members of this House,
that such a state of affairs does exist in some portions of
the southern States.

I am free to say that none can bring the charge to my
door of ever having acted in a manner that would be termed
illiberal.   I am also free to say that I, like other gentlemen
upon the floor of this House, have the honor of representing
a district in which no case of outlawry has ever occurred.
Since the time of reconstruction no outrage has been committed in my district; and I say frankly to you to-day that

until within the last few months no one upon the face of God's earth could have convinced me that any secret organization existed in my State for the purpose of committing murder, arson, or other outrages upon the lives, liberty, and property of the people; and, sir, I sincerely deplore and lament the abundance of that evidence which so plainly proves the existence of such an organization to-day. Would to God, sir, that the fair fame of the State of my birth, and which I have the honor in part to represent, had not been marred by the wicked deeds of these outlaws, who shrink from no cruelty, who spare no sex nor station to carry out their devilish purposes.

But, sir, I cannot shut my eyes to facts; I cannot refuse to yield my faith to tales of horror so fully proven; and I am thoroughly convinced that it is necessary to do something to cure these awful wrongs. I am free to admit that neither the Republicans of my State nor the Democrats of that State can shake their garments and say that they have had no hand in bringing about this condition of affairs. Both parties are responsible for it. As a member of the Republican party I may state, while demanding legislation on behalf of all the citizens there, that both parties to a considerable extent are responsible for this condition of things. Sir, it is necessary that we should legislate upon this subject. The Governor of my State has called upon the Executive of this country for assistance and protection. He has stated distinctly in that call that he is unable to preserve the public peace in some districts of that State. That is something which we must all admit. That is not denied by the Democrats of South Carolina. Some of them doubtless rejoice in this, because they can throw the blame, as they think, upon the administration of the State, which is in the hands of their political foes. It is not now the question, what is the cause which has brought about this condition of affairs? It is useless, except for the purpose of gaining partisan credit or fixing partisan odium, now to charge the blame here or there. But, sir, the naked facts state us in the face, that this condition of affairs does exist, and that it is necessary for the strong arm of the law to interpose and protect the people in their lives, liberty, and property.

Just here allow me to make a suggestion. If the gentlemen on this side of the House propose to legislate for the benefit of the people of the South, I tell them, and say it fully conscious of the responsibility that rests upon me in saying it, that while legislation is necessary, yet unless they

are ready to concede along with this legislation for the protection of the loyal people of the South some accompanying
measure to go hand in hand with this and remove as far as
in our power rests some of the evils that have brought about
the existing condition of things, neither this legislation nor
any other that you may pass from now until the hour of
doom will be of any benefit. I speak knowing what I say.

Mr. Speaker, when the Governor of my State the other
day called in council the leading men of that State, to consider the condition of affairs there and to advise what measure would be best for the protection of the people, whom
did he call together? The major portion of the men whom
he convened were men resting under political disabilities imposed by the fourteenth amendment. In good faith I ask
gentlemen on this side of the House, and gentlemen on the
other side, whether it is reasonable to expect that these men
should be interested, in any shape or form, in using their
influence and best endeavors for the preservation of the public peace, when they have nothing to look for politically in
the future? You say they should have the moral and material interest of their State at heart, though even always to be
denied a participation in its honors. You may insist that the
true patriot seeks no personal ends in the acts of patriotism.
All this is true; but, Mr. Speaker, men are but men everywhere, and you ought not to expect of those whom you daily
call by opprobrious epithets, whom you persistently exclude
from places of the smallest trust in the Government you have
created, to be very earnest to cooperate with you in the work
of establishing and fortifying governments set up in hostility
to the whole tone of their prejudices, their convictions, and
their sympathies. What ought to be is one thing, what in the
weakness and fallibility of human nature will be is quite another thing. The statesman regards the actual and acts upon
it; the desirable, the possible, and even the probable fur-
nishes but poor basis for political action.

If I had time I would enumerate some of the causes
which have brought about the existing state of affairs. I am
not here to apologize for murderers; I am not here to defend anyone who has committed any act of impropriety or
wrong. But, sir, it is a fact, I do not give it as any or
even the slightest excuse for the Democrats of my State, who,
by their influence secretly or by joining in armed organization, have brought about this condition of affairs--it is a
fact, unfortunately for us, that our party has done some
things which give color to the charge that it is responsible
to some degree for the evils which afflict us.

When I heard the gentleman from New York (Mr.
COX) on Tuesday last hurl his shafts against the members of
my race, charging that through their ignorance they had
brought about these excesses, I thought he should have remembered that for the ignorance of that portion of the people
he and his party associates are responsible, not those people
themselves. While there may have been extravagance and
corruption resulting from the placing of improper men in official positions--and this is part of the cause of the existing
state of things--these evils have been brought about by men
identified with the race to which the gentleman from New York
belongs, and not by our race.

Many men like himself, in order to get a better position in society or officially, came down among us, and, not
knowing them, we placed them in position. If we, through
ignorance, have placed them in position, have placed them in
power, and they have deceived us, it is no fault of ours. In
this connection I desire to have read a part of the remarks
of the gentleman from New York on Tuesday last.

The Clerk read as follows:

> South Carolina has been infested by the worst
> local government ever vouchsafed to a people. Ig-
> norance, bribery and corruption are common in her
> Legislature. Bonds by the million are issued, the
> public debt increased, and nothing to show for it.
> The debt in 1860 was but $3,691,574. It was last
> year $11,429,711; and this year no one knows
> whether it is twenty or thirty millions nor how
> much is counterfeit or genuine! Her rulers con-
> trived new burdens in order to blunder more. On
> a full valuation of real and personal property of
> $183,913,367 the people pay this year sixteen mills
> on the dollar as a State tax and four mills county
> tax.
> This is for 1870 and 1871, and amounts in all to
> $4,095,047, to which $300,000 is to be added for
> poll tax. In other words, the value of the property
> is reduced from $489,000,000 before the war to
> $188,000,000 and the tax raised from $400,000 to
> $4,230,000, or ten times as much. It is two and
> a half per cent on a full valuation, and only chronic
> insecurity and disorder as the consideration! This
> is done by those who pay no taxes, who squander
> what is paid, who use the means to arm negro

militia and create a situation of terror, from which
men rush into secret societies for defense of
homes, mothers, sisters, wives, and children.
Add to these grievances the intolerable exactions
of the Federal Government, not only in taxes, but
in laws, and it should give us pause before we
place that people at the mercy of an inferior race,
a vindictive party, a court-martial, and a hostile
President. The people in their agony in that State
actually clamored for United States troops to save
them from the rapacity and murder of the negro
bands and their white allies. Can we not understand why men, born free, should rise, or, if not
rise with safety, that they are compelled to hide in
Ku Klux or other secret clans, and strike against
this ruin and desolation, peculation and violence,
and that, too, when it is done by those who are not
of their race and but lately in their midst?

Mr. DeLARGE. I desire to correct the statement
made by the gentleman from New York, that the State tax of
South Carolina for 1870 is only nine mills on the dollar, for
1871, seven mills, not, as he states, sixteen mills. I have
already alluded to the ignorance referred to in the gentleman's remarks. Before closing I desire to say that I hope
the House will adopt the substitute of the gentleman from
Ohio. I am prepared to vote for that substitute, while I am
free to admit that I did not intend to vote for the bill as
originally reported.

BIBLIOGRAPHY

1. Biographical Directory of the American Congress 1774-
    1971. Washington, D.C.: United States Government
    Printing Office, 1971.

2. U.S. Congress. House. Enforcement of Fourteenth
    Amendment. 42nd Congress, 1st session, 1871.

V. ROBERT BROWN ELLIOT

Elliot, Robert Brown, a Representative from South Carolina; born in Boston, Massachusetts, August 11, 1842; was of the Negro race; attended High Holborn Academy, London, England, in 1853, and was graduated from Eton College, England in 1859; studied law; was admitted to the bar and practiced in Columbia, South Carolina; member of the State constitutional convention in 1868; member of the State house of representatives from July 6, 1868 to October 23, 1870; assistant adjutant general of South Carolina, 1869-1871; elected as a Republican to the 42nd and 43rd Congresses and served from March 4, 1871 until his resignation, effective November 1, 1874; again a member of the State house of representatives, 1874-1878, and served as a speaker; unsuccessful candidate for election as attorney general of South Carolina in 1876; moved to New Orleans, Louisiana in 1881 and practiced law until his death there on August 9, 1884 (1:908).

Robert B. Elliot --"In the Halls of Congress he held the Representatives spellbound by his eloquence. He was a born leader and made so by indomitable will and untiring energy." (South Carolina Plain Dealer, quoted in Moseley, p. 33)

REMOVAL OF POLITICAL DISABILITIES

Sir, I say that this removal would be injurious,
not only to the loyal men of the South, but to the
Government itself. To relieve those men of their
disabilities at this time would be regarded by the
loyal men of the South as an evidence of the weakness of this great Government, and of an intention
on the part of this Congress to foster the men who
to-day are outraging the good and loyal people of
the South. It would be further taken as evidence
of the fact that this Congress desires to hand over
the loyal men of the South to the tender mercies
of the rebels who to-day are murdering and scourging the loyal men of the Southern States. (2:102-
103)

Mr. ELLIOT. Mr. Speaker, the House now has under
consideration a bill of vast importance to the people of the
section that I have the honor in part to represent. It is a
proposition to remove the political disabilities of persons
lately engaged in rebellion against the sovereignty of the
Government of the United States. I believe, sir, that I have
been noted in the State from which I come as one entertain-
ing liberal views upon this very question; but, sir, at a time
like this, when I turn my eyes to the South and see the loyal
men of that section of the country suffering at the hands of
the very men whom it is proposed today by this Forty-
Second Congress of the United States to relieve of their political disabilities, I must here and now enter my solemn
protest against any such proposition.

Sir, it is nothing but an attempt to pay a premium
for disloyalty and treason at the expense of loyalty. I am
not surprised that the gentleman from Kentucky should introduce such a proposition here. It was due to the class of
men that it is proposed to relieve that such a proposition
should come from the gentleman from Kentucky and gentlemen upon that side of the House. I can appreciate the feeling of sympathy that the gentleman from Kentucky entertains

85

for these men in the South who are to-day prohibited from
holding Federal offices. They are his allies. They are his
compatriots. They are to-day disfranchised simply because
they rushed madly into rebellion against this, the best Government that exists under heaven, at their own instance, with
the advice, and with the consent of such gentlemen as the
gentleman from Kentucky. But when I hear gentlemen like
the gentleman from Illionis (Mr. FARNSWORTH), who spoke
upon this question on Friday last, advance views and opinions
such as that gentleman then advanced I must be allowed to
express my surprise, ay, sir, my regret, that at this time
such words should fall from the lips of a man whom I have
been taught long to regard as one of those who are unflinch-
ing in their devotion to the cause of liberty and the preservation and maintenance of this great Government.

The gentleman from Illinois (Mr. FARNSWORTH) took
occasion, in his argument on Friday last, to compare the
condition of the man who is to-day disfranchised and the man
who is allowed to hold office in the South. He drew a parallel between the disfranchised old man and his servant, or
slave, who to-day holds office or may do so. He tells you
that you should take into consideration the condition of this
poor old man who, because he simply happened to join the
rebellion after having taken an oath to support the Constitution of the Government of the United States, is prohibited
from holding office, while his slave is allowed to hold office
under the State and the United States governments. Ay, sir,
the reason of this difference between the political status of
the two is simply this: that while this old man, with whom
the gentleman from Illinois sympathizes in his heart, was
rebellious against the Government which had fostered and
sustained and protected him, his slave was loyal to that Government, loyal to its Army, and loved its flag, which the
man who had been reared under it, who had been fostered
and protected by it, had learned only to despise. The difference is this: that while that "poor old man, " of whom the
gentleman speaks so sympathizingly, would only curse the
Government, would only ill-treat and murder its loyal adherents, the slave was the friend of that Government, and
the protector and defender of those who are endeavoring to
uphold it.

In discussing this question, and as a reason why this
bill should pass, the gentleman from Illinois (Mr. FARNS-
WORTH) stated that the removal of disabilities would do good,
and that to maintain those disabilities could effect no good

purpose.   Sir, I say that this removal would be injurious,
not only to the loyal men of the South, but to the Government itself.   To relieve those men of their disabilities at
this time would be regarded by the loyal men of the South
as an evidence of the weakness of this great Government, and
of an intention on the part of this Congress to foster the men
who to-day are outraging the good and loyal people of the
South.   It would be further taken as evidence of the fact that
this Congress desires to hand over the loyal men of the South
to the tender mercies of the rebels who to-day are murdering
and scourging the loyal men of the southern States.

        The gentleman from Illinois, in his argument, was
pleased to ask this question, which he proposed to answer
himself: are these men who are disfranchised and prohibited
from holding offices the men who commit the murders and
outrages of which complaint is made?   And his answer to that
question was that they are not.   But permit me to say to that
gentleman that those men are responsible for every murder,
responsible for every species of outrage that is committed in
the South.   They are men who, by their evil example, by
their denunciations of Congress, by their abuse of the President of the United States, and of all connected with this Government, have encouraged, aided, and abetted the men who
commit these deeds.   They contribute to this state of things
by their social influence, by their money and the money sent
from the northern States--money furnished by Tammany Hall
for the purpose of keeping up these outrages in order to insure a Democratic triumph in the South in 1872.

        And I am here to-day to tell you, in the name of the
loyal men of the South, that it is the fact that money is sent
to the South by the Democratic party of the North to aid these
men in keeping up this state of lawlessness for the purpose
of overawing the loyal people there and preventing them from
expressing their preferences at the ballot; that the number of
arms shipped to the southern States, and which are brought
there upon every New York steamer that arrives, is an evidence of the fact that these men who have the means, who
have the influence, are responsible for these outrages, and
not the poor, miserable tools who are their instruments in
carrying them out.

        I ask this House, I ask gentlemen on this side es-
pecially, whether they are willing to join hands with those
who propose to-day to relieve these men of their disabilities?
Are they willing to tell the loyal men of the South, whose

only offense is that they have been true to the Government,
that they have sustained Congress in its just and lawful acts,
that they have maintained the authority of Congress; are
gentlemen willing to tell these loyal men that Congress is not
disposed to protect them, but, on the contrary, is willing at
their expense to pay a premium for disloyalty?

Sir, I speak not to-day in behalf of the colored loyalists of the South alone. I wish it to be distinctly understood
that I represent here a constituency composed of men whose
complexions are like those of gentlemen around me as well
as men whose complexions are similar to my own. I represent a constituency as loyal as the constituency of any other
gentleman upon this floor. Those men appeal to you to-day
to do justice to them. They ask you to protect them by
legislation, instead of placing them under the heel of those
men who have ruled in the South with an iron hand since the
reconstruction acts were passed. Sir, I come here backed
up by a majority as large probably as that of any gentleman
on this floor; I come here representing a Republican district; but unless this Congress will aid those loyal men of
the South, unless, instead of passing propositions of this
kind, it will turn its attention, and that speedily, to the protection of property and life in the South, the Republican party
in this House cannot expect the support of those whom I
represent.

ENFORCEMENT OF THE FOURTEENTH AMENDMENT

I do not wish to be understood as speaking for the
colored man alone when I demand instant protection
for loyal men of the South. No, sir, my demand
is not so restricted.... twelve thousand ... white
men ... voted the Republican ticket ... This class
have discovered that the same beneficent system
that emancipates the laborer of the one race secures the freedom of the other. They understand
that the shackle that bound the arms of the black
man threw a deep shadow on the path of the laboring white. The white Republican of the South is
also hunted down and murdered or scourged for his
opinion's sake, and during the past two years more
than six hundred loyal men of both races have
perished.... I trust, sir, that this bill will pass
quickly, and be quickly enforced. (3:389-392)

Mr. ELLIOT. Mr. Speaker, the argument upon the
pending bill has proceeded thus far upon a question of constitutional law and a question of fact. The opponents of the
bill deny that its provisions are warranted by the Constitution
of the United States, and also deny the alleged facts upon
which the proposed bill is founded. The probable efficacy of
the bill, as a measure of relief and protection for the loyal
men of the South from the extraordinary system of oppression
to which they are now subjected, has not been assailed.

I shall therefore confine myself to a necessarily brief
consideration of the law and the facts. I will endeavor to
prove that the pending bill is not obnoxious to the spirit of
the Constitution, and that it is founded in right reason, and
that, as a measure of repression and protection, this bill is
not only fully warranted, but it is imperatively demanded by
the present posture of affairs in the southern States. The
issue of constitutional law evolved thus far by the discussion
of the bill resolves itself into the question, has the Government of the United States the right under the Constitution, to
protect a citizen of the United States in the exercise of his

89

vested rights as an American citizen by the exercise of a
direct force through its Army and Navy, or the assertion of
immediate jurisdiction through its courts, without the appeal
or agency of the State in which the citizen is domiciled?
Those who oppose this bill answer this question in the negative, founding their opposition on section four, article four
of the Constitution, which the gentleman from Indiana (Mr.
KERR) made the burden of his very able and elaborate but
specious argument the other day upon this subject.   This,
then, in the judgment of our opponents, is the pivot upon
which this whole matter revolves, and to this point I shall
address myself at the outset.

The language of the section which the gentleman from
Indiana has made the substratum of his ingenious argument
is as follows:

> The United States shall guaranty to every State in
> this Union a republican form of government, and
> shall protect each of them against invasion, and on
> application of the Legislature, or of the Executive
> (when the Legislature cannot be convened), against
> domestic violence.

Upon this the gentleman from Indiana observes:

> The obligation of the Federal Government to pro-
> tect the States of this Union against invasion is
> clear and obvious; and it interferes with no ques-
> tion of State jurisdiction or of State autonomy. It
> is external to the State itself; it is protection
> against dangers from without, not within.

In this interpretation I fully concur with him, and I
also agree with him that the term "domestic violence" refers
to a force exerted within the State, as the term "invasion"
relates to a power moving from without.   But, sir, I totally
dissent from the conclusion of the gentleman that this clause--

>
> Is intended only to make it the duty of the Federal
> Government to go to the relief of the States of the
> Union against domestic violence when the States ap-
> peal for such aid, being unable by their own powers
> to maintain the public order, to protect themselves
> and their citizens, and enforce their laws in the
> peaceful course of administration.

I deny that it forbids Federal interposition except

upon the call of the Executive or Legislature of the State. It is a sound maxim of the law that where a power is given, the necessary means for its execution are implied. .

In this case the duty imposed upon the Federal Government is to protect the States "against domestic violence." The clause is not inhibitory but mandatory. It was evidently not designed to restrict the rights, but to enlarge the duties of the Government. Hence, when it declares that the Government shall protect the States against domestic violence on application of the Legislature, or of the Executive, when the Legislature cannot be convened, it means not that such "application" shall always be an essential condition-precedent, but simply estops the United States from refusing to give protection when the application is made. Otherwise a faithless and undutiful Executive, giving his personal aid to or covertly bestowing his official sanction upon the insurgent authors of the "domestic violence," might, by withholding his "application," render the Government of the United States a torpid and paralyzed spectator of the oppression of its citizens and the violent dissolution of the State by the overthrow of the authorities constituted pursuant to its organic law.

Those who defend this construction and its logical consequences imitate, in their ideas of governmental duty, but on a grander and graver scale, the rigid etiquette of the Frenchman, who, on being upbraided for not saving the life of a fellow-passenger whom he saw drown before his eyes, attempted to justify himself by pleading that he had "not been introduced to him." No, sir; there are paramount duties devolved upon individuals and upon Governments that in the very nature of things demand prompt performance. No broader or clearer vindication of this view is required than that found in the noble preamble to the Constitution itself, which declares that:

> We, the people of the United States, in order to form a more perfect Union, establish justice, insure domestic tranquility, provide for the common defense, promote the general welfare, and secure the blessings of liberty to ourselves and our posterity, do ordain and establish this Constitution for the United States of America.

How, sir, shall one of the great objects of the Constitution, the securing "the blessings of liberty to ourselves and our posterity," be achieved if it be true, as virtually

contended by the opponents of this bill, that the majority of
the citizens of a State may, by domestic violence, be deprived of "the blessings of liberty, " and yet the Federal
Government, established chiefly for this object, shall remain
as passive observer of the great crime against its fundamental law unless invited to "protect" its own citizens by the
"Executive" of the State?

That it is not a very violent presumption that the majority of the people of a State may be oppressively subordi-
nated to the minority through "domestic violence" is shown
by the following remarks of Justice Story in his comments
upon this very section, in the forty-first chapter of his great
work upon the Constitution, a work to which the gentleman
from Indiana frequently recurred with profound reverence
throughout his cogent effort to "make the worse appear the
better cause. " I think that to quote Justice Story in defense
of the position assumed by the gentleman from Indiana and
his political coactors on this floor is to "steal the livery of
Heaven to serve the devil in. " Says Justice Story:

> At first view it might seem not to square with the
> Republican theory to suppose, either that a majority
> have not the right, or that a minority will have the
> force, to subvert a government, and, consequently,
> that the Federal interposition can never be re-
> quired but when it would be improper. But theo-
> retic reasoning in this, as in most other cases,
> must be qualified by the lessons of practice. Why
> may not illicit combinations for purposes of vio-
> lence be formed, as well by a majority of a State,
> especially a small State, as by a majority of a
> county or a district of the same State; and if the
> authority of the State ought in the latter case to
> protect the local magistracy, ought not the Federal
> authority in the former to support the State author-
> ity? Besides, there are certain parts of the State
> constitutions which are so interwoven with the Fed-
> eral Constitution that a violent blow cannot be given
> to the one without communicating the wound to the
> other. Insurrections in a State will rarely induce
> a Federal interposition, unless the number con-
> cerned in them bear some proportion to the friends
> of government. It will be much better that the
> violence in such cases should be repressed by the
> superintending power than that the majority should
> be left to maintain their cause by a bloody and

obstinate contest. The existence of a right to interpose will generally prevent the necessity of
exerting it.

Is it true that force and right are necessarily on
the same side in republican Governments? May not
the minor party possess such a superiority of
pecuniary resources, of military talents and experience, or of secret succors from foreign Powers as
will render it superior also in an appeal to the
sword? May not a more compact and advantageous
position turn the scale on the same side against a
superior number so situated as to be less capable
of a prompt and collected exertion of its strength?
Nothing can be more chimerical than to imagine
that, in a trial of actual force, victory may be calculated by the rules which prevail in a census of
the inhabitants or which determine the event of an
election. May it not happen, in fine, that the
minority of citizens may become a majority of persons by the accession of alien residents, of a casual concourse of adventurers, or of those whom
the constitution of the State has not admitted to the
rights of suffrage?

****

In cases where it may be doubtful on which side
justice lies, what better umpires could be desired
by two violent factions, flying to arms and tearing
the State to pieces, than the representatives of
confederate States, not heated by the local flame?
To the impartiality of judges they would unite the
affection of friends. Happy would it be, if such a
remedy for its infirmities could be enjoyed by all
free Governments; if a project equally effectual
could be established for the universal peace of
mankind?

It is worthy of remark, Mr. Speaker, that the gentleman from Indiana, in treating this section of the Constitution,
which he has made the text of the most fervid portion of his
able but ill-timed speech, should have omitted all notice of
its opening, and, in this discussion, its most pregnant clause.
I refer to the words:

The United States shall guaranty to every State in
this Union a republican form of government.

Here, then, sir, is a duty imposed without a condition-precedent, even under the very strict construction asserted by the gentleman from Indiana.   The mandate is absolute, recognizing and permitting no discretion, either in the
State or the United States.   It vests in the Federal Government the right to act in the premises, whenever, in its judgment, "a republican form of government" may be endangered
in a "State in this Union" from whatever cause, whether by
"invasion" or "domestic violence. "

To make this clear, let us consider what is "a republican form of government" within the meaning of the Constitution?   To furnish a substantial and comprehensive definition of this term, we need not consult the publicists.   It
must be defined by its attributes.   It is a government having
a written constitution, or organic law, which provides that its
executive and legislative functions shall be exercised by persons elected by the majority of its citizens.   In other words,
it is a government for the people and by the people.

Assuming this definition to be correct in substance, I
ask, how can a republican government be maintained in a
State if the majority of the electors are prevented from exercising the elective franchise by force of arms, or if members of the majority, having thus exercised it according to
their consciences, are, for that cause, put in terror and subjected to murder, exile, and the lash, through "domestic
violence, " organized and operated by the minority for the
sole purpose of acquiring a political domination in the State?
To deny that it would be the absolute and unconditional right
and duty of the United States to intervene for the protection
of its citizens "against domestic violence" thus directed, in
advance of the "application of the Executive" of a State, and
even in defiance of his expressed will, would be to make the
United States an absolute guarantor of a "republican form of
government" "to every State in this Union, " and yet deprive
the United States of the power to determine when to execute
its "guarantee, " or, in other words, when the "republican
form of government, " which it has guaranteed, is endangered.
To argue thus is to violate every sound principle of legal and
logical interpretation, and to suppose a great wrong without a
remedy in our political system.   Upon this point I commend
to the gentleman's attention the following from Story on the
Constitution (chapter forty-one, pages 559, 560).   Says
Justice Story:

The want of a provision of this nature was felt as

a capital defect in the plan of the Confederation, as it might, in its consequences, endanger, if not overthrow, the Union. Without a guarantee the assistance to be derived from the national Government in repelling domestic dangers which might threaten the existence of the State Constitutions could not be demanded as a right from the national Government. Usurpation might raise its standard and trample upon the liberties of the people, while the national Government could legally do nothing more than behold the encroachments with indignation and regret. A successful faction might erect a tyranny on the ruins of order and law, while no succor could be constitutionally afforded by the Union to the friends and supporters of the Government. But this is not all. The destruction of the national Government itself, or of neighboring States might result from a successful rebellion in a single State. Who can determine what would have been the issue if the insurrection in Massachusetts in 1787 had been successful, and the malcontents had been headed by a Caesar or a Cromwell? If a despotic or monarchical government were established in one State, it would bring on the ruin of the whole Republic.

It may possibly be asked, what need there could be of such a precaution, and whether it may not become a pretext for alterations in the State governments, without the concurrence of the States themselves? These questions admit of ready answers. If the interposition of the General Government should not be needed, the provision for such an event will be a harmless superfluity only in the Constitution. But who can say what experiments may be produced by the caprice of particular States, by the ambition of enterprising leaders, or by the intrigues and influence of foreign Powers?

But, sir, if the view that I present, sustained as it is by invincible reasons and fortified by high authority, be not denied, then is the principle that underlies this bill admitted to be constitutionally right.

But the Constitution has not left to implication, however clear, the right of the Federal Government to enforce its "guarantee," for it declares, in article one, section eight, that--

> The Congress shall have power to make all laws
> which shall be necessary and proper for carrying
> into execution the foregoing powers, and all other
> powers vested by this Constitution in the Govern-
> ment of the United States, or in any department or
> officer thereof.

I shall not reiterate the argument already so exhaustively applied, as derived from the fourteenth amendment,
which this bill is declaredly designed to enforce. I would
only call attention to section five of that article, which declares:

> The Congress shall have power to enforce by ap-
> propriate legislation the provisions of this article.

Is not this bill "appropriate legislation?" I appre-
hend, Mr. Speaker, that it is obnoxious to the Democratic
party chiefly because it is "appropriate," and strikes at the
homicidal proclivities which have become chronic among the
active allies of that party in its late exclusive empire, the
so-called confederate States. Indeed, I may say in the apt
language of the poet, without intending any personal dis-
respect--

> No man e'er felt the halter draw
> With good opinion of the law.

But, sir, the right of the loyal people of the South to
have this or some similar measure enacted into a law for
their protection against the perils that environ them is derived from the same consideration in which the Constitution
itself originated, and is founded on an integral principle that
enters in the very idea of government, whether it relates to
subject or citizen. I mean the great paramount duty of the
Republic to protect its citizens wherever its flag has the
right to wave. Indeed, sir, when you abolish or weaken the
right to protection you destroy or diminish the duty of allegiance. I am bound to obey my country and her laws because
I am by them protected. When they cease to protect me I
can rightly cease to obey them. Says Blackstone:

> Allegiance is the duty of all subjects, being the
> reciprocal tie of the people to the prince in return
> for the protection he affords them.

More especially should allegiance and protection be

correlatives when the very danger from which protection is needed is drawn and incurred on the part of the citizens solely because of his loyalty to the Government, at whose hands that protection is demanded.

Sir, the best Government is that under which the humblest citizen is not beneath the protection of the laws, or the highest above the reach of their authority.

But gentlemen, admitting the plain principle of constitutional and governmental law herein enunciated, may deny, and do deny, that the facts exist to warrant an armed intervention of the Federal Government for the protection of its citizens, or any extraordinary legislation investing Federal courts with a novel jurisdiction to enforce that protection through judicial agencies. Thus the gentleman from Indiana, with a skepticism worthy of Zeno himself, declares that--

> It is a gross perversion of truth to assume that any desire or intention to excite rebellion exists anywhere in the country. It is simply dishonest, and is indulged for interested purposes. The utmost extent of insubordination is confined to a very small number of persons, and they are in a few localities. They are merely common criminals, without politics or higher motives of action than the base aims of individual offenders.

Here, then, we have a square issue of fact, and I propose to meet it with incontestable record. In so doing I shall expose the animus of the Democratic party of the South, as evidenced in the utterances of its recognized organs and leaders, as far back as 1868, coincident with the assembly of constitutional conventions in the South, pursuant to the reconstruction acts of Congress. This record, drawn from many States, exhibits the declared purpose to defeat the ballot with the bullet and other coercive means, and also the acts of organized lawlessness perpetrated pursuant to that purpose.

I will now ask you to listen to the words of the Mobile Register, a Democratic witness, whose credibility will not be impeached by gentlemen on the other side of the House. In the month of July, 1868, that paper, in an editorial advocating the election of Seymour and Blair, gave utterance to these words:

> The Radicals are dogs and should be treated as
> dogs.   They should not be permitted to dwell
> among us.

Hear the voice of the central Democratic committee of
Charleston, in their campaign circular of 1868, entitled "An
appeal to the colored people. "   In advising the colored men
of the State to sever their connection with the Republican
party, and join the Seymour and Blair Democratic clubs, they
used these words:

> We know who your leaders are, what they say and
> what they are doing; we have marked them, and we
> know better than you know the sure and swift
> penalty that shall fall on particular heads when the
> conflict begins.

Hearken for a moment to the utterance of ex-United
States Senator Robert Toombs, of Georgia, on the hustings
during that canvass.   He says, in speaking of the Republicans of that State, "Ostracize them; drive them out; spurn
them from your midst. "   Listen, sir, to the following extract
from a communication which appeared in the Newberry (South
Carolina (Herald), signed "Silverstreet Democrat, "   and dated
July 17, 1868:

> Messrs. EDITORS: As a member of a Democratic
> club.   I beg leave, through the Herald, to make a
> suggestion or two to the various clubs throughout
> Newberry district.   Our situation as a people--I
> mean white people--must surely be understood by
> every thinking man; and certainly any suggestion
> that can be made in which there can be any hope of
> advancing our interests ought to be tested.   The
> propositions that I would make are as follows: let
> all members of the different Democratic clubs of
> the district enter into a solemn agreement that from
> the present time forward they will employ no me-
> chanic who does not belong to some Democratic or-
> ganization, neither to patronize any mill, tannery,
> or other place dependent upon the public patronage,
> owned or superintended by any other than an out-
> and-out Democrat.   Let all physicians belonging to
> such organizations have a positive understanding
> with each other that in no case will they attend pro-
> fessionally to any Radical or his family unless the
> medical fee is sent with the messenger; but in case

> the patient be a freedman belonging to some Demo-
> cratic club, let him be attended or half price, and
> if he has not money indulge him until he has.   Let
> lawyers act upon the same principle.   Let all freed-
> men that are not mechanics even, who take an
> active part for the Radical party, be treated as
> suggested above for mechanics.

And, sir, not only was this the sentiment of this individual, "Silverstreet Democrat, " but it was the prevailing
sentiment of Democratic employers and professional men
throughout the State.

Again, sir, let me invite a moment's attention to the
following:

> Frog Level Club. --At a meeting of the Democratic
> club of Frog Level, held July 25, 1868, the follow-
> ing resolutions were presented and adopted:
>   Resolved.   That we do approve the declaration
> of principles as set forth by the national Demo-
> cratic convention at New York, and do cordially
> ratify the nomination of Horatio Seymour for Pres-
> ident, and F. P. Blair for Vice President, and do
> pledge ourselves to support the cause and the men
> that the convention have selected for our standard-
> bearers.
>   Resolved.   That no member of this club shall
> employ, rent lands to, or patronize any Radical
> after the present contracts shall have expired, and
> that from this date we will not give employment to
> any freedmen who are straggling over the country
> as day-laborers who cannot show certificates that
> they are members of some Democratic association.
>   Our club numbers one hundred and thirty-six,
> and still they come.
>   H. C. MOSELY, Secretary

I would also call the attention of this House, Mr.
Speaker, to the following extracts from the report of the investigating committee of the Legislature of South Carolina of
1868 and 1869, appointed to investigate thoroughly the dis-
ordered state of affairs in the third congressional district,
and the causes of the intimidation, outrages, and murders
perpetrated preceding and at the general election of 1868.

ROOMS OF INVESTIGATING COMMITTEE,
THIRD CONGRESSIONAL DISTRICT,
ABBEVILLE COURT-HOUSE, S. C., June 24, 1869.

Pursuant to adjournment, the committee met at
nine a. m.

A quorum being present, the committee proceeded to business, Mr. Wright acting chairman.

Joshua Wardlaw (colored) sworn.

Direct examination by Mr. Elliott:

Question. Are you a resident of this county?

Answer. Yes, sir.

Question. How long have you been a resident of
this country?

Answer. Born and bred here.

Question. In this town?

Answer. Yes.

Question. Do you know of any outrages or any
means of intimidation or threats used to keep persons from voting at the late general election?

Answer. Yes.

Question. Please state what those means of intimidation used were, and who made them?

Answer. I heard Fred Edmunds say that no
colored people should vote at Calhoun Mills except
they voted the Democratic ticket. He said, "I am
going down there now to gather my company and
meet them there." I immediately went to Mr.
Guffin and told him what I had heard. I had to go
to Mr. Bradley's mill myself to vote, and I told
him I was afraid to go on account of the threats
that had been made. Mr. Guffin then told me not
to be afraid, for they dared not interfere with me.
I replied, "I know the people, and will not go, although I am a friend of yours."

Question. Do you know of any other outrage
committed?

Answer. Yes, sir.

Question. Please state what that outrage was?

Answer. Mr. William Richardson, a white man
with whom I resided last year, came to me one
night in August last and said to me, "Get up." (I
was in bed.) I asked him what he wanted. He
said he wanted me to go out with him. I said I
had no particular call out. He said, "Damn you,
you shall go. What have you got in this trunk?"
At this time I arose from the bed. William Har-

mons, Pres. Blackwell, and Mr. Coon were in
company with Mr. Richardson. They took me out
of my house, and went and took my brother-in-law
also. My wife was screaming, and they threatened
her life. Pres. Blackwell kicked one of my little
children that was in the bed. They took my
brother-in-law's gun and broke it against a tree in
the yard. They laid me down on the ground, after
stripping me as naked as when I came into the
world, and struck me five times with a strap before I got away from them. After escaping they
fired four shots at me, but did not hit me. I was
so frightened I laid out in the woods all night,
naked as I was, and suffered from the exposure.
Mr. Richardson afterward told me he was very
sorry that I had escaped from them. My brother-
in-law died from the beating he got that same night;
and my nephew, Harry Durgan, got severely beat
that night by the same party. Mose Martin, another colored man on the place, was also beaten
badly that same night, by the same party, and
Harry Martin, (colored), received about seven
hundred lashes also. My cousin, Ben Pinckney,
was so severely beaten that he was unable to do
any work for a month or so after. I have never
been back to the settlement since that time, being
afraid that they would kill me.
    Question. Had you any difficulty or quarrel with
any of those men before they visited your house
that night?
    Answer. No; but about a week or two before
that William Harmon and William Richardson asked
me whether I was a Radical or Democrat, or what
I intended to be. I replied that I did not desire to
say what I was or what I intended to do, for I had
not decided in my mind. They said, "You will
have to state what you are, or you will have to
quit the place." I told them I would join them
rather than lose my crop. On the day of the general election they called me into the house to vote
the Democratic ticket. They had a keg of whisky
and offered me a drink. I told them no, I would
not drink it. They then asked me whether I was
going to vote the Democratic ticket. I replied no;
that if I could not vote the way I wanted I would
not vote at all. They then said, "Put him out."
They then put me out and slammed the door after

me. One of the party at the polls, named James
Jennings said, "We will take his life before six
months"; and Mr. William Tennent said, "Yes,
damn him, we will do it. " He also said, "Damn
him, he is the damned leader that is keeping the
others from voting the Democratic ticket. " I told
them before leaving that I was a Radical, and did
not care who knew it; and I did prevent a great
many from voting the Democratic ticket, and I will
still do so. The next outrage I witnessed was,
Ellington Searles had a mill burned; a man that
lived with me, named Mack Martin, was accused
by Mr. Searles of breaking into the mill before it
was burned. Mr. Searles came to the place I was
living on with a party of eleven, and took this man
Mack out in the broad daylight and carried him up
the road about a quarter of a mile from the house,
and gave him sixteen hundred lashes, which I saw.
They had a ferocious dog; after they had whipped
him they put the dog on him, and the dog attacked
him, naked as he was, and tore large pieces from
his side and limbs, and they all gathered pine-knots
and placed around the man and said they would
scorch him. Some of the party begged them not to,
and it was not done. This all occurred about
twelve o'clock in the day.

The following are taken from the Charleston News of
November 5, 1870, the leading organ of the Democratic party
of South Carolina, in which they are introduced approvingly,
as showing the spirit of the Democratic press. Speaking of
the unbroken adhesion of the colored people of South Carolina
to the Republican party at the late general election in that
State, the Newberry Herald of November 3 says, addressing
its white Democratic readers:

Remember that we are the white people, and that
they are the negro; that they have chosen their
ground and arrayed themselves against us with a
determination and hate which are unmistakable, and
that our policy is to let them alone and take care
of ourselves. But we must have organization, not
politically, be it remembered, and the views below
are worth consideration. Let us have a thorough
understanding and a union of the whole white people
of the State, not forgetting either the worthy exceptions among the negroes who have identified

themselves with us, or any others who may see fit
to cast their lines in with us.

In the same spirit the Darlington Democrat of the
same date says:

> The time for temporizing, argument, and concilia-
> tion is passed; we shall have no more of it.   A
> straight and severe line must be drawn between the
> races.   The colored people have chosen their
> ground with the advice of the ringleaders, and they
> must follow it out without aid or sympathy from
> their former white friends.   The white people have
> the power and the brains and the determination to
> hold their own and protect themselves, and they
> will do so.   The negroes have followed their devices
> one time too many, and now let them look to others
> for help, assistance, and sympathy.

The Charleston News of November 7, 1870, referring
to the result of the election, declares:

> We understand, therefore, and accept the solid
> black vote cast against the nominees of the Reform
> party as a declaration of war by the negro race
> against the white race, by ignorance against intel-
> ligence, by poverty against actual or potential
> wealth.   This issue we have striven to avoid, but
> the negroes will have nothing else.   They will not
> allow us to work with them.   We must, if neces-
> sary, work against them.   Conciliation, argument,
> persuasion, all have been worse than useless.   The
> white people stand alone.   And they must organize
> themselves, and arm themselves, not as 'a white
> man's party, ' but because the past and present
> prove that decency, purity, and political freedom,
> as well as the preservation of society, are identical
> with the interests of the white people of the State.

The following is an official copy of a Ku Klux order
published in the Charleston News of January 31, 1871, and
vouched for as authentic by the correspondent of that journal,
writing from the State capital.   It was issued from the county
of York, and was posted at the county auditor's office:

HEADQUARTERS K. K. K.
January 22, 1871.

Resolved.   That in all cases of incendiarism
ten of the leading colored people and two white
sympathizers shall be executed in that vicinity.

That if any armed bands of colored people are
found hereafter picketing the roads, the officers of
the company to which the pickets belong shall be
executed.

That all persons reported as using incendiary
language shall be tried by the high court of this
order and be punished at their discretion.

The different officers are charged with the execution of these resolutions.

By order of   K. K. K.
Copy for York.

The same paper, referring to the terrible outrages
practiced upon the unoffending blacks of the up-country, admits the existence of the Ku Klux as a powerful armed organization.   It says:

> We doubt not that Governor Scott, through the
> proper civil officers, will promptly indicate the
> way in which the citizens of York may express,
> in action, their published determination to put an
> end to scenes of violence which disgrace any civil-
> ized community.

To show that the design of the Ku Klux is political,
and that its organization is intended to secure the control of
the State administration by force, I present the following,
from the Spartanburg (South Carolina) Republican of March 22
of the present year:

> Ku Klux in Union. --The Ku Klux last week posted
> a notice on the bulletin-board at the courthouse in
> Union to the effect that the county commissioners,
> the school commissioner, and the members of the
> Legislature must resign their positions by the 27th
> instant.
>
> We understand that the sheriff, the school commis-
> sioner, and the clerk of the county commissioners
> have in obedience to this order, tendered their
> resignations, and it is thought that other officers
> will follow their example.

The following is the document found posted in Union:

K. K. K.
HEADQUARTERS, NINTH DIVISION, S. C.,
SPECIAL ORDERS No. 3, K. K. K.

'Ignorance is the curse of God. '
For this reason we are determined that members of the Legislature, the school commissioner,
and the county commissioners of Union shall no
longer officiate.

Fifteen days' notice from this date is therefore
given, and if they, one and all do not at once and
forever resign their present inhuman, disgraceful,
and outrageous rule, then retributive justice will as
surely be used as night follows day.

Also, 'An honest man is the noblest work of
God. '

For this reason, if the clerk of the said board
of county commissioners and school commissioners
does not immediately renounce and relinquish his
present position, then harsher measures than this
will most assuredly and certainly be used. For
confirmation, reference to the orders heretofore
published in the Union Weekly Times and Yorkville
Enquirer will more fully and completely show our
intention.

By order Grand Chief:

A. O., Grand Secretary.
March 9, A. D. 1871,

I copy, sir, from the <u>Columbia</u> (South Carolina) <u>Daily
Union</u> of March 10, 1871, the following. It is the unimpeach-
able testimony of an officer of your own Army:

The Ku Klux or Council of Safety. --A dispatch-
bearer, Major Whitehead, United States Army,
from the post of United States troops at Yorkville,
brought yesterday the following important intelligence from that locality. The dispatches explain
themselves, and we submit them with the voucher
of bare and naked truth, having tired long ago of
the monotony of chronicling these daily outrages.
The Governor has telegraphed to Washington the
facts, and also to General Terry, commanding the
department, stating that fighting is going on in that
county:

HEADQUARTERS CAMP SHERMAN
YORKVILLE, SOUTH CAROLINA, March 8, 1870.

GOVERNOR: I respectfully state that on Monday
morning last, the company of militia known as the
'Carmel Hill Company' was attacked by a portion of
the organization styled 'Ku Klux,' and after a running flight, lasting nearly three days, arrived in
close proximity to this place. The sheriff of this
county was notified of the coming of this company,
and he at once summoned a posse and proceeded to
arrest and disarm the members thereof. The
company, consisting of two commissioned officers
and sixteen men, were brought into town this evening and are now confined in the county jail, to which
I have sent a guard of United States troops to remain during the night to prevent violence to the
prisoners. At daybreak tomorrow these prisoners
will be turned over by the sheriff to me, and I
shall hold them subject to your orders.

I also respectfully state that the arms taken
from this company are being used this night in
picketing the roads leading from this place.

I respectfully request that thirty days' rations
for twenty men be sent here without delay to subsist the members of the above-mentioned company
until an opportunity offers for their return to their
homes.

Answer by telegram if you intend to subsist
these men until they can go to their homes in safety.

I respectfully suggest that five thousand rounds
of ammunition be sent from your arsenal for the
use of this company, as they must rely upon their
personal courage for that protection which it seems
cannot be obtained in any other manner until civil
law regulates itself in this county.

Very respectfully,

JOHN CHRISTOPHER
Captain Eighth United States Infantry.

His Excellency R. K. SCOTT, Governor South
Carolina, Columbia, South Carolina.

HEADQUARTERS CAMP SHERMAN,
March 9, 1871.

SIR: I have the honor to state for your official

information that the arms taken from the militia
company, now under your custody, were used last
night for the purpose of guarding the principal roads
leading to Yorkville, for the purpose of preventing
the prisoners taken by you from reaching their
homes in safety in case of their discharge; that
this guard consists of the same illegal, unknown,
and armed band that made the raid upon the office
of the county treasurer.

I respectfully suggest that the civil authorities
of York County see that the arms taken by the
posse comitatus be sent to my camp by sunset to-
day, and in addition, I respectfully suggest that the
civil authorities of your county see that the roads
leading to Yorkville are not picketed by the existing
organization that call themselves the 'Ku Klux' or
'Council of Safety, ' I have requested his Excellency, the Governor of this State by a special message, to subsist these men until these roads are
open.

I am, very respectfully, &c.,

JOHN CHRISTOPHER.
Captain Eighteenth United States Infantry

Sheriff R. H. GLENN, York County, South Carolina.

Since the date of the publication of that circular many
of the officers in the upper counties have resigned in obedience to the Ku Klux mandate, while others have fled to the
capital of the State, for security.

Now, sir, I have presented a few of the manifold
proofs that, did time allow, I could at once present in support of the facts warranting the passage of this bill.   I have
shown the declared purpose of the Ku Klux organization, and
I refer to the official records of nearly every southern State
during the past ten months to show how that bloody purpose
has been in part executed.   This bill will tend in some degree to prevent its full achievement.

I do not wish to be understood as speaking for the
colored man alone when I demand instant protection for the
loyal men of the South.   No, sir, my demand is not so restricted.   In South Carolina alone, at the last election,
twelve thousand of the working white men in good faith voted
the Republican ticket, openly arraying themselves on the side

of free government. This class have discovered that the
same beneficent system that emancipates the laborer of the
one race secures the freedom of the other. They understand
that the shackle that bound the arms of the black man threw
a deep shadow on the path of the laboring white. The white
Republican of the South is also hunted down and murdered or
scourged for his opinion's sake, and during the past two
years more than six hundred loyal men of both races have
perished in my State alone.

         Yet, sir, it is true that these masked murderers
strike chiefly at the black race. And here I say that every
southern gentleman should blush with shame at this pitiless
and cowardly persecution of the negro. If the former master
will yield no obedience to the laws of the land he should at
least respect the claims of common gratitude. To him I say
that the negro, whom you now term a barbarian, unfit for
and incapable of self-government, treated you in the day of
your weakness with a forbearance and magnanimity unknown
before in the history of a servile population. In the dark
days of the war, when your strong men were far to the front,
the negro, with no restraint save his own self-control, tilled
your fields and kept watch and ward over your otherwise un-
protected dwellings. He guarded the person of your wife, the
chastity of your daughter, and the helpless infancy of your
children. Nobly suppressing the manhood that burned within
him, he learned "to labor and to wait, " and exhibited through
all his weary years of suffering and unrequited toil--

                 That calm reliance upon God
                 For justice in His own time
                 That gentleness to which belongs
                 Forgiveness for its many wrongs.

         And how do you requite him now? Be it said to the
shame of your boasted chivalry among men of honor in every
land, simply because he exercises his privileges as an
American freeman, you would drive him into exile with the
pitiless lash or doom him to swift murder, seeking your re-
venge for political power lost by moving at midnight along
the path of the assassin!

         It is the custom, sir, of Democratic journals to stig-
matize the negroes of the South as being in a semi-barbarous
condition; but pray tell me, who is the barbarian here, the
murderer or his victim? I fling back in the teeth of those
who make it this most false and foul aspersion upon the negro

of the southern States. I thank God that in the darkest chapters in the history of my race there is no such record as that unfolded by the dread annals that tell the story of the long-protracted horrors of Andersonville.

I trust, sir, that this bill will pass quickly, and be quickly enforced. History teaches us that the adequate policy is the best. In one section of the Union crime is stronger than law. Murder, unabashed, stalks abroad in many of the southern States. If you cannot now protect the loyal men of the South, then have the loyal people of this great Republic done and suffered much in vain, and your free Constitution is a mockery and a snare.

It is recorded that on the entry of Louis XVIII into Paris, after the fall of the great Napoleon, an old marshal of the empire who stood in the vast throng, unknown, was addressed by an ardent Bourbon who expatiated on the gorgeous splendors that marked the scene, and exclaimed: "Is not this grand? Is it not magnificent? What is there wanting to the occasion?" "Nothing, " said the warworn veteran, as his mind wandered over Lodi and Wagram and Austerlitz, and the hundred other fields of victory where he struck beneath the eagles of his now fallen chief. "Nothing, " he answered with tremulous voice; "nothing is wanting to the occasion but the presence of the brave men who died to prevent it. "

Such, sir, will be the bitter reflection of all loyal men in this nation, if the Democratic party shall triumph in the States of the South through armed violence.

His greatest effort was made in a
speech on civil rights when he
participated in debate against
Representatives Beck of Kentucky,
Harris of Virginia and Alexander
H. Stevens of Georgia. (Moseley, p. 33)

CIVIL RIGHTS

The passage of this bill will determine the civil
status, not only of the negro, but of any other
class of citizens who may feel themselves discriminated against. It will form the cap-stone of that
temple of liberty, begun on this continent under
discouraging circumstances, carried on in spite of
the sneers of monarchists and the cavils of pretended friends of freedom, until at last it stands
in all its beautiful symmetry and proportions, a
building the grandest which the world has ever seen,
realizing the most sanguine expectations and the
highest hopes of those who, in the name of equal,
impartial, and universal liberty, laid the foundation
stones.... The last vestiture only is needed--civil
rights. (4:407-410)

Mr. ELLIOT. While I am sincerely grateful for this
high mark of courtesy that has been accorded to me by this
House, it is a matter of regret to me that it is necessary at
this day that I should rise in the presence of an American
Congress to advocate a bill which simply asserts equal rights
and equal public privileges for all classes of American citizens. I regret, sir, that the dark hue of my skin may lend a
color to the imputation that I am controlled by motives personal to myself in my advocacy of this great measure of national justice. Sir, the motive that impels me is restricted
by no such narrow boundary, but is as broad as your Constitution. I advocate it, sir, because it is right. The bill,
however, not only appeals to your justice, but it demands a
response from your gratitude.

In the events that led to the achievement of American
Independence the negro was not an inactive or unconcerned
spectator.   He bore his part bravely upon many battle-fields,
although uncheered by that certain hope of political elevation
which victory would secure to the white man.   The tall
granite shaft, which a grateful State has reared above its
sons who fell in defending Fort Griswold against the attach
of Benedict Arnold, bears the name of Jordan, Freeman, and
other brave men of the African race who there cemented with
their blood the corner-stone of the Republic.   In the State
which I have the honor in part to represent the title of the
black man rang out against the troops of the British crown
in the darkest days of the American Revolution.   Said General Greene, who has been justly termed the Washington of
the North, in a letter written by him to Alexander Hamilton,
on the 10th day of January, 1781, from the vicinity of Cam-
den, South Carolina:

> There is no such thing as national character or
> national sentiment.   The inhabitants are numerous,
> but they would be rather formidable abroad than at
> home.   There is a great spirit of enterprise among
> the black people, and those that come out as vol-
> unteers are not a little formidable to the enemy.

At the battle of New Orleans, under the immortal
Jackson, a colored regiment held the extreme right of the
American line unflinchingly, and drove back the British
column that pressed upon them, at the point of the bayonet.
So marked was their valor on that occasion that it evoked
from their great commander the warmest encomiums, as will
be seen from his dispatch announcing the brilliant victory.

As the gentleman from Kentucky (Mr. BECK), who
seems to be the leading exponent on this floor of the party
that is arrayed against the principle of this bill, has been
pleased, in season and out of season, to cast odium upon the
negro and to vaunt the chivalry of his State, I may be pardoned for calling attention to another portion of the same dispatch.   Referring to the various regiments under his command, and their conduct on that field which terminated the
second war of American Independence, General Jackson says:

> At the very moment when the entire discomfiture of
> the enemy was looked for with a confidence amount-
> ing to certainty, the Kentucky re-enforcements, in
> whom so much reliance had been placed, ingloriously
> fled.

In quoting this indisputable piece of history, I do so
only by way of admonition and not to question the well-at-
tested gallantry of the true Kentuckian, and to suggest to the
gentleman that it would be well that he should not flaunt his
heraldry so proudly while he bears this bar-sinister on the
military escutcheon of his State--a State which answered the
call of the Republic in 1861, when treason thundered at the
very gates of the capital, by coldly declaring her neutrality
in the impending struggle. The negro, true to that patriotism
and love of country that have ever characterized and marked
his history on this continent, came to the aid of the Government in its efforts to maintain the Constitution. To that
Government he now appeals; that Constitution he now invokes
for protection against outrage and unjust prejudices founded
upon caste.

But, sir, we are told by the distinguished gentleman
from Georgia (Mr. STEPHENS) that Congress has no power
under the Constitution to pass such a law, and that the passage of such an act is in direct contravention of the rights of
the States. I cannot assent to any such proposition. The
constitution of a free government ought always to be construed in favor of human rights. Indeed, the thirteenth,
fourteenth, and fifteenth amendments, in positive words, in-
vest Congress with the power to protect the citizen in his
civil and political rights. Now, sir, what are civil rights?
Rights natural, modified by civil society. Mr. Lieber says:

> By civil liberty is meant, not only the absence of
> individual restraint, but liberty within the social
> system and political organism--a combination of
> principles and laws which acknowledge, protect,
> and favor the dignity of man.... Civil liberty is
> the result of man's two-fold character as an indi-
> vidual and social being, so soon as both are equally
> respected. --Lieber on Civil Liberty, page 25.

Alexander Hamilton, the right-hand man of Washington
in the perilous days of the then infant Republic, the great
interpreter and expounder of the Constitution, says:

> Natural liberty is a gift of the beneficent Creator
> to the whole human race; civil liberty is founded on
> it; civil liberty is only natural liberty modified and
> secured by civil society. --Hamilton's History of the
> American Republic, vol. 1, page 70.

In the French constitution of June, 1793, we find this grand and noble declaration:

> Government is instituted to insure to man the free use of his natural and inalienable rights.   These rights are equality, liberty, security, property. All men are equal by nature and before the law.... Law is the same for all, be it protective or penal. Freedom is the power by which man can do what does not interfere with the rights of another; its basis is nature, its standard is justice, its protection is law, its moral boundary is the maxim; 'Do not unto others what you do not wish they should do unto you. '

Arc we then, sir, with the amendments to our Constitution staring us in the face; with these grand truths of history before our eyes; with innumerable wrongs daily inflicted upon five million citizens demanding redress, to commit this question to the diversity of State legislation?   In the words of Hamilton--

> Is it the interest of the Government to sacrifice individual rights to the preservation of the rights of an artificial being, called States?   There can be no truer principle than this, that every individual of the community at large has an equal right to the protection of Government.   Can this be a free Government if partial distinctions are tolerated or maintained?

The rights contended for in this bill are among "the sacred rights of mankind, which are not to be rummaged for among old parchments or musty records; they are written as with a sunbeam, in the whole volume of human nature, by the hand of the Divinity itself, and can never be erased or obscured by mortal power. "

But the Slaughter-house cases!--the Slaughter-house cases!

The honorable gentleman from Kentucky, always swift to sustain the failing and dishonored cause of proscription, rushes forward and flaunts in our faces the decision of the Supreme Court of the United States in the Slaughter-house cases, and in that act he has been willingly aided by the gentleman from Georgia.   Hitherto, in the contests which

have marked the progress of the cause of equal civil rights,
our opponents have appealed sometimes to custom, sometimes to prejudice, more often to pride of race, but they
have never sought to shield themselves behind the Supreme
Court. But now, for the first time, we are told that we are
barred by a decision of that court, from which there is no
appeal. If this be true we must stay our hands. The cause
of equal civil rights must pause at the command of a power
whose edicts must be obeyed till the fundamental law of our
country is changed.

Has the honorable gentleman from Kentucky considered
well the claim he now advances? If it were not disrespectful I would ask, has he ever read the decision which he now
tells us is an insuperable barrier to the adoption of this
great measure of justice?

In the consideration of this subject, has not the judgment of the gentleman from Georgia been warped by the
ghost of the dead doctrines of State-rights? Has he been altogether free from prejudices engendered by long training in
that school of politics that well-nigh destroyed this Government?

Mr. Speaker, I venture to say here in the presence
of the gentleman from Kentucky, and the gentleman from
Georgia, and in the presence of the whole country, that there
is not a line or word, not a thought or dictum even, in the
decision of the Supreme Court in the great Slaughter-house
cases which casts a shadow of doubt on the right of Congress
to pass the pending bill, or to adopt such other legislation
as it may judge proper and necessary to secure perfect
equality before the law to every citizen of the Republic. Sir,
I protest against the dishonor now cast upon our Supreme
Court by both the gentleman from Kentucky and the gentleman
from Georgia. In other days, when the whole country was
bowing beneath the yoke of slavery, when press, pulpit, platform, Congress, and courts felt the fatal power of the slave
oligarchy, I remember a decision of that court which no
American now reads without shame and humiliation. But
these days are past. The Supreme Court of to-day is a tribunal as true to freedom as any department of this Government, and I am honored with the opportunity of repelling a
deep disgrace which the gentleman from Kentucky, backed and
sustained as he is by the gentleman from Georgia, seeks to
put upon it.

What were these Slaughter-house cases? The gentleman should be aware that a decision of any court should be
examined in the light of the exact question which is brought
before it for decision.   That is all that gives authority to any
decision.

The State of Louisiana, by act of her Legislature, had
conferred on certain persons the exclusive right to maintain
stock-landings and slaughter-houses within the city of New
Orleans, or the parishes of Orleans, Jefferson, and Saint
Bernard, in that State.   The corporation which was thereby
chartered were invested with the sole and exclusive privilege
of conducting and carrying on the live-stock, landing, and
slaughter-house business within the limits designated.

The supreme court of Louisiana sustained the validity
of the act conferring these exclusive privileges, and the plaintiffs in error brought the case before the Supreme Court of
the United States for review.   The plaintiffs in error contended that the act in question was void, because, first, it
established a monopoly which was in derogation of common
right and in contravention of the common law; and, second,
that the grant of such exclusive privileges was in violation of
the thirteenth and fourteenth amendments of the Constitution
of the United States.

It thus appears from a simple statement of the case
that the question which was before the court was not whether
a State law which denied to a particular portion of her citizens the rights conferred on her citizens generally, on account of race, color, or previous condition of servitude, was
unconstitutional because in conflict with the recent amendments,
but whether an act which conferred on certain citizens exclusive privileges for police purposes was in conflict therewith, because imposing an involunatry servitude forbidden by
the thirteenth amendment, or abridging the rights and immunities of citizens of the United States, or denying the equal
protection of the laws, prohibited by the fourteenth amendment.

On the part of the defendants in error it was maintained that the act was the exercise of the ordinary and unquestionable power of the State to make regulation for the
health and comfort of society--the exercise of the police
power of the State, defined by Chancellor Kent to be ''the
right to interdict unwholesome trades, slaughter-houses, operations offensive to the senses, the deposit of powder, the

Race is a situation

application of steam-power to propel cars, the building with
combustible materials, and the burial of the dead in the midst
of dense masses of population, on the general and rational
principle that every person ought so to use his own property
as not to injure his neighbors, and that private interests
must be made subservient to the general interests of the
community. "

The decision of the Supreme Court is to be found in
the 16th volume of Wallace's Reports, and was delivered by
Associate Justice Miller. The court hold, first, that the act
in question is a legitimate and warrantable exercise of the
police power of the State in regulating the business of stock-
landing and slaughtering in the city of New Orleans and the
territory immediately contiguous. Having held this, the court
proceeds to discuss the question whether the conferring of
exclusive privileges, such as those conferred by the act in
question, is the imposing of an involuntary servitude, the
abridging of the rights and immunities of citizens of the United
States, or the denial to any person with the jurisdiction of the
State of the equal protection of the laws.

That the act is not the imposition of an involuntary
servitude the court hold to be clear, and they next proceed
to examine the remaining questions arising under the fourteenth amendment. Upon this question the court hold that the
leading and comprehensive purpose of the thirteenth, fourteenth, and fifteenth amendments was to secure the complete
freedom of the race, which, by the events of the war, had
been wrested from the unwilling grasp of their owners. I
know no finer or more just picture, albeit painted in the
neutral tints of true judicial impartiality, of the motives and
events which led to these amendments. Has the gentleman
from Kentucky read these passages which I now quote? Or
has the gentleman from Georgia considered well the force of
the language therein used? Says the court on page 70:

> The process of restoring to their proper relations
> with the Federal Government and with the other
> States those which had sided with the rebellion,
> undertaken under the proclamation of President
> Johnson in 1865, and before the assembling of
> Congress, developed the fact that not withstanding
> the formal recognition by those States of the abo-
> lition of slavery, the condition of the slave race
> would, without further protection of the Federal
> Goverment, be almost as bad as it was before.

Among the first acts of legislation adopted by
several of the States in the legislative bodies
which claimed to be in their normal relations with
the Federal Government, were laws which imposed
upon the colored race onerous disabilities and
burdens, and curtailed their rights in the pursuit
of life, liberty, and property to such an extent
that their freedom was of little value, while they
had lost the protection which they had received
from their former owners from motives both of
interest and humanity.

They were in some States forbidden to appear in
the towns in any other character than menial servants. They were required to reside on and cultivate the soil, without the right to purchase or own
it. They were excluded from any occupations of
gain, and were not permitted to give testimony in
the courts in any case where a white man was a
party. It was said that their lives were at the
mercy of bad men, either because the laws for
their protection were insufficient or were not enforced.

These circumstances, whatever of falsehood or
misconception may have been mingled with their
presentation, forced upon the statesmen who had
conducted the Federal Government in safely through
the crisis of the rebellion, and who supposed that
by the thirteenth article of amendment they had
secured the result of their labors, the conviction
that something more was necessary in the way of
constitutional protection to the unfortunate race
who had suffered so much. They accordingly
passed through Congress the proposition for the
fourteenth amendment and they declined to treat
as restored to their full participation in the Government of the Union the States which had been in
insurrection until they ratified that article by a
formal vote of their legislative bodies.

Before we proceed to examine more critically
the provisions of this amendment, on which the
plaintiffs in error rely, let us complete and dismiss the history of the recent amendments, as
that history related to the general purpose which
pervades them all. A few year's experience satisfied the thoughtful men who had been the authors
of the other two amendments that, notwithstanding
the restraints of those articles on the States and

the laws passed under the additional powers granted to Congress, these were inadequate for the
protection of life, liberty, and property, without
which freedom to the slave was no boon. They
were in all these States denied the right of suffrage. The laws were administered by the white
man alone.

Hence the fifteenth amendment, which declares
that 'the right of a citizen of the United States to
vote shall not be denied or abridged by any State
on account of race, color, or previous condition
of servitude. ' The negro having by the fourteenth
amendment been declared to be a citizen of the
United States, is thus made a voter in every
State of the Union.

We repeat, then, in the light of this recapitula-
tion of events almost too recent to be called history, but which are familiar to us all, and on the
most casual examination of the language of these
amendments, no one can fail to be impressed with
the one pervading purpose found in them all, lying
at the foundation of each, and without which none
of them would have been even suggested: we
mean the freedom of the slave race, the security
and firm establishment of that freedom, and the
protection of the newly-made freeman and citizen
from the oppressions of those who had formerly
exercised unlimited dominion over him. It is true
that only the fifteenth amendment in terms men-
tions the negro by speaking of his color and his
slavery. But it is just as true that each of the
other articles was addressed to the grievances
of that race, and designed to remedy them, as
the fifteenth.

These amendements, one and all, are thus declared to
have as their all-pervading design and end the security to the
recently enslaved race, not only their nominal freedom, but
their complete protection from those who had formerly exercised unlimited dominion over them. It is in this broad light
that all these amendments must be read, the purpose to
secure the perfect equality before the law of all citizens of
the United States. What you give to one class you must give
to all; what you deny to one class you shall deny to all, unless in the exercise of the common and universal police power
of the State you find it needful to confer exclusive privileges
on certain citizens, to be held and exercised still for the
common good of all.

Such are the doctrines of the Slaughter-house cases--
doctrines worthy of the Republic, worthy of the age, worthy
of the great tribunal which thus loftily and impressively enun-
ciates them. Do they--I put it to any man, be he lawyer or
not; I put it to the gentleman from Georgia--do they give
color even to the claim that this Congress may not now legislate against a plain discrimination made by State laws of
State customs against that very race for whose complete
freedom and protection these great amendments were elab-
orated and adopted? Is it pretended, I ask the honorable
gentleman from Kentucky or the honorable gentleman from
Georgia--is it pretended anywhere that the evils of which we
complain, our exclusion from the public inn, from the saloon
and table of the steamboat, from the sleeping-coach on the
railway, from the right of sepulture in the public burial-
ground, are an exercise of the police power of the State? Is
such oppression and injustice nothing but the exercise by the
State of the right to make regulations for the health, comfort, and security of all her citizens? Is it merely enacting
that one man shall so use his own as not to injure another's?
Are the colored race to be assimilated to an unwholesome
trade or to combustible materials, to be interdicted, to be
shut up within prescribed limits? Let the gentleman from
Kentucky or the gentleman from Georgia answer. Let the
country know to what extent even the audacious prejudice of
the gentleman from Kentucky will drive him, and how far
even the gentleman from Georgia will permit himself to be
led captive by the unrighteous teachings of a false political
faith.

If we are to be likened in legal view to "unwholesome
trades, " to "large and offensive collections of animals, " to
"noxious slaughter-houses, " to "the offal and stench which
attend on certain manufactures, " let it be avowed. If that is
still the doctrine of the political party to which the gentlemen
belong, let it be put upon record. If State laws which deny
us the common rights and privileges of other citizens, upon
no possible or conceivable ground save one of prejudice, or
of "taste, " as the gentleman from Texas termed it, and as I
suppose the gentlemen will prefer to call it, are to be placed
under the protection of a decision which affirms the right of
a State to regulate the police of her great cities, then the
decision is in conflict with the bill before us. No man will
dare maintain such a doctrine. It is as shocking to the legal
mind as it is offensive to the heart and conscience of all who
love justice or respect manhood. I am astonished that the
gentleman from Kentucky or the gentleman from Georgia
should have been so grossly misled as to rise here and as-

sert that the decision of the Supreme Court in these cases
was a denial to Congress of the power to legislate against
discriminations on account of race, color, or previous condition of servitude, because that court has decided that exclusive privileges conferred for the common protection of the
lives and health of the whole community are not in violation
of the recent amendments. The only ground upon which the
grant of exclusive privileges to a portion of the community is
ever defended is that the substantial good of all is promoted:
that in truth it is for the welfare of the whole community
that certain persons should alone pursue certain occupations.
It is not the special benefit conferred on the few that moves
the legislature, but the ultimate and real benefit of all, even
of those who are denied the right to pursue those specified
occupations. Does the gentleman from Kentucky say that my
good is promoted when I am excluded from the public inn?
Is the health or safety of the community promoted? Doubtless his prejudice is gratified. Doubtless his democratic instincts are pleased; but will he or his able coadjutor say that
such exclusion is a lawful exercise of the police power of the
State, or that it is not a denial to me of the equal protection
of the laws? They will not so say.

But each of these gentlemen quote at some length
from the decision of the court to show that the court recognizes a difference between citizenship of the United States
and citizenship of the States. That is true, and no man here
who supports this bill questions or overlooks the difference.
There are privileges and immunities which belong to me as
a citizen of the United States, and there are other privileges
and immunities which belong to me as a citizen of my State.
The former are under the protection of the Constitution and
laws of the United States, and the latter are under the protection of the constitution and laws of my State. But what
of that? Are the rights which I now claim--the right to enjoy the common public conveniences of travel on public highways, of rest and refreshment at public inns, of education in
public schools, of burial in public cemeteries--rights which
I hold as a citizen of the United States or of my State? Or,
to state the question more exactly, is not the denial of such
privileges to me a denial to me of the equal protection of
the laws? For it is under this clause of the fourteenth
amendment that we place the present bill, no State shall
"deny to any person within its jurisdiction the equal protection of the laws. " No matter, therefore, whether his rights
are held under the United States or under his particular State,
he is equally protected by this amendment. He is always

and everywhere entitled to the equal protection of the laws.
All discrimination is forbidden; and while the rights of citizens of a State as such are not defined or conferred by the
Constitution of the United States, yet all discrimination, all
denial of equality before the law, all denial of the equal protection of the laws, whether State or national laws, is forbidden.

The distinction between the two kinds of citizenship is
clear, and the Supreme Court have clearly pointed out this
distinction, but they have nowhere written a word or line
which denies to Congress the power to prevent a denial of
equality of rights, whether those rights exist by virtue of
citizenship of the United States or of a State. Let honorable
members mark well this distinction. There are rights which
are conferred on us by the United States. There are other
rights conferred on us by the States of which we are indi-
vidually the citizens. The fourteenth amendment does not
forbid a State to deny to all its citizens any of those rights
which the State itself has conferred, with certain exceptions,
which are pointed out in the decision which we are examining.
What it does forbid is inequality, is discrimination, or, to
use the words of the amendment itself, is the denial "to any
person within its jurisdiction the equal protection of the
laws." If a State denies to me rights which are common to
all her other citizens, she violates this amendment, unless
she can show, as was shown in the Slaughter-house cases,
that she does it in the legitimate exercise of her police
power. If she abridges the rights of all her citizens equally,
unless those rights are specially guarded by the Constitution
of the United States, she does not violate this amendment.
This is not to put the rights which I hold by virtue of my
citizenship of South Carolina under the protection of the national Government; it is not to blot out or overlook in the
slightest particular the distinction between rights held under
the United States and rights held under the States; but it
seeks to secure equality, to prevent discrimination, to confer
as complete and ample protection on the humblest as on the
highest.

The gentleman from Kentucky, in the course of the
speech to which I am now replying, made a reference to the
State of Massachusetts which betrays again the confusion
which exists in his mind on this precise point. He tells us
that Massachusetts excludes from the ballot-box all who cannot read and write, and points to that fact as the exercise
of a right which this bill would abridge or impair. The

honorable gentleman from Massachusetts (Mr. DAWES) answered him truly and well, but I submit that he did not make
the best reply. Why did he not ask the gentleman from Kentucky if Massachusetts had ever discriminated against any of
her citizens on account of color, or race, or previous condition of servitude? When did Massachusetts sully her proud
record by placing on her statute-book any law which admitted
to the ballot the white man and shut out the black man? She
has never done it; she will not do it; she cannot do it so long
as we have a Supreme Court which reads the Constitution of
our country with the eyes of justice; nor can Massachusetts
or Kentucky deny to any man, on account of his race, color,
or previous condition of servitude, that perfect equality of
protection under the laws so long as Congress shall exercise
the power to enforce, by appropriate legislation, the great
and unquestionable securities embodied in the fourteenth
amendment to the Constitution.

But, sir, a few words more as to the suffrage regulation of Massachusetts.

It is true that Massachusetts in 1857, finding that her
illiterate population was being constantly augmented by the
continual influx of ignorant emigrants, placed in her constitution the least possible limitation consistent with manhood
suffrage to stay this tide of foreign ignorance. Its benefit
has been fully demonstrated in the intelligent character of
the voters of that honored Commonwealth, reflected so con-
spicuously in the able Representatives she has to-day upon
this floor. But neither is the inference of the gentleman
from Kentucky legitimate, nor do the statistics of the census
of 1870, drawn from his own State, sustain his astounding
assumption. According to the statistics we find the whole
white population of that State is 1,098,692; the whole colored
population 222,210. Of the whole white population who cannot
write we find 201,077; of the whole colored population who
cannot write, 126,048; giving us, as will be seen, 96,162
colored persons who can write to 897,615 white persons who
can write. Now, the ratio of the colored population to the
white is as 1 to 5, and the ratio of the illiterate colored
population to the whole colored population is as 1 to 2; the
ratio of the illiterate white population is to the whole white
population as 1 is to 5. Reducing this, we have only a pre-
ponderance of three-tenths in favor of the whites as to lit-
eracy, notwithstanding the advantages which they have always
enjoyed and do now enjoy of free-school privileges, and this,
too, taking solely into account the single item of being un-

able to write; for with regard to the inability to read, there
is no discrimination in the statistics between the white and
colored population.   There is, moreover, a peculiar felicity
in these statistics with regard to the State of Kentucky, quoted
so opportunely for me by the honorable gentleman; for I find
that the population of that State, both with regard to its white
and colored populations, bears the same relative rank in regard to the white and colored populations of the United States;
and, therefore, while one negro would be disfranchised were
the limitation of Massachusetts put in force, nearly three
white men would at the same time be deprived of the right
of suffrage--a consummation which I think would be far more
acceptable to the colored people of that State than to the
whites.

Now, sir, having spoken as to the intention of the
prohibition imposed by Massachusetts, I may be pardoned for
a slight inquiry as to the effect of this prohibition.   First, it
did not in any way abridge or curtail the exercise of the suffrage by any person who at that time enjoyed such right.
Nor did it discriminate between the illiterate native and illiterate foreigner.   Being enacted for the good of the entire
Commonwealth, like all just laws, its obligations fell equally
and impartially upon all its citizens.   And as a justification
for such a measure, it is a fact too well known almost for
mention here that Massachusetts had, from the beginning of
her history, recognized the inestimable value of an educated
ballot, by not only maintaining a system of free schools, but
also enforcing an attendance thereupon, as one of the safe-
guards for the preservation of a real republican form of government.   Recurring then, sir, to the possible contingency
alluded to by the gentleman from Kentucky, should the State
of Kentucky, having first established a system of common
schools whose doors shall swing open freely to all, as contemplated by the provisions of this bill, adopt a provision
similar to that of Massachusetts, no one would have cause
justly to complain.   And if in the coming years the result of
such legislation should produce a constituency rivaling that
of the old Bay State, no one would be more highly gratified
than I.

Mr. Speaker, I have neither the time nor the inclination to notice the many illogical and forced conclusions, the
numerous transfers of terms, or the vulgar insinuations
which further incumber the argument of the gentleman from
Kentucky.   Reason and argument are worse than wasted upon
those who meet every demand for political and civil liberty

by such ribaldry as this--extracted from the speech of the
gentleman from Kentucky:

> I suppose there are gentlemen on this floor who
> would arrest, imprison, and fine a young woman
> in any State of the South if she were to refuse to
> marry a negro man on account of color, race, or
> previous condition of servitude, in the event of
> his making her a proposal of marriage, and her
> refusing on that ground. That would be depriving
> him of a right he had under the amendment and
> Congress would be asked to take it up and say,
> 'This insolent white woman must be taught to know
> that it is a misdemeanor to deny a man marriage
> because of race, color, or previous condition of
> servitude'; and Congress will be urged to say after
> a while that that sort of thing must be put a stop
> to, and your conventions of colored men will come
> here asking you to enforce that right.

Now, sir, recurring to the venerable and distinguished
gentleman from Georgia (Mr. STEPHENS), who has added his
remonstrance against the passage of this bill, permit me to
say that I share in the feeling of high personal regard for
that gentleman which pervades this House. His years, his
ability, and his long experience in public affairs entitle him
to the measure of consideration which has been accorded to
him on this floor. But in this discussion I cannot and I will
not forget that the welfare and rights of my whole race in
this country are involved. When, therefore, the honorable
gentleman from Georgia lends his voice and influence to defeat this measure, I do not shrink from saying that it is not
from him that the American House of Representatives should
take lessons in matters touching human rights or the joint
relations of the State and national governments. While the
honorable gentleman contented himself with harmless specu-
lations in his study, or in the columns of a newspaper, we
might well smile at the impotence of his efforts to turn back
the advancing tide of opinion and progress; but, when he
comes again upon this national arena, and throws himself
with all his power and influence across the path which leads
to the full enfranchisement of my race, I meet him only as
an adversary; nor shall age or any other consideration re-
strain me from saying that he now offers this Government,
which he has done his utmost to destroy, a very poor return
for its magnanimous treatment, to come here and seek to
continue, by the assertion of doctrines obnoxious to the true

principles of our Government, the burdens and oppressions which rest upon five millions of his countrymen who never failed to lift their earnest prayers for the success of this Government when the gentleman was seeking to break up the Union of these States and to blot the American Republic from the galaxy of nations. (Loud applause.)

Sir, it is scarcely twelve years since that gentleman shocked the civilized world by announcing the birth of a government which rested on human slavery as its corner-stone. The progress of events has swept away that pseudo-government which rested on greed, pride, and tyranny; and the race whom he then ruthlessly spurned and trampled on are here to meet him in debate, and to demand that the rights which are enjoyed by their former oppressors--who vainly sought to overthrow a Government which they could not prostitute to the base uses of slavery--shall be accorded to those who even in the darkness of slavery kept their allegiance true to freedom and the Union. Sir, the gentleman from Georgia has learned much since 1861; but he is still a laggard. Let him put away entirely the false and fatal theories which have so greatly marred an otherwise enviable record. Let him accept, in its fullness and beneficence, the great doctrine that American citizenship carries with it every civil and political right which manhood can confer. Let him lend his influence, with all his masterly ability, to complete the proud structure of legislation which makes this nation worthy of the great declaration which heralded its birth, and he will have done that which will most nearly redeem his reputation in the eyes of the world, and best vindicate the wisdom of that policy which has permitted him to regain his seat upon this floor.

To the diatribe of the gentleman from Virginia (Mr. HARRIS), who spoke on yesterday, and who so far transcended the limits of decency and propriety as to announce upon this floor that his remarks were addressed to white men alone, I shall have no word of reply. Let him feel that a negro was not only too magnanimous to smite him in his weakness, but was even charitable enough to grant him the mercy of his silence. (Laughter and applause on the floor and in the galleries.) I shall, sir, leave to others less charitable the unenviable and fatiguing task of sifting out of that mass of chaff the few grains of sense that may, perchance, deserve notice. Assuring the gentleman that the negro in this country aims at a higher degree of intellect than that exhibited by him in this debate, I cheerfully commend him to the commiseration of all intelligent men the world over--black men as well as white men.

Sir, equality before the law is now the broad, universal, glorious rule and mandate of the Republic. No State can violate that. Kentucky and Georgia may crowd their statute-books with retrograde and barbarous legislation; they may rejoice in the odious eminence of their consistent hostility to all the great steps of human progress which have marked our national history since slavery tore down the stars and stripes on Fort Sumter; but, if Congress shall do its duty, if Congress shall enforce the great guarantees which the Supreme Court has declared to be the one pervading purpose of all the recent amendments, then their unwise and unenlightened conduct will fall with the same weight upon the gentlemen from those States who now lend their influence to defeat this bill, as upon the poorest slave who once had no rights which the honorable gentlemen were bound to respect.

But, sir, not only does the decision in the Slaughterhouse cases contain nothing which suggests a doubt of the power of Congress to pass the pending bill, but it contains an express recognition and affirmance of such power. I quote now from page 81 of the volume:

'Nor shall any State deny to any person within its jurisdiction the equal protection of the laws. '
In the light of the history of these amendments, and the pervading purpose of them, which we have already discussed, it is not difficult to give a meaning to this clause. The existence of laws in the States where the newly emancipated negroes resided, which discriminated with gross injustice and hardship against them as a class, was the evil to be remedied by this clause, and by it such laws are forbidden.
If, however, the States did not conform their laws to its requirements, then, by the fifth section of the article of amendment, Congress was authorized to enforce it by suitable legislation. We doubt very much whether any action of a State not directed by way of discrimination against the negroes as a class, or on account of their race, will ever be held to come within the purview of this provision. It is so clearly a provision for that race and that emergency, that a strong case would be necessary for its application to any other. But as it is a State that is to be dealt with, and not alone the validity of its laws, we may safely leave that matter until Congress shall

have exercised its power, or some case of State
oppression, by denial of equal justice in its courts
shall, have claimed a decision at our hands.

No language could convey a more complete assertion
of the power of Congress over the subject embraced in the
present bill than is here expressed. If the States do not conform to the requirements of this clause, if they continue to
deny to any person within their jurisdiction the equal protection of the laws, or as the Supreme Court had said, "deny
equal justice in its courts," then Congress is here said to
have power to enforce the constitutional guarantee by appropriate legislation. That is the power which this bill now
seeks to put in exercise. It proposes to enforce the constitutional guarantee against inequality and discrimination by
appropriate legislation. It does not seek to confer new rights,
nor to place rights conferred by State citizenship under the
protection of the United States, but simply to prevent and
forbid inequality and discrimination on account of race, color,
or previous condition of servitude. Never has there a bill
more completely within the constitutional power of Congress.
Never was there a bill which appealed for support more
strongly to that sense of justice and fair-play which has been
said, and in the main with justice, to be a characteristic of
the Anglo-Saxon race. The Constitution warrants it; the
Supreme Court sanctions it; justice demands it.

Sir, I have replied to the extent of my ability to the
arguments which have been presented by the opponents of this
measure. I have replied also to some of the legal propositions advanced by gentlemen on the other side; and now that
I am about to conclude, I am deeply sensible of the imperfect
manner in which I have performed the task. Technically,
this bill is to decide upon the civil status of the colored
American citizen; a point disputed at the very formation of
our present Government, when by a short-sighted policy, a
policy repugnant to true republican government, one negro
counted as three-fifths of a man. The logical result of this
mistake of the framers of the Constitution strengthened the
cancer of slavery, which finally spread its poisonous tentacles
over the southern portion of the body-politic. To arrest its
growth and save the nation we have passed through the har-
rowing operation of intestine war, dreaded at all times, resorted to at the last extremity, like the surgeon's knife, but
absolutely necessary to extirpate the disease which threatened with the life of the nation the overthrow of civil and
political liberty on this continent. In that dire extremity the

members of the race which I have the honor in part to rep-
resent--the race which pleads for justice at your hands to-
day, forgetful of their inhuman and brutalizing servitude at
the South, their degradation and ostracism at the North--flew
willingly and gallantly to the support of the national Government. Their sufferings, assistance, privations, and trials
in the swamps and in the rice-fields, their valor on the land
and on the sea, is a part of the ever-glorious record which
makes up the history of a nation preserved, and might,
should I urge the claim, incline you to respect and guarantee
their rights and privileges as citizens of our common Republic. But I remember that valor, devotion, and loyalty are
not always rewarded according to their just deserts, and that
after the battle some who have borne the brunt of the fray
may, through neglect or contempt, be assigned to a subordinate place, while the enemies in war may be preferred to
the sufferers.

The results of the war, as seen in reconstruction,
have settled forever the political status of my race. The
passage of this bill will determine the civil status, not only
of the negro, but of any other class of citizens who may feel
themselves discriminated against. It will form the cap-stone
of that temple of liberty, begun on this continent under discouraging circumstances, carried on in spite of the sneers
of monarchists and the cavils of pretended friends of freedom, until at last it stands in all its beautiful symmetry and
proportions, a building the grandest which the world has ever
seen, realizing the most sanguine expectations and the highest hopes of those who, in the name of equal, impartial, and
universal liberty, laid the foundation stones.

The Holy Scriptures tell us of an humble hand-maiden
who long, faithfully and patiently gleaned in the rich fields of
her wealthy kinsman; and we are told further that at last, in
spite of her humble antecedents, she found complete favor in
his sight. For over two centuries our race has "reaped
down your fields. " The cries and woes which we have uttered have "entered into the ears of the Lord of Sabaoth, "
and we are at last politically free. The last vestiture only
is needed--civil rights. Having gained this, we may, with
hearts overflowing with gratitude, and thankful that our prayer
has been granted, repeat the prayer of Ruth: "Entreat me
not to leave thee, or to return from following after thee; for
whither thou goest, I will go; and where thou lodgest, I will
lodge: thy people shall be my people, and thy God my God;
where thou diest, will I die, and there will I be buried; the

Lord do so to me, and more also, if aught but death part
thee and me. " (Great applause.)

BIBLIOGRAPHY

1. Biographical Directory of the American Congress 1774-
    1971. Washington, D. C. : United States Government
    Printing Office, 1971.

2. U. S. Congress. House. Removal of Political Disabili-
    ties. 42nd Congress, 1st session, 1871.

3. U. S. Congress. House. Enforcement of the Fourteenth
    Amendment. 42nd Congress, 1st session, 1871.

4. U. S. Congress. House. Civil Rights Bill. 43rd Con-
    gress, 1st session, 1874.

VI. JEREMIAH HARALSON

Haralson, Jeremiah, a representative from Alabama; born on
a plantation near Columbus, Muscogee County, Georgia, April
1, 1846; was of the Negro race and raised as a slave; self-
educated; moved to Alabama and engaged in agricultural pursuits; became a minister of the gospel; member of the State
house of representatives in 1870; served in the state senate
in 1872; unsuccessful candidate for election in 1868 to the
Forty-first Congress; elected as a Republican to the Forty-
fourth Congress (March 4, 1875-March 3, 1877); appointed to
a federal position in the United States custom house in Baltimore, Maryland; later employed as a clerk in the Interior
Department; appointed August 12, 1882, to the Pension Bureau in Washington, D. C., and resigned August 21, 1884;
moved to Louisiana, where he engaged in agricultural pursuits, and thence to Arkansas in 1904; served as pension
agent for a short time; returned to Alabama and settled in
Selma in 1912; moved to Texas and later to Oklahoma and
Colorado and engaged in coal mining in the latter State;
killed by wild beasts near Denver, Colorado, about 1916.
(1:1066)

BIBLIOGRAPHY

1. Biographical Directory of the American Congress 1774-
    1971. Washington, D. C. : United States Government
    Printing Office, 1971.

VII.   JOHN ADAMS HYMAN

Hyman, John Adams, a Representative from North Carolina;
born a slave near Warrenton, Warren County, North Carolina, July 23, 1840; was of the Negro race; was sold and
sent to Alabama; returned to North Carolina in 1865 and engaged in agricultural pursuits; pursued elementary studies;
delegate to the State equal rights convention in 1865 and to
the State constitutional convention in 1868; member of the
State Senate, 1868-1874; elected as a Republican to the Forty-
fourth Congress (March 4, 1875-March 3, 1877); unsuccessful candidate for renomination in 1876; resumed agricultural
pursuits; special deputy collector of internal revenue for the
fourth district of North Carolina from July 1, 1877 to June
30, 1878; died in Washington, D. C. , on September 14, 1891.
(1:1169)

BIBLIOGRAPHY

1.   Biographical Directory of the American Congress 1774-
        1971.   Washington, D. C. :   United States Government
        Printing Office, 1971.

131

Jefferson Franklin Long--"In manner he was perfectly self possessed. His voice is full and powerful, filling the Hall with ease, while his enunciation was quite good. " (New York Tribune, quoted by Moseley, p. 19)

VIII.   JEFFERSON FRANKLIN LONG

Long, Jefferson Franklin, a Representative from Georgia; born near Knoxville, Crawford County, Georgia, March 3, 1836; was of the Negro race; educated himself; became a merchant tailor in Macon, Georgia; elected as a Republican to the 41st Congress to fill the vacancy caused by the House declaring Samuel F. Gove not entitled to the seat and served from December 22, 1870 to March 3, 1872; was not a candidate for renomination in 1870; delegate to the Republican National Convention at Chicago in 1880 which nominated Garfield and Arthur; resumed business in Macon, Georgia, and died there February 5, 1900.   (1:1305)

MODIFICATION OF TEST OATH

... modify the test-oath, and ... give to those
men in the rebel states who are disloyal to-day
to the Government this favor. We propose, sir,
to remove political disabilities from the very men
who were the leaders of the Ku Klux [sic] and
who have committed midnight outrages in that
state.... I think that I am doing my duty to my
constituents and my duty to my country when I
vote against any such proposition. (2:881-882)

Mr. LONG. Mr. Speaker the object of the bill before
the House is to modify the test-oath. As a citizen of the
South, living in Georgia, born and raised in that State, having been there during the war and up to the present time, I
know the condition of affairs in that State. Now, sir, we
propose here to-day to modify the test-oath, and to give to
those men in the rebel States who are disloyal to-day to the
Government this favor. We propose, sir, to remove political disabilities from the very men who were the leaders of
the Ku Klux and who have committed midnight outrages in
that State.

What do those men say? Before their disabilities are
removed they say, "We will remain quiet until all of our
disabilities are removed, and then we shall again take the
lead." Why, Mr. Speaker, in my State since emancipation
there have been over five hundred loyal men shot down by
the disloyal men there, and not one of those who took part
in committing those outrages has ever been brought to justice. Do we, then, really propose here to-day, when the
country is not ready for it, when those disloyal people still
hate this Government, when loyal men dare not carry the
"stars and stripes" through our streets, for if they do they
will be turned out of employment, to relieve from political
disability the very men who have committed these Ku Klux
outrages? I think that I am doing my duty to my constituents
and my duty to my country when I vote against any such proposition.

134

Yes, sir; I do mean that murders and outrages are being committed there. I received no longer ago than this morning a letter from a man in my State, a loyal man who was appointed postmaster by the President, stating that he was beaten in the streets a few days ago. I have also received information from the lower part of Georgia that disloyal men went in the midnight disguised and took a loyal man out and shot him; and not one of them has been brought to justice. Loyal men are constantly being cruelly beaten. When we take the men who commit these outrages before judges and juries we find that they are in the hands of the very Ku Klux themselves who protect them.

Mr. Speaker, I propose, as a man raised as a slave, my mother a slave before me, and my ancestry slaves as far back as I can trace them, yet holding no animosity to the law-abiding people of my State and those who are willing to stand by the Government, while I am willing to remove the disabilities of all such who will support the Government, still I propose for one, knowing the condition of things there in Georgia, not to vote for any modification of the test-oath in favor of disloyal men.

Gentlemen on the other side of the House have complimented men on this side. I hope the blood of the Ku Klux has not got upon this side; I hope not. If this House removes the disabilities of disloyal men by modifying the test-oath, I venture to prophesy you will again have trouble from the very same men who gave you trouble before.

BIBLIOGRAPHY

1. Biographical Directory of the American Congress 1774-1971. Washington, D.C.: United States Government Printing Office, 1971.

2. U. S. Congress. House. Modification of the Test-Oath. 41st Congress, 3rd session, 1871.

JOHN R. LYNCH

IX. JOHN ROY LYNCH

Lynch, John Roy, a Representative from Mississippi; born near Vidalia, Concordia Parish, Louisiana, September 10, 1847; was of the Negro race; after his father's death moved with his mother to Natchez, Mississippi, in 1863, where they were held as slaves; after emancipation engaged in photography and obtained a fair education by attending evening school; appointed by Governor Ames as a justice of the peace in 1869; member of the State house of representatives, 1869-1873, and served the last term as speaker; delegate to the Republican National Conventions in 1872, 1884, 1888, 1892, and 1900; elected as a Republican to the Forty-third Congress (March 4, 1873-March 3, 1877); unsuccessful candidate for re-election in 1876 to the Forth-fifth Congress; successfully contested the election of James R. Chalmers to the Forty-seventh Congress and served from April 29, 1882 to March 3, 1883; unsuccessful candidate for re-election in 1882 to the Forty-eighth Congress; returned to his plantation in Adams County, Mississippi, and engaged in agricultural pursuits; chairman of the Republican State executive committee, 1881-1889; member of the Republican National Committee for the State of Mississippi, 1884-1889; temporary chairman of the Republican National Convention at Chicago in

137

1884; Fourth Auditor of the Treasury for the Navy Department under President Harrison, 1889-1893; studied law; was
admitted to the Mississippi bar in 1896; returned to Washington, D. C. in 1897, where he practiced his profession until
1898, when he was appointed an additional paymaster of Volunteers during the Spanish-American War by President Mc-
Kinley, then as paymaster in the Regular Army with the rank
of captain, 1901, promoted to major in 1906; retired from
the Regular Army 1911; moved to Chicago, Illinois in 1912
and continued the practice of his profession until his death
in that city on November, 1939.

CIVIL RIGHTS

No, Mr. Speaker, it is not social rights that we desire. We have enough of that already. What we ask is protection in the enjoyment of public rights. Rights which are or should be accorded to every citizen alike.... Mr. Speaker, if this unjust discrimination is to be longer tolerated by the American people, which I do not, cannot, and will not believe until I am forced to do so, then I can only say with sorrow and regret that our boasted civilization is a fraud; our republican institutions a failure; our social system a disgrace; and our religion a complete hypocrisy. (2:940-947)

Mr. LYNCH. Mr. Speaker, I was not particularly anxious to take part in this debate, and would not have done so but for the fact that this bill has created a great deal of discussion both in and outside of the halls of Congress. In order to answer successfully the arguments that have been made against the bill, I deem it necessary, if my time will allow me to do so, to discuss the question from three standpoints--legal, social, and political. I confess, Mr. Speaker, that it is with hesitancy that I shall attempt to make a few remarks upon the legal question involved; not that I entertain any doubts as to the constitutionality of the pending bill, but because that branch of the subject has been so ably, successfully, and satisfactorily discussed by other gentlemen who have spoken in the affirmative of the question. The importance of the subject, however, is my apology to the House for submitting a few remarks upon this point in addition to what has already been said.

CONSTITUTIONALITY OF THE BILL

It is a fact well known by those who are at all familiar with the history of our Government that the great question of State rights--absolute State sovereignty as understood by

the Calhoun school of politicians--has been a continuous
source of political agitation for a great many years.   In fact,
for a number of years anterior to the rebellion this was the
chief topic of political discussion.   It continued to agitate the
public mind from year to year and from time to time until
the question was finally settled upon the field of battle.   The
war, however, did not result in the recognition of what may
be called a centralized government, nor did it result in the
destruction of the independent functions of the several States,
except in certain particulars.   But it did result in the recognition, and I hope the acceptance, of what may be called a
medium between these two extremes; and this medium position or liberal policy has been incorporated in the Federal
Constitution through the recent amendments to that instrument.   But many of our constitutional lawyers of to-day are
men who received their legal and political training during the
discussion of the great question of State rights and under the
tutorship of those who were identified with the Calhoun school
of impracticable State rights theorists; they having been taught
to believe that the Constitution as it was justified the construction they placed upon it, and this impression having been
so indelibly and unalterably fixed upon their minds that recent
changes, alterations, and amendments have failed to bring
about a corresponding change in their construction of the Constitution.   In fact, they seem to forget that the Constitution
as it is is not in every respect the Constitution as it was.

We have a practical illustration of the correctness of
this assertion in the person of the distinguished gentleman
from Georgia (Mr. STEPHENS) and I believe my colleague
who sits near me (Mr. LAMAR) and others who agree with
them in their construction of the Constitution.   But believing
as I do that the Constitution as a whole should be so construed as to carry out the intention of the framers of the recent amendments, it will not be surprising to the House and
to the country when I assert that it is impossible for me to
agree with those who so construe the Constitution as to arrive at the erroneous conclusion that the pending bill is in
violation of that instrument.   It is not my purpose, however,
to give the House simply the benefit of my own opinion upon
the question, but to endeavor to show to your satisfaction, if
possible, that the construction which I place upon the Constitution is precisely in accordance with that placed upon it by
the highest judicial tribunal in the land, the Supreme Court
of the United States.   And this brings us to the celebrated
Slaughter-house cases.   But before referring to the decision
of the court in detail, I will take this occasion to remark

that, for the purposes of this debate at least, I accept as
correct the theory that Congress cannot constitutionally pass
any law unless it have expressed constitutional grant of power
to do so; that the constitutional right of Congress to pass a
law must not be implied, but expressed; and that in the absence of such expressed constitutional grant of power the
right does not exist. In other words--

> The powers not delegated to the United States by
> the Constitution, nor prohibited by it to the States,
> are reserved to the States respectively, or to the
> people.

I repeat, that for the purposes of this debate at least,
I accept as correct this theory. After having read over the
decision of the court in these Slaughter-house cases several
times very carefully, I have been brought very forcibly to
this conclusion: that so far as this decision refers to the
question of civil rights--the kind of civil rights referred to
in this bill--it means this and nothing more: that whatever
right or power a State may have had prior to the ratification
of the fourteenth amendment it still has, except in certain
particulars. In other words, the fourteenth amendment was
not intended, in the opinion of the court, to confer upon the
Federal Government additional powers in general terms, but
only in certain particulars. What are those particulars
wherein the fourteenth amendment confers upon the Federal
Government powers which it did not have before? The right
to prevent distinctions and discriminations between the citizens of the United States and of the several States whenever
such distinctions and discriminations are made on account of
race, color, or previous condition of servitude; and that distinctions and discriminations made upon any other ground than
these are not prohibited by the fourteenth amendment. As
the discrimination referred to in the Slaughter-house cases
was not made upon either of these grounds, it did not come
within the constitutional prohibition. As the pending bill refers only to such discriminations as are made on account of
race, color, or previous condition of servitude, it necessarily
follows that the bill is in harmony with the Constitution as
construed by the Supreme Court.

I will now ask the Clerk to read the following extract
from the decision upon which the legal gentlemen on the other
side of the House have chiefly relied to sustain them in the
assertion that the court has virtually decided the pending bill
to be unconstitutional.

The Clerk read as follows:

> Of the privileges and immunities of the citizens
> of the United States, and of the privileges and
> immunities of the citizens of the State, and what
> they respectively are, we will presently consider;
> but we wish to state here that it is only the
> former which are placed by this clause under the
> protection of the Federal Constitution, and that
> the latter, whatever they may be, are not intended
> to have any additional protection by this paragraph
> of the amendment.
>
> If, then, there is a difference between the priv-
> ileges and immunities belonging to a citizen of the
> United States as such, and those belonging to the
> citizen of the State as such, the latter must rest
> for their security and protection where they have
> heretofore rested, for they are not embraced by
> this paragraph of the amendment.

Mr. LYNCH. If the court had said nothing more on
the question of civil rights, then there would probably be
some force in the argument. But after explaining at length
why the case before it did not come within the constitutional
prohibition, the court says:

> Having shown that the privileges and immunities
> relied on in the argument are those which belong
> to citizens of the States as such, and that they
> are left to the State government for security and
> protection, and not by this article placed under
> the special care of the Federal Government, we
> may hold ourselves excused from defining the
> privileges and immunities of citizens of the United
> States which no State can abridge until some case
> involving those privileges may make it necessary
> to do so.

But there are some democrats, and if I am not mistaken the gentleman from Georgia (Mr. STEPHENS) is one
among the number, who are willing to admit that the recent
amendments to the Constitution guarantee to the colored citizens all of the rights, privileges, and immunities that are
enjoyed by white citizens. But they say that it is the province of the several States, and not that of the Federal Government, to enforce these constitutional guarantees. This is

the most important point in the whole argument. Upon its
decision this bill must stand or fall. We will now suppose
that the constitutional guarantee of equal rights is conceded,
which is an important concession for those calling themselves
Jeffersonian democrats to make. The question that now presents itself is, has the Federal Government the constitutional
right to enforce by suitable and appropriate legislation the
guarantees herein referred to? Gentlemen on the other side
of the House answer the question in the negative; but the
Supreme Court answers the question in the following unmistakable language:

> Nor shall any State deny to any person within its
> jurisdiction the equal protection of the laws. In
> the light of the history of these amendments and
> the pervading purpose of them, which we have al-
> ready discussed, it is not difficult to give a mean-
> ing to this clause. The existence of laws, in the
> States where the newly emancipated negroes re-
> sided, which discriminated with gross injustice
> and hardship against them as a class, was the
> evil to be remedied by this clause, and by it such
> laws are forbidden.
>
> If, however, the States did not conform their
> laws to its requirements, then by the fifth section
> of the article of amendment Congress was author-
> ized to enforce it by suitable legislation. We
> doubt very much whether any action of a State not
> directed by way of discrimination against the ne-
> groes as a class, or an account of their race,
> will ever be held to come within the purview of
> this provision.

It will be seen from the above that the constitutional
right of Congress to pass this bill is fully conceded by the
Supreme Court. But before leaving this subject, I desire to
call attention to a short legal argument that was made by a
distinguished lawyer in the other end of the Capitol (if it is
parliamentary to do so) when the bill was under consideration
before that body:

The Clerk will now read the fourth section of the bill;
the section referred to by the distinguished Wisconsin Senator.

The Clerk read as follows:

SEC. 4. That no citizen possessing all other
qualifications which are or may be prescribed by
law shall be disqualified for service as juror in
any court, national or State, by reason of race,
color, or previous condition of servitude; and any
office or other persons charged with any duty in
the selection or summoning of jurors who shall
exclude or fail to summon any citizen for the reason above named shall, on conviction thereof, be
deemed guilty of a misdemeanor and be fined not
less than $1, 000 nor more than $5, 000.

Mr. LYNCH. The position assumed by the eminent
lawyer is so unreasonable, untenable, and illogical that it
would have surprised me had it been taken by an ordinary
village lawyer of inferior acquirements. There is nothing in
this section that will justify the assertion that it contemplates
regulating State juries. It simply contemplates carrying into
effect the constitutional prohibition against distinctions on account of race or color.

There is also a constitutional prohibition against religious proscription. Let us suppose that another section conferred the power on Congress to enforce the provisions of
that article by appropriate legislation; then suppose a State
should pass a law disqualifying from voting, holding office,
or serving on juries all persons who may be identified with
a certain religious denomination; would the distinguished Wisconsin Senator then contend that Congress would have no
right to pass a law prohibiting this discrimination, in the
fact of the constitutional prohibition and the right conferred
upon Congress to enforce it by appropriate legislation? I
contend that any provision in the constitution or laws of any
State that is in conflict with the Constitution of the United
States is absolutely null and void; for the Constitution itself
declares that--

This Constitution and the laws of the United
States which shall be made in pursuance thereof
... shall be the supreme law of the land; and the
judges in every State shall be bound thereby, anything in the constitution or laws of any State to
the contrary notwithstanding.

The Constitution further declares that:

> No State shall make or enforce any law which
> shall abridge the privileges or immunities of cit-
> izens of the United States, ... nor deny to any
> person within its jurisdiction the equal protection
> of the laws.

And that--

> The Congress shall have power to enforce this
> article by appropriate legislation.

As the Supreme Court has decided that the above constitutional provision was intended to confer upon Congress
the power to prevent distinctions and discriminations when
made on account of race or color, I contend that the power
of Congress in this respect is applicable to every office under
the constitution and laws of any State. Some may think that
this is extraordinary power; but such is not the case. For
any State can, without violating the fourteenth or fifteenth
amendments and the provisions of this bill, prohibit any one
from voting, holding office, or serving on juries in their
respective States, who cannot read and write, or who does
not own a certain amount of property, or who shall not have
resided in the State for a certain number of months, days,
or years. The only thing these amendments prevent them
from doing in this respect is making the color of a person
or the race with which any person may be identified a ground
of disqualification from the enjoyment of any of these privileges. The question seems to me to be so clear that further
argument is unnecessary.

CIVIL RIGHTS AND SOCIAL EQUALITY

I will now endeavor to answer the arguments of those
who have been contending that the passage of this bill is an
effort to bring about social equality between the races. That
the passage of this bill can in any manner affect the social
status of anyone seems to me to be absurd and ridiculous.
I have never believed for a moment that social equality could
be brought about even between persons of the same race. I
have always believed that social distinctions existed among
white people the same as among colored people. But those
who contend that the passage of this bill will have a tendency
to bring about social equality between the races virtually and
substantially admit that there are no social distinctions among
white people whatever, but that all white persons, regardless

of their moral character, are the social equals of each other;
for if by cc ıferring upon colored people the same rights and
privileges that are now exercised and enjoyed by whites in-
discriminately will result in bringing about social equality between the races, then the same process of reasoning must
necessarily bring us to the conclusion that there are no social distinctions among whites, because all white persons,
regardless of their social standing, are permitted to enjoy
these rights. See then how unreasonable, unjust, and false
is the assertion that social equality is involved in this legislation. I cannot believe that gentlemen on the other side of
the House mean what they say when they admit as they do,
that the immoral, the ignorants and the degraded of their own
race are the social equals of themselves and their families.
If they do, then I can only assure them that they do not put
as high an estimate upon their own social standing as respectable and intelligent colored people place upon theirs; for
there are hundreds and thousands of white people of both
sexes whom I know to be the social inferiors of respectable
and intelligent colored people. I can then assure that portion
of my democratic friends on the other side of the House
whom I regard as my social inferiors that if at any time I
should meet any one of you at a hotel and occupy a seat at the
same table with you, or the same seat in a car with you, do
not think that I have thereby accepted you as my social equal.
Not at all. But if any one should attempt to discriminate
against you for no other reason than because you are identified with a particular race or religious sect, I would regard
it as an outrage; as a violation of the principles of republicanism; and I would be in favor of protecting you in the exercise and enjoyment of your rights by suitable and appropriate legislation.

        No, Mr. Speaker, it is not social rights that we de-
sire. We have enough of that already. What we ask is protection in the enjoyment of public rights. Rights which are
or should be accorded to every citizen alike. Under our present system of race distinctions a white woman of a questionable social standing, yes, I may say, of an admitted immoral character, can go to any public place or upon any public conveyance and be the recipient of the same treatment,
the same courtesy, and the same respect that is usually accorded to the most refined and virtuous; but let an intelligent,
modest, refined colored lady present herself and ask that the
same privileges be accorded to her that have just been accorded to her social inferior of the white race, and in nine
cases, out of ten, except in certain portions of the country,

she will not only be refused, but insulted for making the
request.

Mr. Speaker, I ask the members of this House in all
candor, is this right? I appeal to your sensitive feelings as
husbands, fathers, and brothers, is this just? You who have
affectionate companions, attractive daughters, and loving sisters, is this just? If you have any of the ingredients of
manhood in your composition you will answer the question
most emphatically, No! What a sad commentary upon our
system of government, our religion, and our civilization!
Think of it for a moment; here am I, a member of your
honorable body, representing one of the largest and wealthi-
est districts in the State of Mississippi, and possibly in the
South; a district composed of persons of different races, re-
ligions, and nationalities; and yet, when I leave my home to
come to the capital of the nation, to take part in the delib-
erations of the House and to participate with you in making
laws for the government of this great Republic, in coming
through the God-forsaken States of Kentucky and Tennessee,
if I come by the way of Louisville or Chattanooga, I am
treated, not as an American citizen, but as a brute. Forced
to occupy a filthy smoking-car both night and day, with drunkards, gamblers, and criminals; and for what? Not that I am
unable or unwilling to pay my way; not that I am obnoxious in
my personal appearance or disrespectful in my conduct; but
simply because I happen to be of a darker complexion. If
this treatment was confined to persons of our own sex we
could possibly afford to endure it. But such is not the case.
Our wives and our daughters, our sisters and our mothers,
are subjected to the same insults and to the same uncivilized
treatment. You may ask why we do not institute civil suits
in the State courts. What a farce! Talk about instituting a
civil-rights suit in the State courts of Kentucky, for instance,
where the decision of the judge is virtually rendered before
he enters the courthouse, and the verdict of the jury substantially rendered before it is impaneled. The only moments
of my life when I am necessarily compelled to question my
loyalty to my Government or my devotion to the flag of my
country is when I read of outrages having been committed
upon innocent colored people and the perpetrators go un-
whipped of justice, and when I leave my home to go traveling.

Mr. Speaker, if this unjust discrimination is to be
longer tolerated by the American people, which I do not, cannot, and will not believe until I am forced to do so, then I
can only say with sorrow and regret that our boasted civili-

zation is a fraud; our republican institutions a failure; our
social system a disgrace; and our religion a complete hypocrisy.   But I have an abiding confidence--(though I must confess that that confidence was seriously shaken a little over
two months ago)--but still I have an abiding confidence in the
patriotism of this people, in their devotion to the cause of
human rights, and in the stability of our republican institutions.   I hope that I will not be deceived.   I love the land
that gave me birth; I love the Stars and Stripes.   This
country is where I intend to live, where I expect to die.   To
preserve the honor of the national flag and to maintain per-
petually the Union of the States, hundreds, and I may say
thousands, of noble, brave, and true-hearted colored men
have fought, bled, and died.   And now, Mr. Speaker, I ask,
can it be possible that that flag under which they fought is to
be a shield and a protection to all races and classes of persons except the colored race?   God forbid!

THE SCHOOL CLAUSE

The enemies of this bill have been trying very hard to
create the impression that it is the object of its advocates to
bring about a compulsory system of mixed schools.   It is not
my intention at this time to enter into a discussion of the
question as to the propriety or impropriety of mixed schools;
as to whether or not such a system is esential to destroy
race distinctions and break down race prejudices.   I will
leave these questions to be discussed by those who have given
the subject a more thorough consideration.   The question that
now presents itself to our minds is, what will be the effect
of this legislation on the public-school system of the country,
and more especially in the South?   It is to this question that
I now propose to speak.   I regard this school clause as the
most harmless provision in the bill.   If it were true that the
passage of this bill with the school clause in it would tolerate
the existence of none but a system of mixed free schools,
then I would question very seriously the propriety of retaining
such a clause; but such is not the case.   If I understand the
bill correctly (and I think I do), it simply confers upon all
citizens, or rather recognizes the right which has already
been conferred upon all citizens, to send their children to
any public free school that is supported in whole or in part
by taxation, the exercise of the right to remain a matter of
option as it now is--nothing compulsory about it.   That the
passage of this bill can result in breaking up the public
school system in any State is absurd.   The men who make

these reckless assertions are very well aware of the fact, or
else they are guilty of unpardonable ignorance, that every
right and privilege that is enumerated in this bill has already
been conferred upon all citizens alike in at least one-half of
the States of this Union by State legislation.   In every Southern State where the republican party is in power a civil-rights
bill is in force that is more severe in its penalties than are
the penalties in this bill.   We find mixed-school clauses in
some of their State constitutions.   If, then, the passage of
this bill, which does not confer upon the colored people of
such States any rights that they do not possess already, will
result in breaking up the public-school system in their respective States, why is it that State legislation has not broken
them up!   This proves very conclusively, I think, that there
is nothing in the argument whatever, and that the school
clause is the most harmless provision in the bill.   My opinion
is that the passage of this bill just as it passed the Senate
will bring about mixed schools practically only in localities
where one or the other of the two races is small in numbers,
and that in localities where both races are large in numbers
separate schools and separate institutions of learning will continue to exist, for a number of years at least.

    I now ask the Clerk to read the following editorial,
which appeared in a democratic paper in my own State when
the bill was under discussion in the Senate.   This is from
the Jackson Clarion, the leading conservative paper in the
State, the editor of which is known to be a moderate, reasonable, and sensible man.

    The Clerk read as follows:

THE CIVIL-RIGHTS BILL AND
OUR PUBLIC-SCHOOL SYSTEM

        The question has been asked what effect will the
    civil-rights bill have on the public-school system
    of our State if it should become a law!   Our
    opinion is that it will have none at all.   The pro-
    visions of the bill do not necessarily break up the
    separate-school system, unless the people inter-
    ested choose that they shall do so; and there is
    no reason to believe that the colored people of
    this State are dissatisfied with the system as it is,
    or that they are not content to let well enough
    alone.   As a people, they have not shown a dis-

position to thrust themselves where they are not
wanted, or rather had no right to go. While they
have been naturally tenacious of their newly acquired privileges, their general conduct will bear
them witness that they have shown consideration
for the feelings of the whites.

The race line in politics never would have been
drawn if opposition had not been made to their enjoyment of equal privileges in the Government and
under the laws after they were emancipated.

As to our public-school system, so far as it
bears upon the races, we have heard no complaint
whatever. It is not asserted that it is operated
more advantageously to the whites than to the
blacks. Its benefits are shared alike by all; and
we do not believe the colored people, if left to
the guidance of their own judgments, will comment
to jeopardize these benefits in a vain attempt to
acquire something better.

Mr. LYNCH. The question may be asked, however,
if the colored people in a majority of the States are entitled
by State legislation to all of the rights and privileges enumerated in this bill, and if they will not insist upon mixing the
children in the public schools in all localities, what is the
necessity of retaining this clause? The reasons are numerous, but I will only mention a few of them. In the first
place, it is contrary to our system of government to discriminate by law between persons on account of their race,
their color, their religion, or the place of their birth. It is
just as wrong and just as contrary to republicanism to provide by law for the education of children who may be identified with a certain race in separate schools to themselves,
as to provide by law for the education of children who may
be identified with a certain religious denomination in separate
schools to themselves. The duty of the law-maker is to
know no race, no color, no religion, no nationality, except
to prevent distinctions on any of these grounds, so far as the
law is concerned.

The colored people in asking the passage of this bill
just as it passed the Senate do not thereby admit that their
children can be better educated in white than in colored
schools; nor that white teachers because they are white are
better qualified to teach than colored ones. But they recognize the fact that the distinction when made and tolerated by

law is an unjust and odious proscription: that you make their color a ground of objection, and consequently a crime. This is what we most earnestly protest against. Let us confer upon all citizens, then, the rights to which they are entitled under the Constitution; and then if they choose to have their children educated in separate schools, as they do in my own State, then both races will be satisfied, because they will know that the separation is their own voluntary act and not legislative compulsion.

Another reason why the school clause ought to be retained is because the negro question ought to be removed from the politics of the country. It has been a disturbing element in the country ever since the Declaration of Independence, and it will continue to be so long as the colored man is denied any right or privilege that is enjoyed by the white man. Pass this bill as it passed the Senate, and there will be nothing more for the colored people to ask or expect in the way of civil rights. Equal rights having been made an accomplished fact, opposition to the exercise thereof will gradually pass away, and the everlasting negro question will then be removed from the politics of the country for the first time since the existence of the Government. Let us, then, be just as well as generous. Let us confer upon the colored citizens equal rights, and, my word for it, they will exercise their rights with moderation and with wise discretion.

CIVIL RIGHTS FROM A POLITICAL STAND-POINT

I now come to the important part of my subject--civil rights from a political stand-point. In discussing this branch of the subject, I do not deem it necessary to make any appeal to the republican members whatever in behalf of this bill. It is presumed, and correctly, too, I hope, that every republican member of the House will vote for this bill. The country expects it, the colored people ask it, the republican party promised it, and justice demands it. It is not necessary therefore for me to appeal to republicans in behalf of a measure that they are known to be in favor of.

But it has been suggested that it is not necessary for me to make an appeal to the democratic, conservative, or liberal republican members in behalf of this measure; that they will go against it to a man. This may be true, but I prefer to judge them by their acts. I will not condemn them in advance. But I desire to call the attention of the demo-

cratic members of the House to one or two things in connection with the history of their organization. Your party went
before the country in 1872 with a pledge that it would protect
the colored people in all of their rights and privileges under
the Constitution, and to convince them of your sincerity you
nominated as your standard-bearer one who had proved himself to be their life-long friend and advocate. But the colored
people did not believe that you were sincere, and consequently
did not trust you. As the promise was made unconditionally,
however, their refusal to trust you does not relieve you from
the performance of the promise. Think for a moment what
the effect of your votes upon this bill will be. If you vote in
favor of this measure, which will be nothing more than re-
deeming the promises made by you in 1872, it will convince
the colored people that they were mistaken when they supposed that you made the promise for no other purpose than
to deceive them. But if you should vote against this bill,
which I am afraid you intend to do, you will thereby convince
them that they were not mistaken when they supposed that you
made the promise for no other purpose than to deceive them.
It can have no other effect than to increase their suspicion,
strengthen their doubts, and intensify their devotion to the
republican party. It will demonstrate to the country and to
the world that you attempted in 1872 to obtain power under
false pretenses. I once heard a very eminent lawyer make
the remark that the crime of obtaining money or goods under
false pretenses is in his opinion the next crime to murder.
I ask the democratic and conservative members of the House,
will you, by voting against this bill, convict yourselves of
attempting in 1872 to obtain power under false pretenses?

I will take this occasion to say to my democratic
friends, that I do not wish to be understood as endeavoring
to convey the idea that all of the prominent men who were
identified with the so-called liberal movement in 1872 were
actuated by improper motives, that they made promises
which they never intended to redeem. Far from it. I confess, Mr. Speaker, that some of the best and most steadfast
friends the colored people in this country have ever had were
identified with that movement. Even the man whom you selected, from necessity and not from choice, as your standard-bearer on that occasion is one whose memory will ever
live in the hearts of the colored people of this country as one
of their best, their strongest, and most consistent friends.
They will ever cherish his memory, in consequence of his
life-long devotion to the cause of liberty, humanity, and jus-
tice--for his earnest, continuous, persistent, and consistent

advocacy of what he was pleased to term manhood suffrage.
In voting against him so unanimously as the colored voters
did, it was not because they questioned his honesty, or his
devotion to the cause of equal rights, but they recognized the
fact he made the same mistake that many of our great men
have made--he allowed his ambition to control his better
judgment.   While the colored voters would have cheerfully
supported him for the Presidency under different circumstances, they could not give their votes to elevate him to that
position through such a questionable channel as that selected
by him in 1872.   But since he has passed away, they are
willing to remember only his virtues and to forget his faults.
I might refer to several other illustrious names that were
identified with that movement and whose fidelity to the cause
of civil rights can never be questioned, but time will not allow me to do so.

        I will now refer to some of the unfortunate remarks
that were made by some gentlemen on the other side of the
House during the last session-especially these made by the
gentleman from North Carolina (Mr. ROBBINS) and those
made by the gentleman from Virginia (Mr. HARRIS).   These
two gentlemen are evidently strong believers in the exploded
theory of white superiority and negro inferiority.   But in
order to show what a difference of opinion exists among men,
with regard to man's superiority over man, it gives me pleasure to assure those two gentlemen that if at any time either
of them should become so generous as to admit that I, for
instance, am his equal, I would certainly regard it as anything else but complimentary to myself.   This may be regarded as a little selfish, but as all of us are selfish to
some extent, I must confess that I am no exception to the
general rule.   The gentleman from North Carolina admits,
ironically, that the colored people, even when in bondage and
ignorance, could equal, if not excel, the whites in some
things--dancing, singing, and eloquence, for instance.   We
will admit, for the sake of the argument, that in this the
gentleman is correct, and will ask the question, Why is it
that the colored people could equal the whites in these respects, while in bondage and ignorance, but not in others?
The answer is an easy one: You could not prevent them from
dancing unless you kept them continually tied; you could not
prevent them from singing unless you kept them continually
gagged; you could not prevent them from being eloquent unless you deprived them of the power of speech; but you could
and did prevent them from becoming educated for fear that
they would equal you in every other respect; for no educated

people can be held in bondage.   If the argument proves anything, therefore, it is only this: That if the colored people
while in bondage and ignorance could equal the whites in
these respects, give them their freedom and allow them to
become educated and they will equal the whites in every other
respect.   At any rate I cannot see how any reasonable man
can object to giving them an opportunity to do so if they can.
It does not become southern white men, in my opinion, to
boast about the ignorance of the colored people, when you
know that their ignorance is the result of the enforcement of
your unjust laws.   Anyone would suppose, from the style and
the manner of the gentleman from North Carolina, that the
white man's government of the State from which he comes is
one of the best States in the Union, for white men to live in
at least.   But I will ask the Clerk to read, for the information of that gentleman, the following article from a democratic
paper in my own State.

            The Clerk read as follows:

            The following from the Charlotte Democrat is a
        hard hit: 'The Legislature of Mississippi has just
        elected a negro to represent that State in the
        United States Senate.   The white men who re-
        cently moved from Cabarrus County, North Caro-
        lina, to Mississippi, to better their condition, will
        please report the situation and say   which they
        like best, white rule in North Carolina or black
        rule in Mississippi. '
            We do not see the point of the joke.   The
        'white men who moved from Cabarrus will doubt-
        less report' that they have not realized, and do
        not expect to, any serious inconvenience from the
        election of Bruce.   It is better to be endured
        than the inconvenience of eking out a starveling
        existence in a worn-out State like North Carolina.
        Besides, when we look to the executive offices of
        the two States we will find that the governor of
        North Carolina claims to be as stanch a republican
        as his excellency of Mississippi.   And then con-
        trast the financial condition of the two States.
        There is poor old North Carolina burdened with a
        debt of $30, 000, 000, with interest accumulating
        so rapidly that she is unable to pay it much less
        the principal.   The debt of Mississippi, on the
        other hand, is but three millions, and with her

wonderful recuperative powers it can be wiped out
in a few years by the economical management
solemnly promised by those in charge of her State
government.

The men 'who moved from Cabarrus' will 'look
upon this picture, and on this,' and conclude that
they have bettered their condition, notwithstanding
affairs are not entirely as they would have them.
A warm welcome to them.

Mr. LYNCH. So far as the gentleman from Virginia
is concerned, the gentleman who so far forgot himself as to
be disrespectful to one of his fellow-members, I have only
this remark to make: Having served in the Legislature of
my own State several years, where I had the privilege of
meeting some of the best, the ablest, and I may add, the
bitterest democrats in the State, it gives me pleasure to be
able to say, that with all of their bitterness upon political
questions, they never failed to preserve and maintain that degree of dignity, self-respect, and parliamentary decorum
which always characterized intelligent legislators and well-
bred gentlemen. Take, for instance, my eloquent and distinguished colleague (Mr. LAMAR) on the other side of the
House, and I venture to assert that he will never declare
upon this floor or elsewhere that he is only addressing white
men. No, sir; Mississippians do not send such men to
Congress, nor even to their State Legislature. For if they
did, it would not only be a sad and serious reflection upon
their intelligence, but it would be a humiliating disgrace to
the State.

Such sentiments as those uttered by the gentleman
from North Carolina and the gentleman from Virginia are
certainly calculated to do the southern white people a great
deal more harm than it is possible for them to do the colored
people. In consequence of which I can say to those two gentlemen, that I know of no stronger rebuke than the language
of the Saviour of the world when praying for its persecutors:

Father, forgive them; for they know not what they
do.

THE SOUTH NOT OPPOSED TO CIVIL RIGHTS

The opposition to civil rights in the South is not so

general or intense as a great many would have the country
believe. It is a mistaken idea that all of the white people in
the South outside of the republican party are bitterly opposed
to this bill. In my own State, and especially in my own district, the democrats as a rule are indifferent as to its fate.
It is true they would not vote for it, but they reason from
this stand-point: The civil-rights bill does not confer upon
the colored people of Mississippi any rights that they are not
entitled to already under the constitution and laws of the State.
We certainly have no objection, then, to allowing the colored
people in other States to enjoy the same rights that they are
entitled to in our own State. To illustrate this point more
forcibly, I ask the Clerk to read the following article from
the ablest conservative paper in the State, a paper, however,
that is opposed to the White League. This article was published when the civil-rights bill was under discussion in the
Senate last winter.

The Clerk read as follows:

A civil-rights bill is before the Senate. As we
have civil-rights here in Mississippi and elsewhere
in the South, we do not understand why southern
representatives should concern themselves about
applying the measure to other portions of the
country; or what practical interest we have in the
question. On the 29th, Senator NORWOOD, of
Georgia, one of the mediocrities to whom expedi-
ency has assigned a place for which he is unfitted,
delivered himself of a weak and driveling speech
on the subject in which he did what he was able
to keep alive sectional strife and the prejudices of
race. We will venture to say that his colleague,
General GORDON, who was a true soldier when
the war was raging, will not be drawn into the
mischievous controversy which demagogues from
both sections, and especially latter-day fire-eaters
who have become intensely enraged since the sur-
render, take delight in carrying on.

Mr. LYNCH. What is true of Mississippi in this respect is true of nearly every State where a civil-rights bill
is in force. In proof of this, I ask the Clerk to read the
following remarks made by the present democratic governor
of Arkansas during his candidacy for that office:

The Clerk read as follows:

> But I hear it whispered round and about that the
> Southern States, and Arkansas among them, are
> to be overhauled by Congress this winter had in
> some way reconstructed, because the colored man
> has no law giving him civil-rights in those States.
> Upon this pretext we are to be upset and worked
> over. My fellow-citizens, one and all, upon this
> proposition Arkansas is at home and comfortable.
> In the acts of the Legislature of 1873, pages 15-
> 19 (No. 19), a 'civil-rights bill,' which is now in
> force--almost a copy, if I mistake not, of the bill
> Mr. Sumner shortened his life in vainly trying to
> get Congress to pass. If Congress next winter
> can get up one more definite, more minute, and
> more specific in giving rights to the colored man,
> I would be pleased to look upon and observe it.
> That act is now in force, as I said, and I know
> of no one who wants to repeal it, and certainly I
> do not want it repealed; and will not favor its re-
> peal; and I do hope, if our opponents do start in
> this direction before Congress, they will call at-
> tention to it directly. If there is any complaint
> with and among our colored friends as to the
> terms of this act, or as to its not being enforced,
> I have not heard of them, and I am persuaded
> there have been none.

Mr. LYNCH. It will be seen from the above that if
Mr. Garland means what he says, which remains to be seen,
the democratic or conservative party in Arkansas is in favor
of civil rights for the colored people. Why? Simply because, the republican Legislature having passed the bill, democrats now see that it is not such a bad thing after all. But
if the Legislature had failed to pass it, as in Alabama for
instance, White League demagogues would have appealed to
the passions and prejudices of the whites, and made them believe that this legislation is intended to bring about a revolution in society. The opposition to civil rights in the South
therefore is confined almost exclusively to States under democratic control, or States where the Legislature has failed or
refused to pass a civil-rights bill. I ask the republican
members of the House, then, will you refuse or fail to do
justice to the colored man in obedience to the behests of
three or four democratic States in the South? If so, then

the republican party is not made of that material I have always supposed it was.

PUBLIC OPINION

Some well-meaning men have made the remark that
the discussion of the civil-rights question has produced a
great deal of bad feeling in certain portions of the South, in
consequence of which they regret the discussion of the question and the possibility of the passage of the pending bill.
That the discussion of the question has produced some bad
feeling I am willing to admit; but allow me to assure you,
Mr. Speaker, that the opposition to the pending bill is not
half so intense in the South to-day as was the opposition to
the reconstruction acts of Congress. As long as congressional action is delayed in the passage of this bill, the more
intense this feeling will be. But let the bill once pass and
become a law, and you will find that in a few months reasonable men, liberal men, moderate men, sensible men, who
now question the propriety of passing this bill, will arrive at
the conclusion that it is not such a bad thing as they supposed it was. They will find that democratic predictions
have not and will not be realized. They will find that there
is no more social equality than before. That whites and
blacks do not intermarry any more than they did before the
passage of the bill. In short, they will find that there is
nothing in the bill but the recognition by law of the equal
rights of all citizens before the law. My honest opinion is
that the passage of this bill will have a tendency to harmonize the apparently conflicting interests between the two races.
It will have a tendency to bring them more closely together
in all matters pertaining to their public and political duties.
It will cause them to know, appreciate, and respect the rights
and privileges of each other more than ever before. In the
language of my distinguished colleague on the other side of
the house, "They will know one another, and love one another. "

CONCLUSION

In conclusion, Mr. Speaker, I say to the republican
members of the House that the passage of this bill is expected of you. If any of our democratic friends will vote
for it, we will be agreeably surprised. But if republicans
should vote against it, we will be sorely disappointed; it will

be to us a source of deep mortification as well as profound
regret. We will feel as though we are deserted in the house
of our friends. But I have no fears whatever in this respect.
You have stood by the colored people of this country when it
was more unpopular to do so than it is to pass this bill. You
have fulfilled every promise thus far, and I have no reason
to believe that you will not fulfill this one. Then give us
this bill. The white man's government negro-hating democracy will, in my judgment, soon pass out of existence. The
progressive spirit of the American people will not much
longer tolerate the existence of an organization that lives
upon the passions and prejudices of the hour. But when that
party shall have passed away, the republican party of to-day
will not be left in undisputed control of the Government; but
a young, powerful, and more vigorous organization will rise
up to take the place of the democracy of to-day. This organization may not have opposition to the negro the principal
plank in its platform; it may take him by the right hand and
concede him every right in good faith that is enjoyed by the
whites; it may confer upon him honor and position. But if
you, as leaders of the republican party, will remain true to
the principles upon which the party came into power, as I am
satisfied you will, then no other party, however just, liberal,
or fair it may be, will ever be able to detach any considerable number of colored voters from the national organization.
Of course, in matters pertaining to their local State affairs,
they will divide up to some extent, as they sometimes should,
whenever they can be assured that their rights and privileges
are not involved in the contest. But in all national contests,
I feel safe in predicting that they will remain true to the
great party of freedom and equal rights.

        I appeal to all the members of the House--republicans
and democrats, conservatives and liberals--to join with us in
the passage of this bill, which has for its object the protection of human rights. And when every man, woman, and
child can feel and know that his, her, and their rights are
fully protected by the strong arm of a generous and grateful
Republic, then we can all truthfully say that this beauftiful
land of ours, over which the Star Spangled Banner so tri-
umphantly waves, is, in truth and in fact, the "land of the
free and the home of the brave."

POLITICAL CONDITION OF THE SOUTH

... the political status of the colored race of this country is in some respect an unfortunate one. In my humble judgment it is unfortunate that the status of that race is necessarily made the subject of political discussion. I had hoped that after the last three amendments to the Constitution had been ratified, and the colored people invested with all their rights, civil and political, so far as constitutional declarations and statutory enactments could fix them, that all political parties would acquiesce in these results to such an extent as to remove from the politics of the country this race question. I had hoped that the elevation, the advancement, and the protection of this race would be the aim, the object, and the aspiration of all political parties. This race issue will not be removed from the politics of the country, in my judgment, until that is done, and that it should be done I believe every honest man must admit.
... I am satisfied that the people of this great Republic, realizing the necessities of the situation, will see to it that this grand and glorious union of ours must, shall, and will be preserved. (3:5540-5543)

Mr. LYNCH. Mr. Speaker, I am very grateful to the House for its courtesy in allowing me to occupy the floor for an hour. It is not my purpose to reply to the speech which was made by my colleague from the fifth district (Mr. HOOKER), but to reply to some of the points which were so ably and so eloquently presented by my colleague from the first district (Mr. LAMAR). It is not my purpose, however, to refer to the first part of his speech, as I have no disposition or inclination to discuss the theory of our Government, the constitutional limitations of power, the propriety or impropriety of Federal interference in the domestic affairs of a State. I shall endeavor to confine myself to what I believe to be the living issues of to-day--those which are now agitating the public mind.

Now, sir, the political status of the colored race of
this country is in some respects an unfortunate one. In my
humble judgment it is unfortunate that the status of that race
is necessarily made the subject of political discussion. I
had hoped that after the last three amendments to the Constitution had been ratified, and the colored people invested with
all of their rights, civil and political, so far as constitutional
declarations and statutory enactments could fix them, that all
political parties would acquiesce in these results to such an
extent as to remove from the politics of the country this race
question. I had hoped that the elevation, the advancement,
and the protection of this race would be the aim, the object,
and the aspiration of all political parties. This race issue
will not be removed from the politics of the country, in my
judgment, until that is done, and that it should be done I believe every honest man must admit.

Before proceeding to answer the points which were so
forcibly made by my colleague from the first district, I hope
I will be pardoned for digressing a little, for the purpose of
explaining to the House and the country why it is that the
colored people in the State of Mississippi are in favor of
general amnesty. I have been desirous of making a remark
or two on this point ever since the amnesty debates of last
winter, but have not had an opportunity to do so. As this
question has a direct bearing on the Southern situation, I presume it will not be inappropriate for me to do so now.

After the passage of the reconstruction acts by Congress conferring upon the colored people the right to vote,
we found ourselves in a very peculiar position. The voting
population of the South was composed of three distinct elements: the ex-confederate soldiers and those who sympa-
thized with them, the ex-Federal soldiers who had concluded
to locate at the South, and the colored race. These elements
have been, and were at that time, politically antagonistic to
each other. The colored men could not be expected to identify themselves with any other than the republican party, and
yet they could not fail to see and realize the fact that that
party, to have a permanent existence and a firm and solid
foundation, must include in its membership a large percent-
age of the wealth and the intelligence of the State, some of
those who fought on the side of the confederacy.

How to bring the republican party into existence in
that State upon such a basis as would render possible a harmonious union of these conflicting elements and at the same

time be in harmony with the great republican party of the
Union, was the task we had before us. To make this union
possible, the colored men very generously and magnanimously,
traits for which I presume all will admit they are particularly characterized, declared in language which could not be
misunderstood that if those who had fought and upheld the
"lost cause" would renounce all allegiance to that cause, announce it as their determination to stand by and defend the
Union, and concede to the colored men every right and privilege they claimed for themselves--in other words, identify
themselves with the great republican party--if they would do
this, that they, the colored men, would support them just as
heartily, just as earnestly, and just as enthusiastically as
they would support those who fought for the cause of the
Union; and to give emphasis to this declaration they were
willing to incorporate in the platform of the republican party
of that State, and did incorporate, a plank pledging the party
to this doctrine of equal rights for every man and amnesty
for the late rebels.

This was done. Upon this platform the republican
party of Mississippi was brought into existence; and I stand
upon the floor of the House of Representatives to-day for the
purpose of declaring what I know to be true, that this party
as thus organized, including in its membership as it does not
less than nineteen-twentieths of the colored men of the South;
including in its membership as it does not less than nineteen-
twentieths of the ex-Federal soldiers in the State; including
in its membership as it does not less than one-fifth and
possibly more of the ex-confederate soldiers in the State; this
party as thus organized includes in its membership a majority of not less than thirty thousand of the qualified voters
of that State. It was so strong, so powerful, so overwhelming in numbers that nothing short of organized terrorism and
armed violence, such as was unfortunately resorted to by the
democratic party of that State last year, could crush it out
of existence or defeat it at the polls.

I may be pardoned, Mr. Speaker, for remarking here
that the white men who are identified with the republican
party of the State of Mississippi, not northern men merely
but southern men, ex-confederates, represent a large per-
centage of the wealth, the intelligence, and the moral worth
of the white people of that State. They are as a class men
who would be accepted in any community as high-toned,
honest, honorable citizens and valuable members of society.
They are as a class men whom the democracy in former

days delighted to honor with the highest positions in the gift
of the people of the State.   They are admitted to be men of
character, men of ability, men of standing and of unquestionable reputation.   None of my democratic colleagues, I venture to assert, will deny this; for they know it to be true.
Consequently, Mr. Speaker, this is why we have placed ourselves upon this broad, liberal, and conservative platform in
addition to the fact that the colored people are particularly
desirous of showing to their white brethren that they have no
disposition to oppress them or deprive them of a single right
they claim for themselves.

        I will now refer to some of the points made by my
honorable colleague.   In giving his reasons for the present
unfortunate condition of affairs at the South, there was one
remark made by him that touched my sensitive feeling.   And
that was the comparison, apparently at least, of the colored
people with the Mongolian race, that has been imported from
China to America.   It is certainly known by southern as well
as northern men that the colored people of this country are
thoroughly American; born and raised upon American soil and
under the influence of American institutions; not American
citizens by adoption, but by birth; worshiping the same God
that the white men worship; identified with the same religious
denominations that the white race is identified with; imbued
with every sentiment of love of country, devotion to the Constitution, and loyalty to the flag that the white race is imbued
with; identified in every conceivable particular with American
institutions and with American liberty.   For my honorable
colleague, unwittingly as I believe, to compare this race with
the untutored, the uncivilized, the unchristianized, and the un-
Americanized Mongolian, that has been imported from China
to America, was unjust, ungenerous, and unfair.   I do not
wish to be understood as detracting anything from that great
and powerful race, but it is known that they are not American; and that cannot be said of the colored race, for they are.

RECONSTRUCTION

        Now, sir, let me say something with regard to the
policy of reconstruction.   It will be remembered by those who
heard the speech of my colleague that he made the remark
that the reconstruction policy of the Government was the
foundation of all of the political evils at the South; that that
was the foundation of the color-line in politics, because the
reconstruction policy of the Government enfranchised the

colored men and disfranchised the white men; and that therefore there was a gulf between the two races, and that was
the cause of the race struggles of the South and all the evils
of which we complain.   Before answering that argument let
us see what are the logical deductions to be drawn from it.
If it be true, as he asserted, that the enfranchisement of the
colored men at the South was the cause of all of our troubles
there, it seems to me that we can draw no other deduction
from that argument (if there is anything in it) than that the
only effectual remedy is to remove the cause; that you cannot remove it unless you disfranchise them and remand them
back to their former condition.   That seems to me to be the
logical deduction to be drawn from the argument, though he
did not say so, and I do not wish to be understood as placing
him in the attitude of advocating that proposition.   I am
merely stating what seems to me the only conclusion to be
arrived at as the logical result of the argument.

Let us inquire whether there is anything in that view
of the case.   I take issue with my honorable colleague in that
respect, and will endeavor to show by referring to my own
State that he is entirely mistaken.   Why, sir, my colleague
seems to have forgotten that in the State of Mississippi we
have never had any serious troubles between the two races
since the re-admission of that State into the Union until the
latter part of 1874 and during the campaign of 1875.   Until
then we never had any serious troubles whatever.   The two
races got along well together and never had any serious difficulty of any kind, the democratic party sometimes putting
colored men on their own ticket.   If, then, the enfranchisement of the colored men was the cause of all the troubles in
the South, is it not remarkably strange that it took the democratic party from five to eight years to find it out?   Is it
not remarkably strange that we could get along so well together for five or eight years without finding out that the incorporation of the colored element into the body-politic was
the cause of our difficulties?   No, sir; I will tell you what
was the cause.   The democratic victories at the North in
1874 so encouraged and exasperated the lawless and turbulent
elements at the South as to give them the entire control of
the party machinery in the democratic party.   That was the
cause of it.

The democratic victories at the North so strengthened
this element of lawlessness as to give them power to control
the democratic organization and to shape its policy; and therefore the color line was drawn in politics, not because the

colored men first drew it, as is sometimes charged, but because this element felt that they would be sustained by the
public sentiment of the country in resorting to violent measures for the purpose of accomplishing what they could not
accomplish by peaceful means.   The incorporation of the
colored element into the body-politic had nothing to do with
it, because the two races had lived as peaceful, as quietly,
as orderly together prior to that time as they possibly could
have done.   Every election held in Mississippi since the re-
admission of the State was peaceable, quiet, orderly and, except possibly in one or two localities which were not general
in their character, fair.   We never had occasion to call on
the Federal Government for Federal interference; we never
had an occasion to bring up charges for violence in any election held in the State until the general election last year and
in a local election the fall previous.

Is it not strange that the argument is now brought forward that what was done five or eight years ago was the
foundation of the violence of last year?   Why, the argument
is fallacious, it is unsound, it is unreasonable, and cannot
be substantiated.

DEMOCRATIC RULE IN MISSISSIPPI

Now, sir, let us see what has been done in the State
of Mississippi under this policy that has been inaugurated.   It
will be remembered that my honorable colleague in his very
eloquent speech referred to the State of Louisiana, and in so
doing he held up republican rule in that State as typical of
republican rule in the other Southern States.   But he did not
make any allusion to Mississippi especially.

Now, then, when holding up republican rule in the
State of Louisiana as typical of republican rule in other southern States, he certainly must have known that republican rule
in Louisiana, as understood and explained by himself, is not
typical of republican rule in Mississippi.   But I presume that
none of our democratic friends will object to having democratic rule in the State of Mississippi under the new order of
things held up as typical of democratic government in the
other Southern States.

Now let us see what it is.   I cannot speak of all of
it, for I have not the time to do so.   As the result of the
election in the State of Mississippi in November last we had

a Legislature brought into existence which has characterized
its proceedings by greater blunders than any that were ever
complained of by any of its republican predecessors. This
Legislature having been brought into existence through questionable channels--that is a mild phrase, for I have too much
respect for the feelings of my colleagues to use harsh phrases
in their presence--but that Legislature having been brought
into existence through questionable channels, what did it do?

Among the first of its proceedings was to revolutionize
the entire State government, by taking forcibly the possession
of the other two departments--the executive and judicial--by
turning out of office every man who stood as a stumbling-
block in the way of a complete democratic ascendency in the
State. Well, they say they did it in a legal and constitutional
way. Let us see about that. To get control of the executive
and judicial departments of the government, it was necessary
for them to impeach and remove from office both the governor
and lieutenant-governor, so that the democratic president of
the senate could become the acting governor. The first thing
then was to get rid of the lieutenant-governor. He was impeached and removed from office on a charge of bribery. He
was charged with having been bribed by two eminent lawyers
to pardon a convict out of the State penitentiary; a very grave
offense, for which he deserved impeachment, if true. Under
the laws of Mississippi a man who proposes a bribe is just
as guilty as the one who accepts it.

Those two lawyers who were charged with having
bribed the lieutenant-governor happened to be very eminent
and able democrats. The charge was made several months
before the election and several months before the assembling
of the Legislature. During that time the grand jury of
Lowndes County, the county in which all three of the parties
resided, thoroughly we are told, investigated this matter.
This grand jury, composed of a majority of democrats, made
a report to the court that all the parties to the transaction
were innocent. No evidence could be produced to establish
the guilt of any of them. The Legislature had no jurisdiction
over the two democratic lawyers, they being private citizens.
But they did have jurisdiction over the lieutenant-governor,
he being a civil officer of the State. They then proceeded to
investigate his conduct upon the charges upon which he had
been acquitted by a democratic grand jury, no other charge
being preferred against him, and pronounced him guilty, and
he was accordingly impeached and removed. Now I do not
say he was innocent, for I do not know; I did not investigate

the matter and I am not prepared to express an opinion upon
that subject.   Perhaps he was guilty; it is not necessary to
answer my purpose to defend him.   But the point I make is
that either the democratic grand jury failed to discharge its
duty for the purpose of shielding the two democratic lawyers
from justice or else the Legislature was guilty of persecuting
an officer for political purposes; one of the two is true, and
it is not very favorable to the democratic party either way.

Now, after having got rid of the licutenant-governor,
the next thing was to get rid of the governor.   Charges of
impeachment were preferred against him.   My time will not
permit me to go over all of them, but I will give a skeleton
of some of them.   He was impeached in one article for failing to remove a man from office who in the judgment of the
Legislature ought to have been removed.   In another article
he was impeached for failing to remove a man from office
who in the judgment of the Legislature ought to have been removed.

He was impeached in another article because he called
on the President of the United States for troops to put down
what he believed to be domestic violence.   He was impeached
in another article because he leased out the penitentiary con-
victs to his partisan friends.   The law expressly authorized
him to lease them out; there was no crime at all in leasing
them out; the offense was in leasing them out to his partisan
friends.   The inference of course is that if he had leased
them out to his partisan enemies no offense would have been
committed.

These were the principal charges that were preferred
against him.   He was impeached on these articles and driven
from his office for the sole purpose of getting a democrat in
his place.   After the articles had been drawn up, some of
the democratic members of the Legislature had some conscientious scruples on the subject.   They did not desire to
vote for these articles, and therefore a public pressure had
to be brought to bear upon them for the purpose of whipping
them into the traces.

What was done now to accomplish that?   The leading
democratic paper published at the capital of the State came
out with flaming head-lines: "This man must be impeached
and removed from office!"   How?   Upon the law and the evidence that may be presented?   Not at all.   Upon principles
of equity and justice?   By no means.   Then how are you to

get rid of him? He must be impeached and removed, said the democratic paper, "as a party measure." I defy any of my colleagues to deny that.

      Mr. SINGLETON.   What paper have you got there?

      Mr. LYNCH.   The Clarion, of Jackson, Mississippi.

      Mr. SINGLETON.   Produce that paper and let me see it.

      Mr. LYNCH.   Certainly, I will take great pleasure in doing so.   This paper said that the governor must be impeached and removed from office as a party measure.   No matter what the constitution may declare, no matter what the law may provide, no matter what the evidence may be, the people demand it at their hands, and they must obey the command of the people.   I ask the Clerk to read what I have marked, and to be careful and emphasize the words I have underscored.   (Laughter)

The Clerk read as follows:

> We cannot see that any lesson for our guidance in this matter of Governor Ames is to be drawn from the case of Andrew Johnson cited by the South.   He was impeached for upholding the Constitution and laws.   If Ames is impeached it will be for trampling them under foot.   Nor does it follow that proceedings against the latter will fail because they failed in the case of the former. Johnson had justice on his side; Ames has not. Johnson was a republican President on trial before a democratic senate; and therefore no apprehensions need be felt that partisan influence will shield him from the penalty of his crimes.   It is idle for The South to say that these proceedings 'cannot be carried on as a party measure.'   They cannot be carried on in any other way.
>
> ... It is not time for sentimentalism; practical work is needed.   The democratic and other opposers of radical misrule 'carried' the election, and if the fall benefits of the victory are to be realized they will have to arraign Governor Ames and the other radical officeholders who have abused

their trusts, and visit upon them the consequences
of their crimes as 'a party measure. '

Mr. LYNCH.   The South referred to in that article is
a democratic paper that was opposed to impeaching the governor "as a party measure, " and this article was in reply to
The South.

Mr. FOSTER.   And this Clarion is the official organ
of the party?

Mr. LYNCH.   Yes, sir; it is the official organ of the
party, and its proprietors are the public printers of the State.
I suppose my colleague (Mr. SINGLETON) has had some experience in the matter of public printing.   Now, having demanded the impeachment of this man as a party measure, of
course the articles of impeachment were put through the
House, but one democrat, I believe, dissenting.

After the impeachment articles had gone through the
house, it was found out that there were some conscientious
democrats in the senate who were not altogether prepared to
vote for conviction.   So the next thing was to prepare the
senate for conviction.   But the only way to do that was to
turn out enough republicans and put in enough democrats to
make conviction sure.

They then proceeded to turn out republican senators.
They turned out one man upon the ground that he was a
foreigner, although he was ready to swear that he was born
in New York.   But it made no difference where he was born;
a democratic vote was needed and they must have it.   Therefore the republican was turned out and a democrat put in his
place, who had not been elected even in the peculiar manner
by which they carried the elections there last fall.   He had
not been elected, and had no right or title to the seat.   Yet
they turned out the republican and put in the democrat.

After having prepared the senate for conviction we are
told that a committee waited on the governor.   And I suppose
some such conversation as this took place: "Governor, you
have been impeached; your conviction is but a question of
time.   If you will resign your office, then you will save
money to the State and some money to yourself. "   To that I
suppose the governor replied something like this: "If I resign, will you withdraw your articles of impeachment?"

Judging from the result the reply to that was, "Yes, certainly we will. " And that was agreed upon.

The committee went back, made their report, and the articles of impeachment were immediately withdrawn, the resignation was sent in, and the proceedings thereupon came to an end. Now, in what attitude does this place them? I am not a lawyer, but it seems to me that the democratic party in that Legislature proved itself guilty of one or two things: they either acknowledged that the charges were groundless and false, without a shadow of foundation in fact, or else they were guilty of what the lawyers would call compounding a felony. I would like any democrat to deny that. One of the two must be true. Either that Legislature was guilty of compounding a felony by allowing this man to escape as a consideration for his office, or else it was a confession on their part that he was innocent of the charges brought against him. They said: "All that we want is your office; it is immaterial to us what you may have been guilty of; the sole objective point we have in view is to get a republican out and a democrat in. "

Now, in a speech of my honorable colleague (Mr. LAMAR), which he delivered here when some proposition relative to the impeachment of the late Secretary of War was before the House, he took the very strong ground that the object of impeachment is not merely to get rid of an objectionable officer, but to punish him besides. He did not represent his Legislature in that sentiment, for they took the position that the object of an impeachment with them is to get a republican out and a democrat in. I would like to know whether the democrats on the other side of this House from the Southern States are willing to have the Mississippi democracy held as typical of the democracy in their States. I hope for their sakes that they are not.

THE COLOR LINE--VIOLENCE

In referring to this question of the prevalence of violence and the drawing of the color line in politics, I am willing for one to give my colleague credit for everything that he says on that point. I am willing to give him credit for sincerity in deprecating the drawing of the color line and the inauguration of brute force and violence. The only thing upon which I take issue with him in that respect is this: He believes, honestly, no doubt, that in giving utterance to con-

servative sentiments here and elsewhere, in deprecating the
drawing of the color line and the inauguration of violence, he
represents the controlling element in the ranks of the democratic party in Mississippi. I believe (and I presume he will
give me credit for honesty and sincerity in this opinion) that
he does not.

I am willing to admit, as I said upon a former occasion, that there are in the State of Mississippi numbers of
white men who are not identified with the republican party and
whom I believe to be honestly opposed to these violent measures and to drawing the color line in politics. I may be
pardoned for mentioning the names of one or two of these
gentlemen, because their names are somewhat national; they
are known to the country. I will mention for instance the
present speaker of the house of representatives of Mississippi,
Hon. H. M. Street. I will also mention Hon. J. W. C. Wat-
son, of Marshall, the editor of the paper that opposed the
impeachment of the governor upon party grounds; General A.
M. West, of the same town; ex-Governor Charles Clarke, and
ex-Governor and ex-United States Senator Albert G. Brown,
of Hinds. These men, I believe, are honestly opposed to this
policy of violence and the drawing of the line in politics. I
have always believed that my colleague (Mr. LAMAR) was one
of that number; I am willing to give him credit for it; but
when he asserts that in his conservative utterances he reflects the sentiments of the controlling element of his party,
I take issue with him. His position cannot be substantiated,
for it is not correct.

It is sometimes said that these violent measures are
sometimes necessary to get rid of bad government, heavy
taxes, and dishonest officials. I have asserted on this floor
more than once that this cannot be truthfully said of Mississippi. I did not make groundless assertions and empty declarations, but presented facts and figures to substantiate what
I said. Not one of my democratic colleagues has denied or
can deny my position on this question. In that State there
was no occasion whatever for the inauguration of violent measures on the ground that bad, incompetent, or dishonest men
had control of the government.

INEFFICIENCY OF STATE GOVERNMENTS

One other point which has been made very forcibly is
the inefficiency of republican State governments at the South.

It is very often said that we have violence only in the States
under republican rule. Without admitting that there is any
foundation for this statement (for it is not altogether true), I
say that admitting it for the sake of argument, what does it
prove? It proves that the democrats will obey the laws only
when made and enforced by men of their own choice, while
republicans will obey the laws whether they are made and enforced by men of their own choice or by democrats. Let us
admit that violence exists only in republican localities; why
is it so? Simply because democrats say, "Let us have the
government and we will obey the laws; if you do not, we will
not." That is precisely the argument upon which the rebellion
was inaugurated.

I presume no gentleman in this Hall who is familiar
with the history of our Government will deny for a moment
that had Fremont been elected President instead of Buchanan
in 1856, the war would have inaugurated four years sooner
than it was. And I presume no one familiar with our history
will deny that had Breckinridge, or even Douglas, been
elected in 1860 instead of Lincoln, the war would have been
postponed at least four years later.

Did not the southern democrats say, "We will stay in
the Union if you let us control it; if you do not, we will
not?"

Why, sir, my colleague might just as well come before the American people and contend that the election of
Tilden and Hendricks is essential to the peace of the country;
he might just as well say, "Elect Tilden and Hendricks and
you will have peace; elect Hayes and Wheeler and you will
have war." If the argument is good as applicable to a single
State, it must be equally good as applicable to the nation.

If the country is ready to accept this condition of
affairs, then it can do so, but it seems to me that it would
be death and destruction to what are recognized as the results of the war.

CIVIL-SERVICE REFORM

My colleague lays great stress upon civil-service reform in the Government. That is the controlling idea, he
says. Let me say to the House and the country that civil-
service reform does not occupy one-twentieth part of the

consideration of the southern democrats. Civil-service reform does not enter into their composition. They have not
got it to think about. The sole objective point with the democratic party of the South, and I presume at the North, is
democratic success. It is immaterial to them what the attitude of their candidate may be on any of the public questions
now before the people. It is immaterial to them whether
their candidate for the Presidency be in favor of contracting
the currency or expanding it. It is immaterial to them
whether he be in favor of free trade or protection. It is
immaterial to them whether he be really in favor of administrative reform or whether he be, as their candidate for the
Presidency is now believed to be, the earnest advocate of
gigantic corporations. They are willing to subordinate all
other questions to the one great object of democratic success.
They are willing to subordinate all other questions, without
excepting the honor, the integrity, and the plighted faith of
the nation. They only ask, "Give us the democratic party;
that is what we want. The sole objective point with us is to
get the Government into our hands and let us get our fingers
on the purse-strings of the Treasury. "

They have not only drawn the color line in politics for
the purpose of appealing to the passions and prejudices of
race, but they have drawn the sectional line for the purpose
of rolling up the southern vote in behalf of the Saint Louis
nominees. Civil-service reform amounts to nothing in the
estimation of the democratic party south of Mason and Dixon's
line. I speak of them knowingly. It may be true of those
north of it also; but I speak of those south, for I know where-
of I speak. The order has already gone forth from Tammany Hall, as represented by the chiefs of that organization,
saying to the democratic party of the South, "Put this party
into power, elect the ticket nominated at Saint Louis, and
all things else will be added unto you. "

I tell you that it is the only issue in the South to-day.
No other public question agitates the public mind there. You
may be divided at the North on questions of currency or of
administrative reform, but they do not enter into politics at
the South, because the democrats do not care anything about
them.

CONCLUSION

Now, sir, let me say that the South is proposed to be

carried by the democratic party.   Every Southern State they
propose to carry as they carried Mississippi last year; a
State with 30, 000 republican majority reversed by giving
30, 000 democratic majority nominally.   They propose to
carry all the others the same way, not by the power of the
ballot, but by an organized system of terrorism and violence.
That is the way they propose to do it.

Now let me say, in conclusion, that I am satisfied, I
am convinced, that the public sentiment of the people of this
country is sufficiently aroused now to see the danger we are
in.   I am satisfied that the people of this country are beginning to realize the importance of the situation we are in.
I am satisfied that when these questions are known, when
they are fully understood, the people will be determined to
rise in their might and declare in language which cannot be
misunderstood that this great, grand, glorious Republic must
and shall be preserved.

Mr. Speaker, it is no pleasure for me to be compelled to admit the violence which exists in my own State.   I
would be happy if I could say truthfully that such is not the
case.   It gives me no pleasure to be compelled to acknowledge perfect toleration of opinion does not exist in the State
of Mississippi.   I have friends there on both sides.   My home
is there.   My interests are there.   My relatives are there;
and I want to see the State prosperous and happy.

I want to see perfect toleration of opinion everywhere,
and especially in the State where I live.   I am anxious for
that to be the case, and nothing would give more pleasure
than to be able to declare on the floor of the House of Representatives that perfect toleration of opinion is allowed to
all classes.   The fact that I am compelled to acknowledge
that such is not the case in many counties in the State fills
me with pain, mortification, and regret, for I want to see
the two races living in harmony and in peace, and friendly
relations existing between both parties.   That is the object of
my aspiration, and it is what I hope the better judgment of
the whole body of the people of that State will see is for the
general good.   For I can realize the fact that since the State
of Mississippi has been in its present condition of turmoil
our commerce has been practically destroyed, the friendly
relations between the two races arrested, emigration to the
State retarded, and the State itself almost in a disorganized
condition, with a lawless class controlling it to a great extent.

(Here the hammer fell.)

Mr. LYNCH.   I should like to have two minutes more.

Mr. RANDALL.   I do not want more than two minutes.

Mr. LYNCH.   I do not want more than two minutes.

There being no objection, Mr. LYNCH's time was extended.

Mr. LYNCH.   In conclusion let me warn the House and the country, not with any feeling of malice, not with any feeling of hatred, for I have none, that if you expect to preserve the constitutional liberties of the people as well as to uphold the perpetuity of republican institutions you must see to it that lawlessness is crushed out at the South.   I say to the northern democrats, you must see to it, with my honorable friend from New York (Mr. LORD), that your party stands upon the platform which that gentleman made in the resolutions introduced here yesterday to crush out mob law and violence at the South, whether proceeding from political friends or from political enemies.   If the democratic party has a legitimate majority in the State of Mississippi or any other State, it is entitled to the vote of that State and ought to have it.   If the republican party has a legitimate majority in that State or in any other State, it is entitled to the vote of that State and ought to have it.   This is what honest men of all parties ought to be willing to say.   And now, sir, I am satisfied that the people of this great Republic, realizing the necessities of the situation, will see to it that this grand and glorious Union of ours must, shall, and will be preserved.   (Applause)

BIBLIOGRAPHY

1.   Biographical Directory of the American Congress 1774-1971.   Washington, D. C. :   United States Government Printing Office, 1971.

2.   U. S. Congress.   House.   Civil Rights.   43rd Congress, 2nd session, 1875.

3.   U. S. Congress.   House.   Political Condition of the South. 44th Congress, 1st session, 1876.

JOHN WILLIS MENARD

X. JOHN WILLIS MENARD

Menard, John Willis (1838-1893), First of the Reconstruction politicians to be elected to Congress, was born of French Creole parents in Kaskaskia, Illinois. He was educated in Sparta, Illinois, and at Iberia College in Ohio. During the Civil War, he was a clerk in the Department of the Interior in Washington, D. C. At the close of the War, he moved to New Orleans to work for the Republican Party's Reconstruction policies. Nominated for a seat in the 40th Congress in 1868, he ran against Caleb S. Hunt and received the greater number of votes in the election; but, when he claimed his place in Congress, the defeated Hunt contested the seating of a Negro. The case was referred to the committee on election, where it was decided that it was "too early" to admit a Negro to the United States Congress. The seat was again declared vacant, but Menard was awarded the full salary that was normally paid to its holder. In 1869, after the 40th Congress refused to seat Menard, he was appointed inspector of customs of the port of New Orleans and, later, commissioner of streets. (1:99-100)

CONTESTING HIS REJECTED SEATING

> It was certainly not my intention at first to take
> any part in this case at all, but as I have been
> sent here by the votes of nearly nine thousand
> electors I would feel myself recreant to the duty
> imposed upon me if I did not defend their rights
> on this floor. (2:1684)

Mr. MENARD (the contestant). Mr. Speaker, I appear here more to acknowledge this high privilege than to
make an argument before this House. It was certainly not
my intention at first to take any part in this case at all; but
as I have been sent here by the votes of nearly nine thousand
electors I would feel myself recreant to the duty imposed
upon me if I did not defend their rights on this floor. I wish
it to be well understood before I go any further that in the
disposition of this case I do not expect nor do I ask that
there shall be any favor shown me on account of my race or
the former condition of that race. I wish the case to be decided on its own merits and nothing else. As I said before
the Committee of Elections, Mr. Hunt, who contests my
seat, is not properly a contestant before this House for the
reason that he has not complied with the law of Congress in
serving notice upon me of his intention to contest my seat.
The returns of the board of canvassers of the State of Louisiana were published officially on the 25th of November, and
the gentleman had sufficient time to comply with the law of
Congress if he had chosen to do so. When Congress convened on the 7th of December he presented to the Speaker of
this House a protest against my taking my seat. I did not
know the nature of that protest until about the middle of January, when the case was called up before the committee.

Upon this point of notice I desire to call the attention
of the House to this fact: that General Sheldon, who ran on
the same ticket that I did as a candidate for the Forty-First
Congress was declared to be elected upon the same grounds
that I was, and he wrote to the chairman of the Committee
of Elections to find out his opinion with regard to this ques-

tion of notice. Mr. Hunt, it seems, failed to give him
notice also, and I understood when I was last in New Orleans
that it is the opinion of the chairman of the Committee of
Elections that the case of Mr. Sheldon is a very clear one.
I am very sorry that the chairman of the Committee of Elections did not give the benefit of that opinion.

I am of opinion that when Congress enacted that law it
certainly intended that every contestant should comply with its
requirements, and I can see no reason why the law should be
set aside in this case any more than in any other, and I think
that if Mr. Hunt did not know the law of Congress he was a
very poor subject to be sent to Congress. (Laughter)

Now, sir, the Committee of Elections, in their report, have cited the New Hampshire case of Perkins vs.
Morrison, but they take as a precedent the action of the
minority of the committee in that case, which is very strange
indeed, and they give us no benefit from the report of the
majority of that committee. I ask the Clerk to read from
that majority report the passage which I have marked.

Mr. MENARD. Mr. Speaker, in the matter of redis-
tricting the State of Louisiana the Governor had no authority
of law whatever to send his precept for an election to fill
this vacancy to any other district than the new one made by
the Legislature on the 22nd of August, 1868. He could not
have ordered an election to fill this vacancy under a law
which had been repealed.

There is another point to which I wish to call the attention of this House. The State was redistricted before
Colonel Mann died. Therefore, at the time when he died his
district was intact, and no change was made in it after his
death. And the voters in that portion of the new district
which were formerly within the districts that elected Mr.
NEWSHAM and Mr. VIDAL to this House were no longer constituents of those gentlemen, but had become the constituents
of Mr. MANN. So far as the law is concerned Mr. Mann
represented the new district as it now stands. And when he
died, and there was a vacancy in that new district, the Governor of the State had no power whatever to order an election
in the old district to fill the vacancy, but the election had to
be held by law within the territorial limits of the new district. The Legislature of Louisiana, according to the Constitution of the United States, had the power to change the

districts. Therefore the Governor was by the new redis-
tricting act to order an election to fill the vacancy within the
new district.

Now, I would call attention to another point. If it be
admitted that the election was legal, and that the Legislature
had full power to create new districts, I ask a moment's
attention while I compare the vote on the 3rd of November
with the vote cast in the preceding April election on the ratification of the constitution. In the first, second, third,
tenth, and eleventh wards of the city of New Orleans, which
are included in the new second congressional district, the
vote for the constitution in April was 7, 373. In the same
wards on the 3rd of November there were only 125 votes,
showing a falling off of 7, 248 votes in the space of six
months. In the parish of Jefferson, on the 17th and 18th
days of April, 1868, the votes for the constitution were
3, 133. On the 3rd of November following, the Republican
votes in that parish were only 662; showing a falling off in
six months of 2, 470 votes. This is sufficient to show to any
reasonable person that the loyal voters in this portion of the
district were deprived of the right to go to the polls and cast
their ballots. Now, this falling off was caused by the intim-
idations and threats made and the frauds practiced in those
parishes. And I now ask Congress on behalf of the loyal
people of my district to set aside the returns of votes from
those parishes, so as to give the rebels there no more encouragement for their systematic plan of fraud and intimidation. And if the votes of those two parishes are thrown out
I will then have, in the remainder of the district, a majority
over Mr. Hunt, my contestant, of 3, 341 votes. And as I
hold the certificate of election from the Governor I hold that
I should be recognized and admitted to this body as the legal
Representative of the district in which a vacancy was created
by the death of my predecessor, Mr. Mann. There is no
evidence whatever that there was any fraud in the election in
the remaining five parishes of the district. Our vote in November compares favorably with the vote cast in April for
the constitution. And I think that Congress should recognize
the right of the voters of those parishes to be represented
here. Had the same Republican vote been cast in November
that was cast in April in the parishes of Orleans and Jefferson I would still have a majority over Mr. Hunt of several
hundred votes.

It will be noticed that under the new registration for
the election of November there were 20, 314 voters registered

in the five wards of the city of New Orleans comprised in
the second congressional district of Louisiana. The total
votes in those wards cast at the election, admitting all of
them to have been legal, were 11, 660, showing that over
8, 500 legal voters were deprived of the right to vote in consequence of the condition of things then existing in Louisiana,
and I have every reason to believe, judging from the election
in April previous, that those 8, 500 were Republican voters.
I ask this House to give these men--most of whom were
colored--some consideration, and not allow the rebel votes
to be counted against them. If this is done, it is possible
that at the next election loyal men will have a chance to express their will through the ballot-box. And according to the
registration for the parish of Jefferson there were then 5, 969
voters, while the total number of votes cast on the 3rd of
November was 2, 886, showing that in that parish alone there
were 3, 083 loyal voters who were deprived of their right to
vote in consequence of the intimidation and lawlessness there.

BIBLIOGRAPHY

1.   Robinson, Wilhelmena S.   International Library of Negro
     Life and History: Historical Negro Biographies.   New
     York: Publishers, Inc., 1967.

2.   U. S. Congress.   House.   In Defense of His Seat in
     Congress.   40th Congress, 3rd session, 1868.

XI. CHARLES EDMUND NASH

Nash, Charles Edmund, a Representative from Louisiana; born in Opelousas, St. Landry Parish, Louisiana, May 23, 1844; was of the Negro race; attended the Common schools; was a brick layer by trade; during the Civil War enlisted in 1863 as a private in the Eighty-second Regiment, United States Volunteers, and was promoted to the rank of Sergeant-major; lost a leg at Fort Blakely and was honorably discharged; appointed night inspector of customs in 1865; elected as a Republican to the Forty-fourth Congress (March 4, 1875-March 3, 1877); unsuccessful candidate for re-election in 1876 to the Forty-fifth Congress; postmaster at Washington, St. Landry Parish Louisiana, from February 15, 1882 until May 1882; died in New Orleans, Louisiana, June 21, 1913. (1:1460)

POLITICAL CONDITION OF THE SOUTH

When the thirteenth amendment, abolishing slavery,
was proposed, the democratic party, both in
Congress and throughout the country, opposed it;
when the fourteenth amendment was proposed the
democratic party opposed it; when the fifteenth
amendment was proposed the democratic party,
with a vehemence only equal to its assaults upon
the life of the nation, opposed it.... when arming the negroes was proposed, the democratic
party opposed it   when giving the right of suffrage to the colored people of the District of Columbia was proposed as an experiment, the democratic party came forward with its usual philanthropy and opposed it.   (2:3667-3669)

Mr. NASH.   Mr. Chairman, it was not my purpose to
crave the indulgence of the House during the present session,
in view of my inexperience in public legislation, and especially in public speaking, but the recent speech of the honorable member from North Carolina (Mr. YEATES) is such an
extraordinary production in its reflections upon the existing
State government of Louisiana and the character of many of
its citizens that I feel that I would be false to my public trust
were I to remain silent and fail to refute the many glaring
misrepresentations of the distinguished gentleman's production.   The gentleman from North Carolina has given the caption to his speech, "Economy, Retrenchment, and Reform, "
and the House now being in Committee of the Whole on the
state of the Union I shall follow with a like caption as the
text for my remarks.

The gentleman from North Carolina in his speech says:

I could go through the Southern States and select
leading secessionists of the country whom the republican party has hugged to its bosom long ago.
There is one distinguished hero and leader, General Longstreet, whose fiery columns were felt on

every battle-field but a few years since, and
whose name was worth a thousand men to the
cause of secession. Where is he to-day? and
where has he been for the last eight years? He
is on that side, and they think him a marvelously
proper and good patriot.

Now, sir, General Longstreet needs no defense at my
hands, being a representative man of that class of our reconstructed citizens who immediately after the close of hos-
tilities patriotically came to the front, accepted the situation,
put their shoulders to the burdens and responsibilties of
bringing order out of chaos by re-establishing the practical
relations of the insurrectionary States and the people to the
Federal Government. He had political sagacity and independence of character to be among the advanced guards in
this patriotic labor of reconstruction. The democratic party
in like spirit and for like purposes as evidenced by the remarks of the gentleman from North Carolina have made General Longstreet a target of their displeasure and attack. The
gentleman admits that General Longstreet performed valiant
services for the confederacy, and I will tell him that he has
done equal service for the reconstruction of the Federal
Union; and I do not understand why he should be specially
assaulted for the performance of his duties as a citizen. But
it seems the special pleasure of the democratic party to assault the character and impugn the motives of all white men
who act in concert with the policy of the republican party in
the Southern States, as well as to doubt the integrity and
ability of the few colored men called to the performance of
the public trusts therein. I can better explain my position
to the House by reading a portion of the recent report to this
House made at the last session of Congress bearing on the
subject, and known as the Hoar Louisiana report, in which
the honorable chairman of the committee (Mr. HOAR) used
the following language:

> Charges of corruption are made by the conserva-
> tives against republican officials without the
> slightest discrimination. They assume that the
> acceptance of office is a badge of fraud. No
> matter how high the position hitherto occupied
> socially, how spotless the reputation, the moment
> of acceptance of office witnesses an entire re-
> verse. The gentleman suddenly becomes a black-
> guard, the honest man a thief.

Mr. Chairman, comment by me is unnecessary. The language of this report gives to the world the true secret of the ostracism and menaces of the democratic party against such worthy citizens of the South as General Longstreet; so I will dismiss all further reference to that portion of the debate.

Again, the member from North Carolina (Mr. YEATES), further along in his speech, uses the following language:

> Now, Mr. Chairman, to be perfectly serious, we all know that the republican party did not start out in the war with the aim of freeing the colored people. It declared in its resolutions in Congress and in the proclamations of its President that that was not the object. But, sir, the colored man was freed, in spite both of the northern and southern men, by the will of God; and the colored people are learning that. Another thing: the republican party did not willingly give the colored man his right to vote.
>
> A MEMBER. Who did?
>
> Mr. YEATES. I will answer that question. They undertook to pass the fourteenth amendment to the Constitution of the United States, and said to the southern people, 'Vote for that, ' You are fresh out of the war, now turn around and abuse and curse your friends and let them die. We would not do that. If the republicans could have got the white people of the South to have voted with them they would have let the colored man go on forever without a vote. But when they found out that the southern people, though defeated in arms, still rose pure and strong in virtue and could not be beaten down in that way, they threatened us that they would let the colored people vote. Is not that the history of the times?
>
> So, in due course of time, when they could not get our votes then they turned the colored people loose and let them vote. What else did they do? They multiplied offices and filled those offices with ten thousand carpet-baggers, who came down and prejudiced the colored people against us.... They poisoned the minds of the colored people; they left the country a howling waste and wilderness; they destroyed liberty in Louisiana ... and

in all the States where they had the power to
do it.

Mr. Chairman, I am willing to admit with this gentleman that the colored race owe their freedom rather to the
providence of Almighty God, who took His own good time and
adopted His own means to accomplish this great result, than
to any party. Being one of that proscribed race which has
been benefited by the results of the war of the rebellion in
the providence of God, I take this occasion to publicly offer
up my thanksgiving and heartfelt prayer of gratitude to Him
who is the Giver of all good for the emancipation of my race
in view of the anticipated future which I trust awaits them as
citizens of this Republic. But, sir, I cannot agree with the
gentleman in that portion of his speech where he announces
that the colored race owes nothing to the republican party for
the enjoyment of the political rights conferred upon us. I
may be no historian, but this much of history do I know, because I have been an actor in its scenes. Let me remind the
gentleman what the democratic party have done for us in the
past. When the thirteenth amendment, abolishing slavery,
was proposed, the democratic party, both in Congress and
throughout the country, opposed it; when the fourteenth amendment was proposed the democratic party, with a vehemence
only equal to its assaults upon the life of the nation, opposed
it. Why, sir, when arming the negroes was proposed, the
democratic party opposed it; when paying pensions to negroes
was proposed, the democratic party opposed it; when giving
the right of suffrage to the colored people of the District of
Columbia was proposed as an experiment, the democratic
party came forward with its usual philanthropy and opposed it.

Now, sir, tell me where any measure of constitutional
law or general legislation has been proposed or enacted for
the benefit of the emancipated black race which the democra
cratic party has not strenuously opposed; and, not satisfied
after the popular verdict had been rendered in favor of the
rights which we have thus far secured, this same demo-
party in the South, encouraged and backed by its brethren of
the North, has kept a continual warfare upon the advancement, peace, and prosperity of our people. Therefore, I
propose to give a timely warning to these stirrers up of
strife, what they may expect if they continue this war of
races. Ex-Governor Pinchback, of my State, hit the nail
squarely on the head in his recent address before the colored
convention at Jackson, Mississippi. Said Mr. Pinchback:

I tell you my white friends, that this killing off
our people must be stopped, and I intend to help
in putting a stop to it.   Not by force of arms,
not by use of needleguns and Remington rifles, by
breaking up this issue of race and by breaking up
your whiteline democratic party.   The colored
people are bound to have their rights, and I advise you who are gentlemen to be the ones to
guarantee them those rights; for if you do not, in
sober earnestness I warn you to beware of the
day when the ruffian class of whites shall unite
with the more ignorant class of colored people!
I leave you to imagine the result.

Sir, it is not difficult to comprehend the effect of a
combination like that named by Mr. Pinchback.   When it
shall be made, if it ever shall be, the day will be a sorry
one for southern society.   So far it has been for the interests
of the ruffians and outlaws of the South to work with the
white-leaguer.   But the moment of the scramble for spoils
shall have fairly commenced there will be a division, and in
that division white respectability must be re-enforced by
colored decency, or the cotton States will be handed over to
a rule as shameless and scandalous as the imagination can
conceive.   There has been a great deal of opposition manifested by the native southern whites to the education of the
colored people.   Wherever the republicans have had control,
as in Texas, Louisiana, and Mississippi, a system of schools
has been put in operation that would have honored the New
England States themselves.   But the moment any of them fall
into the hands of the democracy, that moment public education
meets with discouragement.   This is such egregious folly that
it is surprising that the people of the South do not see it.
The danger to that section is and has been in the ignorance
of the masses.   Designing demagogues can influence the uneducated and thus compass their ends; whereas, if intelligence
were universal, any combination of vice and ignorance would
be impossible.   Let the South realize this fact and encourage
popular education.   The race issue is the issue of ignorance.
Education dispels narrow prejudices as the sun dispels the
noxious vapors of the night.   The South needs more and better
schools than the North, for she has a wider field for them.
Not only has she a large colored population groveling in the
dust of intellectual squalor, but a majority of her white citizens are without the facilities for mental improvement.   Reform this altogether.   Let a spirit of progress in this respect
be manifested, and the southern people will find the North

giving them a helping hand and bidding them Godspeed in
the work.

Mr. Chairman, there are other portions of the gentleman's speech that I might take notice of, but I hardly deem
it necessary, inasmuch as I have already noticed those parts
of it which apply more particularly to the interests and
people of my State.

As to a defense of the whole republican party, which
he has seen fit to arraign, there need little be said. We
have before us to-day a living and useful illustration of the
wise forethought and broad philanthropy of the men of 1776.
To-day it is the boast of the republican party that every man
born in this country or naturalized, no matter what his condition in life, his race, or color, is an American citizen,
and, as such, is entitled to equal rights before the law, and
to a participation in the elective franchise.   The republican
party, which has achieved much for the country, has wrought
no greater work than this.   It is a proud day for us.   Although we have passed through a sanguinary struggle in which
thousands of our brave and patriotic citizens have yielded up
their lives, yet we cannot lose sight of the fact that at the
close of the conflict the immortal principles so happily announced in the Declaration of Independence have not only been
preserved, but have grown into practical and living reality.
This is the essential creed of the republican party.   It is
true we have not yet seen unqualified acquiescence in this
grand result on the part of our democratic fellow-citizens,
but the time is not far distant when even the people of the
South must lay aside the prejudices engendered by the late
war, and accept in its fullest sense the freedom of citizenship and equality before the law of all men.   Democratic conventions may be silent on this subject, and a democratic
House may be criminally neglectful of its highest duty; the
people themselves may be misled and deceived by political
leaders; the "still, small voice" of reason may be hushed
and silenced by the turbulent passions of the hour, yet the
day is not far distant when this underlying principle of the
republican party will be fully acknowledged and accepted by
all the people.   When this shall be done, the first great purpose of the republican party will have been accomplished; and
it will then be the duty of that party to preserve intact its
own great power.

The mission of the republican party is not yet ended.
The loyal people of this country, who preserved the Govern-

ment in war and have maintained its honor in peace, are not
yet ready to hand it over to the party that conspired to destroy it and has resisted every effort to make it indestruct-
ible.   At no time in our history has the cause of civil and
religious liberty made such progress as in this decade under
the fostering care of the republican party.   In giving freedom
with civil and political rights to one race it has not been unmind-
ful of the rights and liberties of the other.   The same constitutional provision that gave freedom to the black man makes
it forever impossible to enslave any portion of the white race.
The citizenship secured by the fourteenth article of amendment to all persons born or naturalized in the United States
applies alike to all persons, rich and poor, white and black.
The inhibition upon the States to make or enforce any law
which shall abridge the privileges or immunities of the citizens of the United States, or to deprive any person of life,
liberty, or property without due process of law, or to deny
to any person within their jurisdiction the equal protection of
the laws, is a bulwark of safety to every citizen and a protection against the oppressors that might otherwise be created
by sectional jealousy or local hate.   All these constitutional
provisions were passed in the interest of personal liberty and
individual security.   The love of liberty is inherent in human
nature.   It may be stifled, but not without much difficulty.
Whenever it is not gratified there is danger to the state.
Gratify it and you insure the safety of society.   Neither those
constitutional provisions nor any statute passed in conjunction
with them oppresses or harms any human being.   A government which cannot protect its humblest citizens from outrage
and injury is unworthy the name and ought not to command
the support of a free people.

These are the works of the great republican party of
the nation, which saved the country in war and is able to
preserve it in peace.   This is the party which must control
the destinies of this free country for years to come.

The awful scenes of the late war are passed, and forever.   The battle-cry is no longer sounded; war's thunder-
clouds have rolled muttering away, and the skies are bright
after the storm.   The heroes of one side are sleeping side
by side with those whom they withstood in battle, and they
sleep in peace.   The grave has closed over their animosities
and a truce has been proclaimed between them forever.   Let
the living strike hands also, for we are not enemies but
brethren.   A man with the noblest instincts may succumb to
a temporary madness, but he is nevertheless a man, and

when the cloud has passed away he is to be restored to a
man's loves and rights and privileges. Brother, late our foe
in battle but our brother still, this country is our joint inheritance, this flag has always been our joint banner. The
glories of our past belong to both of us. This purified land,
this great, united people, these broad acres stretching from
ocean to ocean, yet bound by the cord of commerce, which
makes of oceans near neighbors and of mountains level plains
--this boundless wealth, this tireless energy, this hunger for
progress, this thirst for knowledge--it is yours, it is ours,
and no power can despoil us of it. We alone by our dissen-
sions can destroy this rich inheritance. Over brothers'
graves let brothers' quarrels die. Let there be peace between us, that these swords which we have learned to use so
well, may if used again strike only at a common foe. Let
us sing anthems of peace; let the song be taken up throughout
the land; by the shores of the great lakes, by the waters of
the Gulf, in the land of the loom and spindle, in the land of
gold, on broad prairies, on sunny savannas, let the chorus
again and again break forth, "Peace on earth, good will toward men. " We have had enough war. Too many widows'
weeds are scattered in this land; too many orphan children
are gazing upon and lamenting the past. It was a just and
righteous war, bravely fought and nobly won. Thank God it
is over; and let us hope it will be revived only in memory.

    I think the time has arrived for the ravages of this
war to entirely disappear. Where any turbulent elements
still exist the law should have its just sway, however much
we may dread such necessities. And unto every citizen is
there a duty assigned. As to what that is no honest patriot
can doubt. The elimination of bias and bigotry and the general education of the high and low of every section will be
found the true source of our national prosperity; and as the
mind is expanded, reason will come forth from the dark ob-
scurity of ignorance to balance with a nice hand the scales
of justice.

    America will not die. As the time demands them
great men will appear, and by their combined efforts render
liberty and happiness more secure. The people will be ready
and answer in every emergency that may arise. If they have
been able to direct and manage affairs wisely in the past,
how much additional power will they have in the future with
which to mold and invigorate the mighty fabric of the Republic. The union of national prosperity with social harmony,
which is sure to come, will be indicated by one rapid recon-

struction. Wisdom and knowledge from their highest pinnacles
must no longer view the progress of national greatness, but
its perfection. From Maine to Alaska will resound the shouts
of rejoicing which will arise from millions of intelligent and
happy freemen. With such watchwords as freedom, equality,
and fraternity no factor of discord will be apparent. The
seed has been sown and the harvest shall be reaped, and
such a one as has never been known before in the history of
nations--a harvest of peace, prosperity, and virtue.

But before this millennium dawns there will be still
much to accomplish. However, we may comfort ourselves
with the reflection that the path of virtue is sometimes dark;
if we follow it steadily difficulties and embarrassments will
melt away. The cloud will one day roll off, and the bow of
hope and promise will be found in its place. Let us sur-
render no vital principle; neither let us waste precious time
in the idle discussion of obsolete issues. The policy to be
adopted must be one that will build up our waste places,
cover our broad acres with waving grain, send our ships into
every sea, start our factories, bridge our streams, and
make the hum of industry resound on all sides. Let us go
on as an orderly, law-abiding people, and wait patiently for
the time when the reward cometh; for the time when a sense
of justice shall once more animate the hearts of all, and
malice and hate shall give place to brotherly love.

With the ardent prayer that our Government may remain an everlasting unit, and that the great Commonwealth of
Louisiana regain and then maintain her lofty position among
the sisterhood of States, I shall close with the prediction that
this Government "of the people, for the people, and by the
people" will not perish from the face of the earth.

BIBLIOGRAPHY

1. Biographical Directory of the American Congress 1774-
      1971. Washington, D.C.: United States Government
      Printing Office, 1971.

2. U.S. Congress. House. Political Condition of the South.
      44th Congress, 1st session, 1876.

JOSEPH HAYNE RAINEY

XII.   JOSEPH HAYNE RAINEY

Rainey, Joseph Hayne, a Representative from South Carolina; born in Georgetown, Georgetown County, South Carolina, June 21, 1832; was of the Negro race; received a limited schooling; followed the trade of barber until 1862, when upon being forced to work on the Confederate fortifications in Charleston, South Carolina, he escaped to the West Indies and remained there until the close of the war; delegate to the State Constitutional Convention in 1868; member of the State senate in 1870 but resigned; elected as a Republican to the Forty-first Congress to fill the vacancy caused by the action of the House of Representatives in declaring the seat of B. Franklin Whittemore vacant, and was the first Negro elected to the National House of Representatives to be re-elected to the 42nd and to the three succeeding Congresses-- he served from December 12, 1870 to March 3, 1879; appointed internal-revenue agent of South Carolina in May 22, 1879, and served until July 15, 1881, when he resigned; engaged in banking and the brokerage business in Washington, D. C.; retired from all business activities in 1886, returned to Georgetown, South Carolina, and died there August 2, 1887.   (1:1581)

SUPPORT OF FOURTEENTH AMENDMENT

In the dawn of our freedom our young Republic
was widely recognized and proudly proclaimed to
the world the refuge, the safe asylum of the oppressed of all lands.   Shall it be said that at this
day, through mere indifference and culpable neglect, this grand boast of ours is become a mere
form of words, an utter fraud? ... and yet, if
we stand with folded arms and idle hands, while
the cries of our oppressed brethren sound in our
ears, what will it be but a proof to all men that
we are utterly unfit for our glorious mission, unworthy our noble privileges, as the greatest of
republics, the champions of freedom for all men?
(2:393-395)

Mr. RAINEY.   Mr.'Speaker, in approaching the subject now under consideration I do so with a deep sense of its
magnitude and importance, and in full recognition of the fact
that a remedy is needed to meet the evil now existing in
most of the southern States, but especially in that one which
I have the honor to represent in part, the State of South
Carolina.   The enormity of the crimes constantly perpetrated
there finds no parallel in the history of this Republic in her
very darkest days.   There was a time when the early settlers
of New England were compelled to enter the fields, their
homes, even the very sanctuary itself, armed to the full extent of their means.   While the people were offering their
worship to God within those humble walls their voices kept
time with the tread of the sentry outside.   But, sir, it must
be borne in mind that at the time referred to civilization had
but just begun its work upon this continent.   The surroundings were unpropitious, and as yet the grand capabilities of
this fair land lay dormant under the fierce tread of the red
man.   But as civilization advanced with its steady and resist-
less sway it drove back those wild cohorts and compelled
them to give way to the march of improvement.   In course
of time superior intelligence made its impress and established its dominion upon this continent.   That intelligence,

194

with an influence like that of the sun rising in the east and spreading its broad rays like a garment of light, gave life and gladness to the dark and barbaric land of America.

Surely, sir, it were but reasonable to hope that this sacred influence should never have been overshadowed, and that in the history of other nations, no less than in our own past, we might find beacon-lights for our guidance. In part this has been realized, and might have reached the height of our expectations if it had not been for the blasting effects of slavery, whose deadly pall has so long spread its folds over this nation, to the destruction of peace, union, and concord. Most particularly has its baneful influence been felt in the South, causing the people to be at once restless and discontented. Even now, sir, after the great conflict between slavery and freedom, after the triumph achieved at such a cost, we can yet see the traces of the disastrous strife and the remains of disease in the body-politic of the South. In proof of this, witness the frequent outrages perpetrated upon our loyal men. The prevailing spirit of the Southron is either to rule or to ruin. Voters must perforce succumb to their wishes or else risk life itself in the attempt to maintain a simple right of common manhood.

The suggestions of the shrewdest Democratic papers have proved unavailing in controlling the votes of the loyal whites and blacks of the South. The people emphatically decline to dispose of their rights for a mess of pottage. In this particular the Democracy of the North found themselves foiled and their money needless. But with a spirit more demon-like than that of a Nero or a Caligula, there has been concocted another plan, destructive, ay, diabolical in its character, worthy only of hearts without regard for God or man, fit for such deeds as those deserving the name of men would shudder to perform. Is it asked, what are those deeds? Let those who liberally contributed to the supply of arms and ammunition in the late rebellious States answer the question. Soon after the close of the war there had grown up in the South a very widely-spread willingness to comply with the requirements of the law. But as the clemency and magnanimity of the General Government became manifest once again did the monster rebellion lift its hydra head in renewed defiance, cruel and cowardly, fearing the light of day, hiding itself under the shadow of the night as more befitting its bloody and accursed work.

I need not, Mr. Speaker, recite here the murderous

deeds committed both in North and South Carolina. I could
touch the feelings of this House by the story of widows and
orphans now wandering amid the ravines of the rural counties
of my native State seeking protection and maintenance from
others who are yet unable, on account of their own poverty,
to grant them aid. I could dwell upon the sorrows of poor
women, with their helpless infants, cast upon the world,
homeless and destitute, deprived of their natural protectors
by the red hand of the midnight assassin. I could appeal to
you, members upon this floor, as husbands and fathers, to
picture to yourselves the desolation of your own happy firesides should you be suddenly snatched away from your loved
ones. Think of gray-haired men, whose fourscore years are
almost numbered, the venerated heads of peaceful households,
without warning murdered for political opinion's sake. In
proof I send to the desk the following article and ask the
Clerk to read. It is taken from the Spartanburg (South Carolina) Republican, March 29, 1871.

      The Clerk read as follows:

            Horrible Attempt at Murder by Disguised Men.
            - One of the most cowardly and inhuman attempts
            at murder known in the annals of crime was made
            last Wednesday night, the 22d instant, by a band
            of disguised men upon the person of Dr. J. Win-
            smith at his home about twelve miles from town.
            The doctor, a man nearly seventy years of age,
            had been to town during the day and was seen and
            talked with by many of our citizens. Returning
            home late, he soon afterward retired, worn out
            and exhausted by the labors of the day. A little
            after midnight he was aroused by someone knock-
            ing violently at his front door. The knocking was
            soon afterward repeated at his chamber door,
            which opens immediately upon the front yard. The
            doctor arose, opened the door, and saw two men
            in disguise standing before him. As soon as he
            appeared one of the men cried out, 'Come on,
            boys! Here's the damned old rascal.' The doc-
            tor immediately stepped back into the room,
            picked up two single-barreled pistols lying upon
            the bureau, and returned to the open door. At
            his reappearance the men retreated behind some
            cedar trees standing in the yard. The doctor, in
            his night clothes, boldly stepped out into the yard

and followed them. On reaching the trees he
fired, but with what effect he does not know. He
continued to advance, when twenty or thirty shots
were fired at him by men crouched behind an
orange hedge. He fired his remaining pistol and
then attempted to return to the house. Before
reaching it, however, he sank upon the ground exhausted by the loss of blood, and pain, occasioned
by seven wounds which he had received in various
parts of his body. As soon as he fell the assas-
sins mounted their horses and rode away.

The doctor was carried into the house upon a
quilt, borne by his wife and some colored female
servant. The colored men on the premises fled
on the approach of the murderers, and the colored
women being afraid to venture out, Mrs. Winsmith
herself was obliged to walk three-quarters of a
mile to the house of her nephew, Dr. William
Smith, for assistance. The physician has been
with Dr. Winsmith day and night since the difficulty occurred, and thinks, we learn, that there
is a possible chance of the doctor's recovery.

The occasion of this terrible outrage can be only
the fact that Dr. Winsmith is a Republican. One
of the largest land-holders and tax-payers in the
county, courteous in manner, kind in disposition,
and upright and just in all his dealings with his
fellow-men, he has ever been regarded as one of
the leading citizens of the county. For many years
prior to the war he represented the people in the
Legislature, and immediately after the war he was
sent to the senate. Because he has dared become
a Republican, believing that in the doctrines of
true republicanism only can the State and country
find lasting peace and prosperity, he has become
the doomed victim of the murderous Ku Klux Klan.

The tragedy has cast a gloom over the entire
community, and while we are glad to say that it
has generally been condemned, yet we regret to
state that no step has yet been taken to trace out
and punish the perpetrators of the act. The judge
of this circuit is sitting on his bench; the machinery of justice is in working order; but there can
be found no hand bold enough to set it in motion.
The courts of justice seem paralyzed when they
have to meet such issues as this. Daily reports
come to us of men throughout the country being

whipped; of school-houses for colored children
being closed, and of parties being driven from
their houses and their families.   Even here in
town there are some who fear to sleep at their
own homes and in their own beds.   The law affords no protection for life and property in this
county, and the sooner the country knows it and
finds a remedy for it, the better it will be.
Better a thousand times the rule of the bayonet
than the humiliating lash of the Ku Klux and the
murderous bullet of the midnight assassin.

Mr. RAINEY.   The gentleman to whom reference is
made in the article read, is certainly one of the most inoffensive individuals I have ever known.   He is a gentleman
of refinement, culture, and sterling worth, a Carolinian of
the old school, an associate of the late Hon. John C. Calhoun, being neither a pauper nor a pensioner, but living in
comparative affluence and ease upon his own possessions, respected by all fair-minded and unprejudiced citizens who knew
him.   Accepting the situation, he joined the Republican party
in the fall of 1870; and for this alliance, and this alone, he
has been vehemently assailed and murderously assaulted.   By
all the warm and kindly sympathies of our common humanity,
I implore you to do something for this suffering people, and
stand not upon the order of your doing.   Could I exhume the
murdered men and women of the South, Mr. Speaker, and
array their ghastly forms before your eyes, I should not need
remove the mantle from them, because their very presence
would appeal, in tones of plaintive eloquence, which would be
louder than a million tongues.   They could indeed---

A tale unfold whose lightest word
Would harrow up thy soul.

It has been asserted that protection for the colored
people only has been demanded; and in this there is a certain
degree of truth, because they are noted for their steadfast-
ness to the Union and the cause of liberty as guaranteed by
the Constitution.   But, on the other hand, this protection is
equally desired for those loyal whites, some to the manner
born, others who, in the exercise of their natural rights as
American citizens, have seen fit to remove thither from
other sections of the States, and who are now undergoing persecution simply on account of their activity in carrying out
Union principles and loyal sentiments in the South.   Their

efforts have contributed largely to further reconstruction and the restoration of the southern States to the old fellowship of the Federal compact.   It is indeed hard that their reward for their well-meant earnestness should be that of being violently treated, and even forced to flee from the homes of their choice.   It will be a foul stain upon the escutcheon of our land if such atrocities be tamely suffered longer to continue.

In the dawn of our freedom our young Republic was widely recognized and proudly proclaimed to the world the refuge, the safe asylum of the oppressed of all lands.   Shall it be said that at this day, through mere indifference and culpable neglect, this grand boast of ours is become a mere form of words, an utter fraud?   I earnestly hope not!   And yet, if we stand with folded arms and idle hands, while the cries of our oppressed-brethren sound in our ears, what will it be but a proof to all men that we are utterly unfit for our glorious mission, unworthy our noble privileges, as the greatest of republics, the champions of freedom for all men? I would that every individual man in this whole nation could be aroused to the sense of his own part and duty in this great question.   When we call to mind the fact that this persecution is waged against men for the simple reason that they dare to vote with the party which has saved the Union intact by the lavish expenditure of blood and treasure, and has borne the nation safely through the fearful crisis of these last few years, our hearts swell with an overwhelming indignation.

The question is sometimes asked, Why do not the courts of law afford redress?   Why the necessity of appealing to Congress?   We answer that the courts are in many in-stances under the control of those who are wholly inimical to the impartial administration of law and equity.   What benefit would result from appeal to tribunals whose officers are secretly in sympathy with the every evil against which we are striving?

But to return to the point in question.   If the negroes, numbering one-eighth of the population of these United States, would only cast their votes in the interest of the Democratic party, all open measures against them would be immediately suspended, and their rights, as American citizens, recog-nized.   But as to the real results of such a state of affairs, and speaking in behalf of those with whom I am conversant, I can only say that we love freedom more, vastly more, than slavery; consequently we hope to keep clear of the Demo-crats!

In most of the arguments to which I have listened the
positions taken are predicated upon the ground of the uncon-
stitutionality of the bill introduced by the gentleman from
Ohio (Mr. SHELLABARGER). For my part I am not prepared, Mr. Speaker, to argue this question from a constitutional standpoint alone. I take the ground that, in my opinion, lies far above the interpretation put upon the provisions
of the Constitution. I stand upon the broad plane of right; I
look to the urgent, the importunate demands of the present
emergency; and while I am far from advocating any step not
in harmony with that sacred law of our land, while I would
not violate the lightest word of that chart which has so well
guided us in the past, yet I desire that so broad and liberal
a construction be placed upon its provisions as will insure
protection to the humblest citizen, without regard to rank,
creed, or color. Tell me nothing of a constitution which
fails to shelter beneath its rightful power the people of a
country!

I believe when the fathers of our country framed the
Constitution they made the provisions so broad that the humblest, as well as the loftiest citizen, could be protected in
his inalienable rights. It was designed to be, and is, the
bulwark of freedom, and the strong tower of defense, against
foreign invasion and domestic violence. I desire to direct
your attention to what is imbodied in the preamble, and would
observe that it was adopted after a liberal and protracted discussion on every article composing the great American Magna
Charta. And like a keystone to an arch it made the work
complete. Here is what it declares:

> We, the people of the United States, in order to
> form a more perfect Union, establish justice, in-
> sure domestic tranquillity, provide for the com-
> mon defense, promote the general welfare, and
> secure the blessings of liberty to ourselves and
> our posterity, do ordain and establish this Consti-
> tution for the United States of America.

If the Constitution which we uphold and support as the
fundamental law of the United States is inadequate to afford
security to life, liberty, and property--if, I say, this inadequacy is proven, then its work is done, then it should no
longer be recognized as the Magna Charta of a great and free
people; the sooner it is set aside the better for the liberties
of the nation. It has been asserted on this floor that the Republican party is answerable for the existing state of affairs

in the South. I am here to deny this, and to illustrate, I
will say that in the State of South Carolina there is no disturbance of an alarming character in any one of the counties
in which the Republicans have a majority. The troubles are
usually in those sections in which the Democrats have a pre-
dominance in power, and, not content with this, desire to be
supreme.

I say to the gentlemen of the Opposition, and to the
entire membership of the Democratic party, that upon your
hands rests the blood of the loyal men of the South. Dis-
claim it as you will, the stain is there to prove your crimi-
nality before God and the world in the day of retribution which
will surely come. I pity the man or party of men who would
seek to ride into power over the dead body of a legitimate
opponent.

It has been further stated that peace reigned in the
rebellious States from 1865 until the enactment of the reconstruction laws. The reason of this is obvious. Previous to
that time they felt themselves regarded as condemned trait-
ors, subject to the penalties of the law. They stood awaiting
the sentence of the nation to be expressed by Congress. Subsequently the enactments of that body, framed with a spirit
of magnanimity worthy a great and noble nation, proved that,
far from a vindictive course, they desired to deal with them
with clemency and kindness. This merciful plan of action
proved to be a mistake, for cowardice, emboldened by the
line of policy of the President, began to feel that judgment
long delayed meant forgiveness without repentance. Their
tactics were changed, and again a warlike attitude was assumed, not indeed directly against the General Government,
but against those who upon southern soil were yet the staunch
supporters of its powers. Thus is it evident that if only the
props which support such a fabric could be removed the
structure must necessarily fall, to be built again by other
hands. This is the animus of the Ku Klux Klan, which is
now spreading devastation through the once fair and tranquil
South.

If the country there is impoverished it has certainly
not been caused by the fault of those who love the Union, but
it is simply the result of a disastrous war madly waged
against the best Government known to the world. The murder of unarmed men and the maltreating of helpless women
can never make restitution for the losses which are the
simply inevitable consequence of the rebellion. The faithful-

ness of my race during the entire war, in supporting and
protecting the families of their masters, speaks volumes in
their behalf as to the real kindliness of their feelings toward
the white people of the South.

In conclusion, sir, I would say that it is in no spirit
of bitterness against the southern people that I have spoken
to-day. There are many among them for whom I entertain a
profound regard, having known them in former and brighter
days of their history. I have always felt a pride in the
prestige of my native State, noted as she has been for her
noble sons, with their lofty intellect or tried statesmanship.
But it is not possible for me to speak in quiet and studied
words of those unworthy her ancient and honorable name, who
at this very day are doing all they can do to deface her fair
records of the past and bring the old State into disrepute.

I can say for my people that we ardently desire peace
for ourselves and for the whole nation. Come what will, we
are fully determined to stand by the Republican party and the
Government. As to our fate, "we are not wood, we are not
stone, " but men, with feelings and sensibilities like other
men whose skin is of a lighter hue.

When myself and colleagues shall leave these Halls
and turn our footsteps toward our southern homes we know
not but that the assassin may await our coming, as marked
for his vengeance. Should this befall, we would bid Congress
and our country to remember that 'twas--

Bloody treason flourish'd over us.

Be it as it may, we have resolved to be loyal and
firm, "and if we perish, we perish!" I earnestly hope the
bill will pass.

NATIONAL EDUCATION

I feel confident in saying that the populace is
eager for education, and are looking with an
ardent desire to the General Government to aid
them in this particular. Educational facilities
are needed alike by all classes, both white and
black. There is an appalling array of the illiterate ... ignorance is widespread; it is not confined to any one state. This mental midnight,
we might justly say, is a national calamity, and
not necessarily sectional. We should therefore
avail ourselves of every laudable means in our
power to avert its direful effects. The great
remedy, in my judgment, is free schools, established and aided by the Government throughout
the land. (3:Appendix)

Mr. RAINEY. Mr. Speaker, I have been an attentive
listener to the discussions on House bill No. 1043. This
bill, as you are aware, has for its object the education of
the people, and proposes to that end that the proceeds accruing from the sale of all public lands should be set apart
as a sacred fund for that object. Viewing it in this light,
one may well be surprised at the manner in which the entire
subject has been treated by the Opposition. It is truly marvelous to observe the manifest antipathy exhibited toward
measures that are brought before this House having for their
purpose the amelioration and improvement of the masses.

It ought not to be forgotten that we are the custodians
of the interests of the whole people, sent here direct from
their hands to represent their claims and interests before
Congress, and, I may add, the whole country. Why, sir,
those illiterate and somewhat neglected people are the actual
bone and sinew of the country, and at this time may be
safely numbered among the stanchest supporters of its institutions. Their efficiency, bravery, and power were known
to the country in its darkest days and dire necessities, the
testimony of which is stamped in bloody stains upon many a

battle field. These gallant and true men, many of whom have
passed away, have left their fatherless children as a heritage
and trust to this Government. Yea, the whole people are
deeply interested in this subject of education; therefore, we
should endeavor to reflect as best we can their opinions,
wishes, and desires in this regard.

I feel confident in saying that the populace is eager
for education, and are looking with an ardent desire to the
General Government to aid them in this particular. Educational facilities are needed alike by all classes, both white
and black. There is an appalling array of the illiterate made
in the admirable report of the Commissioner of Education, a
forcible tabular statement of which has been brought to the
notice of this House by the distinguished gentleman from
Massachusetts (Mr. HOAR). Surely this ought to be sufficient
to disarm all hostility to this laudable and much-needed measure; but instead of that, it meets with every conceivable objection and opposition from those who profess to be the
friends and advocates of universal education. By some the
bill under consideration is said to be unconstitutional; by
others, centralizing power in the hands of the General Government which by right belongs to individual States.

The gentleman from Georgia (Mr. McINTYRE) expressed his apprehensions that this was a plan to mix the
schools throughout the country. What of that? Suppose it
should be so, what harm would result therefrom? Why this
fear of the negro since he has been a freedman, when in the
past he was almost a household god, gamboling and playing
with the children of his old master? And occasionally it was
plain to be seen that there was a strong family resemblance
between them.

Now, since he is no longer a slave, one would suppose
him a leper, to hear the objections expressed against his
equality before the law. Sir, this is the remnant of the old
proslavery spirit, which must eventually give place to more
humane and elevating ideas. Schools have been mixed in
Massachusetts, Rhode Island, and other States, and no detriment has occurred. Why this fear of competition with a
negro? All they ask for is an equal chance in life, with
equal advantages, and they will prove themselves to be worthy
American citizens. In the southern States it was a pride in
the past to exult in the extraordinary ability of a few representative men, while the poorer classes were kept illiterate
and in gross ignorance; consequently completely under the
control of their leaders, all of whom were Democrats.

The Republican party propose by this measure now
pending to educate the masses so that they will be enabled
to judge for themselves in all matters appertaining to their
interests, and by an intelligent expression of their manhood
annihilate the remnant of that oligarchical spirit of exclusive-
ness which was so prominent in the past. Sir, it appears
to me as though gentlemen on this floor have lost sight of
the fact that the besom of war has swept over this country,
and that there is a change in the condition of affairs; that
the people are the rightful rulers, and those in power are
but their servants.

During the last Congress we had under consideration
a bill for the establishing of a system of national education,
but adverse arguments were urged against the proposition,
which resulted in its defeat. It was said then, as now, that
it was unwise and inexpedient for such a bill to pass Congress, because it looked forward to centralization of Government, and an eventual invasion and trespass upon State rights.
In my opinion, if the doctrine of State rights was not destroyed in the heated conflict of the late war, there are
little or no apprehensions of such a contingency in the passage of this bill.

The decision of the sword is conceded to be the most
arbitrary of all decisions which we have on record, and it
might be added that they are written in blood and will assuredly withstand, all corrosive arguments to the contrary
notwithstanding. The results of the rebellion have decided
some things, and, in my judgment, defined the boundaries of
State rights. Sir, speaking of centralization, all powerful
Governments have a tendency in that direction, and those who
have not are showing this day their sad want of power to
control their internal affairs, and at the same time exercise
a salutary influence on the actions and affairs of other nations.

In the old Roman empire, proud though it was, boasting of its many conquests, and its almost unlimitable extent
of territory, feeling themselves secured by a supposed high
order of civilization, they grew indifferent to their best interests in this regard, and as a natural sequence their power
waned, and they are only known to us as a nation through the
pages of history. The nations of modern Europe most respected are those which have succeeded partly in centralizing
their power, and I can see no difference in this respect with
republics and monarchical governments. I am confident--

yea, it is inevitable--that if this Government expects to control this vast extent of territory now in its possession, with
an almost annual augmentation thereto, it must, of necessity,
become somewhat centralized or it cannot stand.

Mr. Speaker, I have no argument to advance for or
against the constitutionality of this bill; that I cheerfully submit to abler hands.   It was said, however, by the gentleman
from Pennsylvania (Mr. STORM) and others, that it is
grossly unconstitutional; therefore more objectionable than
the Ku Klux bill was.   Such strictures are frequently heard
from the Democracy.   Nothing, in fact, appears to be constitutional to them that emanates or originates with the Republicans; consequently, the force of the argument is not felt
to any extent.   But admitting the assertion with all of the
force and potency with which it is constantly uttered, I ask
if it is a perversion of the spirit of the Constitution to invoke
the sanction of that sacred instrument upon such a laudable
measure as this, having for its aim the advancement of the
whole people intellectually; thereby raising them to a higher
plane, from which they may observe the beneficent workings
of this, the greatest and most magnanimous of Governments.

The natural result of this mental improvement will be
to impart a better understanding of our institutions, and thus
cultivate a loyal disposition and lofty appreciation for them.
The military prowess and demonstrative superiority of the
Prussians, when compared to the French, especially in the
late war, is attributable to the fact that the masses of the
former were better educated and trained than those of the
latter.   The leavening spirit of the German philosophers has,
apparently, pervaded all classes of the population of that entire empire.   It is not necessary to detail the result that has
passed into history, the lesson of which should not be lost on
this continent.   With these truths confronting us what is best
to be done?   Why, educate the people to a higher standard of
citizenship.   If this is done by the aid of the General Government its fruits will be seen in every department, and its
power felt in every emergency.

Now, I am in favor of Government aid in this respect,
for it will materially assist and eventually succeed in oblit-
erating sectional feeling and differences of opinion, and thus
foster a unit of sentiment that is so desirable by all true
patriots, who are ever ready to acknowledge its essentiality
to harmony, concord, and perpetual peace; thereby aiding the
industries of our country and developing our vast national

resources. If this had been done years ago there would have
been a better understanding and more fraternal feeling between the North and the South, which would have annihilated
that obstinate, hostile spirit which engendered the late "un-
pleasantness. " The recent trials of the Ku Klux at Columbia,
South Carolina, furnish a striking proof, which is beyond con-
troversion, for the criminals themselves confessed an utter
destitution of general information that did not fail to excite
the commiseration of the presiding judges.

This lamentable condition of things demands a remedy
at the hand of our powerful and generous Government. The
evidence is conclusive; therefore it is not necessary that
arguments should be multiplied on this point. The report of
the Commissioner of Education presents an astonishing ano-
maly in its tabular statements setting forth the illiterate of
all classes in the United States. We find that out of a population of over thirty-eight millions, over two and one half
millions in the southern States over twenty-one years old are
unable to read and write, and over one million in the northern States.

I find in the report of the superintendent of education
of the State which I have the honor in part to represent the
following interesting statement: there are 206, 610 school
children between the ages of six and sixteen, with a total attendance of only 66, 056, the greater portion of the remainder
being unable to attend for the want of educational facilities,
although there has been one hundred and four school-houses
erected during the year 1871, at a cost of $13, 254, and
fifty-two rented in addition thereto. There are employed in
that State 1, 898 teachers, at a cost of over two hundred and
sixty-one thousand dollars per annum.

Sir, I now ask is not this statement of sufficient force
to baffle opposition, and awaken a lively interest on the part
of this House favorable to this great popular necessity?
Think of it, only 66, 056 children attending school out of a
school population of 206, 610 in one State in this Union. What
must be the exhibit of all the States? But for all this the
people are not to blame for their insufficiency of information.
They are eager for knowledge, and the cry is still for more.
I have seen, much to my admiration, old gray-headed men,
formerly slaves, learning the alphabet, and straining their
blunted senses in quest of knowledge, and this, too, after the
hard toils of the day. The delight with which they behold
their little children striving to read while seated around their

humble firesides is pleasurable to behold, as a hopeful sign
of what the once oppressed will be when they shall have drunk
deep from the perennial stream of knowledge. What we want
is schools, and more of them. We want them strung along
the highways and by-ways of this country.

Mr. Speaker, I would have it known that this ignorance
is widespread; it is not confined to any one State. This
mental midnight, we might justly say, is a national calamity,
and not necessarily sectional. We should therefore avail ourselves of every laudable means in our power to avert its
direful effects. The great remedy, in my judgment, is free
schools, established and aided by the Government throughout
the land. The following statistics will demonstrate what I
have said:

In Illinois, in the year 1870, the number of white
pupils was 826, 829; number of colored pupils, 6, 210; number
of school-houses, 10, 381; number of school districts with no
schools, 390; number of scholars attending school, 706, 780.
By this you will perceive that there are over 126, 000 children not attending school in this State.

In Indiana, in the years 1867 and 1868, the number of
school children was 591, 661; number attending school,
436, 736; average daily attendance 283, 340; amount expended
for tuition, $1, 474, 832. 40.

The population of Maine, in 1870, was 630, 423; number of school children, 228, 167; number enrolled, 126, 946;
number not enrolled, 90, 335; average attendance, 100, 815.
Average duration of schools only four months and twenty days.

The population of Louisiana, in 1870, was 716, 394;
school population, 254, 533; number enrolled, 50, 000; average
attendance, 40, 000; number not registered, 204, 533; making
a total absence from school in that State of 214, 533.

The school population of Arkansas, in 1870, was
180, 000; number enrolled, 100, 000; average attendance,
60, 000; number not enrolled, 80, 000; average absence of
those enrolled, 40, 000; total average absence, 120, 000.

Can we look at these facts unmoved? Do they not
call for our deliberate and earnest action? Surely they do.

There is another fact which should not be lost sight

of: our country is comparatively new; the want of skilled
labor is felt in all the branches of its progressive industries.
If the Government can utilize any portion of its immense domain for the furtherance of these ends, it will thus be dis-
pensing its benefits and wealth to another class besides railroad corporations, who already have too much of what in
right and equity belongs to the people. Millions of fertile
acres have been disposed of in a prodigal manner to these
opulent, dictatorial corporations. At present they have too
much power and influence at their command, and in certain
States in this Union they shape and control legislation to a
great extent. My fears are that if Congress continues to
assist them by further grants of the public domain, they will
eventually become the dictators of national legislation.

The plan embraced in this bill thwarts their designs,
and will in a measure protect the Government from such a
misfortune, and the people from such a catastrophe. In fact
the people have long since rendered a verdict on this sub-
ject--"No more public lands to corporations. " If this verdict
holds good, the public possessions, henceforth, will be held
in fee simple for the sole benefit of the people.

I shall remind the House of one thing more, then I
shall have done. The youth now springing up to manhood
will be the future lawmakers and rulers of our country. That
they should be intelligent and thoroughly educated is a prime
necessity and of great importance, which is admitted by all
and denied by none. All that may be done with this end in
view will be returned with an increased interest.

I truly hope that those who oppose this bill will re-
consider their opposition, and give it their vote when the
question shall again be before the House. For one, I shall
give it my hearty support, believing it to be just and beneficial in its provisions.

CIVIL RIGHTS (March 5, 1872)

If the colored people ... had had the same wealth
and surroundings ... they would have shown to
this nation that their color was no obstacle to
their holding positions of trust, political or otherwise. Not having had those advantages, we cannot at the present time compete with the favored
race of this country; but perhaps if our lives are
spared ... if the House will only accord to us
right and justice, we shall show to them that we
can be useful, intelligent citizens of this country.
But if they continue to proscribe us, if they will
continue to cultivate prejudice against us, if they
will continue to decry the negro and crush him
underfoot, then you cannot expect the negro to
rise ... We ask you, sir, to do by the negro as
you ought to do by him in justice. (4:1439-1443)

Mr. RAINEY. I move to strike out the last word. I
regret, Mr. Chairman, very much that at this time a discussion of this character has been opened on this floor. I
believe the time will come when the atrocities committed in
the southern States will be fairly exhibited here, and also
made known to the country by records and other official declarations. I congratulate the gentleman from Virginia (Mr.
DUKE) on being able to say to the House that the State of
Virginia is in a condition of peace and quiet; that throughout
her broad domain quietude and safety are extended to each
and every citizen. I would, sir, that I could say as much
for the State that I have the honor in part to represent.

Sir, that State has not enjoyed a peace and quiet com-
mensurate with that of Virginia, and I could only attribute the
difference to the fact that we have got there a large loyal
element, an element of men who are determined to stand by
the General Government, who are determined to stand by the
interests of the great party which we have espoused in our
political infancy. I say, sir, that because we have thus acted,
and have dared as men, on the establishment of our man-

hood, to declare our sentiments to the country and cast our
ballots as we think best, we have been persecuted, mal-
treated, murdered, and in every way abused, not only men,
but helpless women and children, be it said to the shame of
these white citizens of South Carolina who perpetrated these
atrocities.

I, sir, for one, stand here in favor of voting every
dollar that may be necessary to carry on these prosecutions
until every man in the southern States shall know that this
Government has a strong arm, and that there is a power here
that will make them feel that if they will not obey the statutes of the country they shall be made to bow submissively
to those enactments at the point of the bayonet, be they white
or black.

Mr. Chairman, I have not time allowed me to enter
fully into a discussion of this question. If I had thought it
would have come up to-day, I would have had facts and figures here to substantiate every assertion that I make; but it
so happens that the question has been sprung upon us here,
not because it is germane to the subject under consideration,
but to allow the gentleman from Virginia (Mr. DUKE) to give
vent to his pent-up spleen, and express his opposition to the
enactments of the first session of this Congress.

I hope, sir, that his amendment will not prevail. I
trust that Congress will feel it to be its duty sternly, strenuously, and unflinchingly to see that the laws be enforced in
every part of this country. We have provided that men
charged with violating the laws of the land shall be tried. If
not guilty, they will go "scot-free"; but if they are guilty
then let them be put in the penitentiary, or otherwise punished, whether white or black, southern or northern men.

The assertion that it is the carpet-baggers who are
bringing about all the trouble in the South is untrue. The
great trouble has been brought about by the fact that the
southern people have failed to obey the laws giving equal protection to all; and because we have presumed to be loyal to
the Government, and support the laws, they have been trying
to exterminate us.

In conclusion, I hope this amendment will not be
adopted, and that an appropriation of $1,000,000 will be
adopted by the committee.

* * *

Mr. RAINEY. Mr. Chairman, I renew the amendment. The remarks made by the gentleman from New York
(Mr. COX) in relation to the colored people of South Carolina
escaped my hearing, as I was in the rear of the Hall when
they were made, and I did not know that any utterance of
that kind had emanated from him. I have always entertained
a high regard for the gentleman from New York, because I
believed him to be a useful member of the House. He is a
gentleman of talent and of fine education, and I have thought
heretofore that he would certainly be charitable toward a race
of people who have never enjoyed the same advantages that
he has. If the colored people of South Carolina had been accorded the same advantages--if they had had the same wealth
and surroundings which the gentleman from New York has
had, they would have shown to this nation that their color
was no obstacle to their holding positions of trust, political
or otherwise. Not having had those advantages, we cannot at
the present time compete with the favored race of this
country; but perhaps if our lives are spared, and if the
gentleman from New York and other gentlemen on that side
of the House will only accord to us right and justice, we
shall show to them that we can be useful, intelligent citizens
of this country. But if they will continue to proscribe us, if
they will continue to cultivate prejudice against us, if then
will continue to decry the negro and crush him under foot,
they you cannot expect the negro to rise while the Democrats
are trampling upon him and his rights. We ask you, sir, to
do by the negro as you ought to do by him in justice.

If the Democrats are such staunch friends of the negro,
why is it that when propositions are offered here and elsewhere looking to the elevation of the colored race, and the
extension of right and justice to them, do the Democrats
array themselves in unbroken phalanx, and vote against every
such measure? You, gentlemen of that side of the House,
have voted against all the recent amendments to the Constitution, and the laws enforcing the same. Why did you do it?
I answer, because those measures had a tendency to give to
the poor negro his just rights, and because they proposed to
knock off his shackles and give him freedom of speech, freedom of action, and the opportunity of education, that he might
elevate himself to the dignity of manhood.

Now you come to us and say that you are our best
friends. We would that we could look upon you as such. We

would that your votes as recorded in the Globe from day to day could only demonstrate it. But your votes, your actions, and the constant cultivation of your cherished prejudices prove to the negroes of the entire country that the Democracy are in opposition to them, and if they (the Democrats) could have sway our race would have no foot-hold here.

Now, sir, I have not time to vindicate fully the course of action of the colored people in South Carolina. We are certainly in the majority there; I admit that we are as two to one. Sir, I ask this House, I ask the country, I ask white men, I ask Democrats, I ask Republicans, whether the negroes have presumed to take improper advantage of the majority they hold in that State by disregarding the interest of the minority? They have not. Our convention which met in 1868, and in which the negroes were in a large majority, did not pass any proscriptive or disfranchising acts, but adopted a liberal constitution, securing alike equal rights to all citizens, white and black, male and female, as far as possible. Mark you, we did not discriminate, although we had a majority. Our constitution towers up in its majesty with provisions for the equal protection of all classes of citizens. Notwithstanding our strong majority there, we have never attempted to deprive any man in that State of the rights and immunities to which he is entitled under the Constitution of this Government. You cannot point me to a single act passed by our Legislature, at any time, which had a tendency to reflect upon or oppress any white citizen of South Carolina. You cannot show me one enactment by which the majority in our State have undertaken to crush the white men because the latter are in a minority.

I say to you, gentlemen of the Democratic party, that I want you to deal justly with the people composing my race. I am here representing a Republican constituency made up of white and colored men. I say to you, deal with us justly; be charitable toward us. An opportunity will soon present itself when we can test whether you on that side of the House are the best friends of the oppressed and ill-treated negro race. When the civil rights bill comes before you, when that bill comes up upon its merits asking you to give civil rights to the negro, I will then see who are our best friends on that side of the House. (Laughter and applause on the Republican side of the House.)

I will say to the gentleman from New York that I am sorry I am constrained to make these remarks. I wish to say to him that I do not mind what he may have said against the negroes of South Carolina. Neither his friendship nor his enmity will change the sentiment of the loyal men of that State. We are determined to stand by this Government. We are determined to use judiciously and wisely the prerogative conferred upon us by the Republican party. The Democratic party may woo us, they may court us and try to get us to worship at their shrine, but I tell the gentleman that we are Republicans by instinct, and we will be Republicans so long as God will allow our proper senses to hold sway over us. I withdraw the amendment.

REMOVAL OF PERSONAL DISABILITIES

It is not the disposition of my constituency that
those disabilities should longer be retained on
them. We are desirous, sir, of being magnanimous; it may be that we are so to fault; never-
less, we have open and frank hearts toward those
who were our former oppressors and task masters.
We foster no enmity now, and we desire to foster
none for their acts in the past to us, nor to the
Government we love so well. (5:3382-3383)

Mr. RAINEY. Mr. Speaker, there is no member on
this floor who hails with greater satisfaction and gratification
than myself a bill of this description, having for its avowed
purpose the removal of those disabilities imposed by the
fourteenth article of the amendments to the Constitution of
the United States upon those lately in rebellion. There are
many who are under these disabilities for whom I entertain
the highest respect and esteem. I regretted that their course
of action in the past made it necessary for Congress to impose on them any disabilities whatever. It is not the disposition of my constituency that those disabilities should
longer be retained on them. We are desirous, sir, of being
magnanimous; it may be that we are so to a fault; nevertheless, we have open and frank hearts toward those who were
our former oppressors and task masters. We foster no
enmity now, and we desire to foster none for their acts in
the past to us, nor to the Government we love so well. But
while we are willing to accord them their enfranchisement,
and here to-day give our votes that they may be amnestied;
while we declare our hearts open and free from any vindictive feelings toward them, we would say to those gentlemen
on the other side, and also to those on this side who are
representing more directly the sentiment and wishes of our
disfranchised fellow citizens, that there is another class of
citizens in this country who have certain dear rights and immunities which they would like you, sirs, to remember and
respect.

215

The Republican members of this House will give their votes for the passage of this amnesty bill. The majority of them are also in favor of civil rights, which my people, the colored people, are desirous of having. We are in earnest about this matter. We are earnest in our support of the Government. We were earnest in the hour of the nation's perils and dangers, and now, in our country's comparative peace and tranquillity, we are in earnest for our rights. We now invoke you, gentlemen, to show the same magnanimity and kindly feeling toward us--a race long oppressed; and in demonstration of this humane and just feeling give, I implore you, give support to the civil rights bill, which we have been asking at your hands, lo! these many days.

You will observe that when a bill is introduced for the purpose of removing political disabilities, no parliamentary manueverings are resorted to by the Republicans to impede the passage of such a bill.

I want the House further to understand, and especially the gentlemen on the other side, that this apparent indiffer- ence and reticence on our part is not from any want of the knowledge of parliamentary tactics by which legislation is often retarded, and salutary measures hindered, but it is be- cause we are disposed to facilitate and assist the furtherance of those measures we believe equitable and just to our fellow- man; thus doing unto others as we would they should do unto us. Now, in respect to the action of the Democrats, I re- gret very much to say that whenever a bill comes up here which is designed to relieve and benefit the outraged and op- pressed negro population of this country, those whom I may strictly call my constituency, their apparent eagerness to de- feat such desirable measures is perceptible on every hand, and is known to all. No vigilance or efforts were spared on their part to defeat the civil rights bill whenever it came up in its regular order. I hope, in the future, gentlemen, you will deal with us justly and generously as we now propose to deal with the late rebels. I hope you will assist us in se- curing our civil rights. I need not say to you that we fought for the maintenance of this Government while those who are about to be amnestied fought to destroy it. I thank the House for this courtesy.

CIVIL RIGHTS (December 19, 1873)

... the negro will never rest until he gets his
rights. We ask them because we know it is
proper, not because we want to deprive any other
class of the rights and immunities they enjoy, but
because they are granted to us by the law of the
land. Why this discrimination against us when we
enter public conveyances or places of public
amusement: Why is a discrimination made against
us in the churches; and why in the cemeteries
when we go to pay that last debt of nature that
brings us all upon a level? ... I say to you this
discrimination must cease. (6:343-344)

Mr. RAINEY. Mr. Speaker, I did not expect to participate in this debate at this early period; and I would have
preferred to wait until I should have had a full exposition of
the opinions entertained by the other side of the House. I
know, sir, that gentlemen on the other side have professed
a great deal of friendship for the race to which I belong; and
in the last presidential election they pledged themselves that
they would accord to the negroes of this country all the rights
that were given to other citizens. I am somewhat surprised
to perceive that on this occasion, when the demand is made
upon Congress by the people to guarantee those rights to a
race heretofore oppressed, we should find gentlemen on the
other side taking another view of the case from that which
they professed in the past. The gentleman from Kentucky
(Mr. BECK) has taken a legal view of this question, and he
is undoubtedly capable of taking that view. I am not a lawyer,
and consequently I cannot take a legal view of this matter, or
perhaps I cannot view it through the same optics that he does.
I view it in the light of the Constitution--in the light of the
amendments that have been made to that Constitution; I view
it in the light of humanity; I view it in the light of the progress and civilization which are now rapidly marching over
this country. We, sirs, would not ask of this Congress as
a people that they should legislate for us specifically as a
class if we could only have those rights which this bill is designed to give us accorded us without this enactment. I can

very well understand the opposition to this measure by gentlemen on the other side of the House, and especially of those
who come from the South.   They have a feeling against the
negro in this country that I suppose will never die out.   They
have an antipathy against that race of people, because of
their loyalty to this Government, and because at the very
time when they were needed to show their manhood and valor
they came forward in defense of the flag of the country and
assisted in crushing out the rebellion.   They, sir, would not
give to the colored man the right to vote or the right to enjoy any of those immunities which are enjoyed by other citizens, if it had a tendency to make him feel his manhood and
elevate him above the ordinary way of life.   So long as he
makes himself content with ordinary gifts, why it is all well;
but when he aspires to be a man, when he seeks to have the
rights accorded him that other citizens of the country enjoy,
then he is asking too much, and such gentlemen as the
gentleman from Kentucky are not willing to grant it.

      The gentleman from Kentucky says that the Constitu-
tion has prescribed what rights we ought to have and to enjoy.   I ask the gentleman, in the light of the Constitution,
if he can say to the House to-day conscientiously, if he can
say to the country conscientiously, that the rights which are
guaranteed by the Constitution are given to the negroes in
the State of Kentucky?   I should like to know if they enjoy
those immunities and those rights there.   Why, I saw not
long since a measure pending--and it was pending during the
last Congress--to deprive the negroes of Kentucky of the
right of suffrage.   They do not want any enactment by Congress that will have a tendency to elevate the negro and make
him feel that he is a man and an American citizen.   Just so
long as you will let Kentucky and the other Southern States,
and some of the Northern and Western States, mete out to
us what they think we ought to have, and we receive it without objection, we are good, clever fellows; but just as soon
as we begin to assert our manhood and demand our rights we
are looked upon as men not worthy to be recognized, we become objectionable, we become obnoxious, and we hear this
howl about social equality.

      Now, gentlemen, let me say the negro is not asking
social equality.   We do not ask it of you, we do not ask of
the gentleman from Kentucky that the two races should intermarry one with the other.   God knows we are perfectly content.   I can say for myself that I am contented to be what I
am so long as I have my rights; I am contented to marry one

of my own complexion, and do not seek intercourse with any
other race, because I believe that the race of people I represent, to the extent of the opportunities which they have had,
and considering how recently they have escaped from the oppression and wrongs committed upon them, are just as virtuous and hold just as many high characteristics as any class
in the country. I think the statistics will prove that there is
as much virtue among the negroes as among the whites. Sir,
we are not seeking to be put on a footing of social equality.
I prefer to choose my own associates, and all my colleagues
here and the whole race I belong to prefer to make that
choice. We do not ask the passage of any law forcing us
upon anybody who does not want to receive us. But we do
want a law enacted that we may be recognized like other men
in the country. Why is it that colored members of Congress
cannot enjoy the same immunities that are accorded to white
members? Why cannot we stop at hotels here without meeting objection? Why cannot we go into restaurants without
being insulted? We are here enacting laws for the country
and casting votes upon important questions; we have been sent
here by the suffrages of the people, and why cannot we enjoy
the same benefits that are accorded to our white colleagues
on this floor?

I say to you, gentlemen, that this discrimination
against the negro race in this country is unjust, is unworthy
of a high-minded people whose example should have a salutary
influence in the world. I am very much surprised at the
gentleman from Kentucky (Mr. BECK) making these objections
and urging them upon this House. I had supposed that, having had an opportunity during the past summer to return to
the land that gave him birth, and to breathe the free atmosphere among the hills of Old Scotland, he would return to the
land of his adoption with a generous spirit and open heart,
ready to accord to the negro in this country the rights that
belong to him as a citizen. But, returning as he does to the
soil of America, he comes back with the same deep-rooted
prejudice against the race to which I belong, and stands up
here to-day and declares that if we be permitted to enter
free schools or the public institutions in this country it can
only be by the power of the bayonet, because it would create
insurrection and rebellion in the Southern States.

Sir, why does it not create insurrection and rebellion
in the East? Why not in Ohio and in other parts of the
country where these rights are now accorded to us? We
have a great many, but not all, of our rights in South Caro-

lina, and there is no rebellion there.   In the Legislature of
South Carolina I find democrats voting for the civil-rights
bill.   It is upon this floor that I find men who talk about the
South being oppressed, rather than those who have an opportunity at home to give an expression to their opinion.

I say to you, gentlemen, that you are making a mistake.   Public opinion is aroused on this question.   I tell you
that the negro will never rest until he gets his rights.   We
ask them because we know it is proper, not because we want
to deprive any other class of the rights and immunities they
enjoy, but because they are granted to us by the law of the
land.   Why this discrimination against us when we enter public conveyances or places of public amusement?   Why is a
discrimination made against us in the churches; and why in
the cemeteries when we go to pay that last debt of nature
that brings us all upon a level?

Gentlemen, I say to you this discrimination must
cease.   We are determined to fight this question; we believe
the Constitution gives us this right.   All of the fifteen amendments made to the Constitution run down in one single line of
protecting the rights of the citizens of this country.   One
after another of those amendments give these rights to citizens; step by step these rights are secured to them.   And
now we say to you that if you will not obey the Constitution,
then the power is given by that Constitution for the enactment
of such a law as will have a tendency to enforce the provisions thereof.

Mr. Speaker, I will reserve much that I have to say
upon this question for another time.   I feel grateful to the
gentleman from New York (Mr. WOODFORD) for having accorded to me so much of his time and to the House for its
indulgence.

ESTABLISHMENT OF NATIONAL MONUMENT

> Fort Moultrie has clustering around it a great
> many historical associations. Its history is in-
> timately connected with that of this Government
> in its very incipiency, when the American people
> were struggling for their nationality; and it stands
> now as one of the monuments of the bravery of
> the men of that memorable era.   (7:1441-1443)

Mr. RAINEY. I renew the amendment, pro forma.
Mr. Chairman, I hope that the motion made by the gentleman from Pennsylvania (Mr. STORM) will not prevail. The
amount asked to keep Fort Moultrie in repair and in proper
condition is certainly very small when compared with the
amount asked for some other fortifications in the country.
If there were no other reason why this appropriation ought to
be made, a sufficient one is this: Fort Moultrie has clustering around it a great many historical associations. Its history is intimately connected with that of this Government in
its very incipiency, when the American people were struggling for their nationality; and it stands now as one of the
monuments of the bravery of the men of that memorable era.
I say, sir, that it should be kept as nearly as possible intact, if it be only that strangers may go there and satisfy
their curiosity by looking at it, if it be only that the children
of the present generation may go and look at a fortification
in which their fathers fought for the liberties of this country.
I say, sir, this fort should be kept not only in repair but in
good condition, so as to command the respect of all who may
be disposed to examine it, and of the country at large.

I am well aware that General Sherman in his testimony before the Military Committee said, "Let Fort Moultrie slide. " I would not like to suggest the reason why General Sherman may have made that statement; but it must be
borne in mind that he was speaking in behalf of the Army; he
was not speaking particularly in behalf of the engineers; but
he wanted the Army to be kept intact, and he knew very well
that if the fortifications were allowed to sink into neglect, the

Army must, of necessity, be maintained in a strong condition.
If the fortifications of this country be allowed to crumble into
dust, we shall have one broad frontier that will need to be
defended by the Army, and which will admit no possibility of
a reduction of our military force without the greatest detriment to the nation.   Now, while it may be necessary to re-
duce the Army in the interest of economy to meet the present
exigency of national affairs and the requirements of the people,
I think we should not forget we are a nation and must command respect abroad.   When we begin to neglect our fortifications, to neglect our Army, and to neglect our Navy, we
will lose that respect of other nations which we should have
if we kept ourselves always prepared for any emergency
which might arise.

        One moment more.   I have spoken about historical
associations.   There are a great many historical associations
clustering about Fort Sumter.   Only call to mind what was
done at Fort Sumter during the past war of the rebellion.
Whether in defense of the southern cause or in defense of
the Union cause, the associations of that fortification are intimately interwoven with the history of this Republic.   I hope,
therefore, this appropriation will be made.

        And I might add, before taking my seat, that the
appropriations in all of these bills for the Southern States
have been much neglected in reference to appropriations.
I do not like to see curtailments made in the appropriation
for these fortifications in the Southern States.   In my judgment the appropriations should be made equal, no larger for
one section than for another, and no smaller.   The people of
the North and South have been knitted more closely together
by the results of the war.   They are now united, never again,
I trust, to be separated, and one section ought not to be
neglected while another is favored by these appropriation
bills.   Appropriations are needed in the South, too, and I
hope they will be made.

        (Here the hammer fell.)

CIVIL RIGHTS (February 3, 1875)

We do not intend to be driven to the frontier as
you have driven the Indian. Our purpose is to
remain in your midst an integral part of the body-
politic. We are training our children to take our
places when we are gone....
Sir, it is not within the scope of reason to expect
that any people will continue to be legal and faithful to a government that disregards their rights
and treats with indifference their earnest appeal
for the accordment of those privileges and immunities enjoyed by other citizens within its confines; but more especially is this true when they
are aware that the only ground upon which these
privileges and immunities are withheld is because
of complexional differences. (8:958-960)

Mr. RAINEY. Mr. Speaker, it was my original intention to have submitted some remarks to night upon this
bill. But upon further reflection I had made up my mind to
wait until to-morrow morning, when I hoped to have an opportunity to speak at some length and to my better satisfaction; yet I cannot permit this opportunity to pass without a
few words in reply to the gentleman from Virginia (Mr.
WHITEHEAD). I regret that some others on that side of the
House have not seen fit to participate in the debate to-night,
for it looks a little uncharitable to direct all our arguments
from this side against a single honorable opponent. But it so
happens that he is the only one who has said anything in regard
to the bill at this time. I did not come in the Hall this evening
early enough to hear all the gentleman had to say. I wish I had
heard his entire speech, for I might have been able then to form
a better judgment of the course of his argument.

I must say, judging from what I have heard, that the gentleman has made no argument that, in my opinion, can do the civil-
rights bill any harm. He has attempted to ridicule the same; he
has attempted to ridicule the people whom it is designed to benefit; but he has not adduced any strong argument, logical nor

legal, why the bill should not pass and become a law; why
the class of people against whom he has raised his opposing
voice to-night should not have their constitutional rights. His
premises are erroneous altogether, consequently his conclusions are fallacious and void of force. He said the common
law now provides all of the remedies this bill is intended to
afford; therefore he could not see the necessity for its passage. He further adds that it was intended to create strife
and not benefit the colored people. I want to say to the member from Virginia that so far as the common law is concerned, although I am not a lawyer, I am aware, however,
that it contains remedial provisions; but they are so general
in their character as frequently to lose specific application
and force unless wrought into statutory enactment. Hence the
necessity for this bill, which sets forth specifically the offenses and the means of redress. That I believe to be why,
among other reasons, we enact statutory law; otherwise we
would appeal to the common law and obtain our ends independent of the statutes.

The fact of the determined and earnest opposition to
which this measure has been subjected is an additional argument in favor of its passage in order that we may have the
constitutional rights guaranteed us, being citizens. The time
has come under this Government when we must no longer be
looked upon and judged by the color of our skins. Yes, the
time is at hand when you must cease to take us for cringing
slaves. We may have been such in the past, but you should
not fail to remember that we are freemen now, and citizens
of this great country in common with yourselves; therefore
entitled to the full enjoyment of all the privileges and immunities incidental to that condition.

But, as I said before, the gentleman remarked that
this bill is intended to create or provoke strife, and in the
next breath he contradicted himself by saying if this was the
intention and purpose of the republican party for political
effect it would be deceived, at least so far as Virginia was
concerned, as there would be no strife there. If that would
be the case in Virginia, namely, that there would be no
strife, why then the gentleman's argument falls to the ground,
inasmuch as he admits that in his own State there would be
no trouble in event of its becoming a law. Whether this admission was intentional or not I have no means whereby to
determine; the gentleman will therefore have to reconcile it
to himself.

Now I take the ground that there will be no difficulty in any of the States on account of this bill. There is no argument offered by the opposition to it that was not presented here years ago. True it was not upon this subject, of a kindred nature affecting the Government more vitally than this ever will. I assert that this "genus" in argument has gnawed at the vitals of this Republic for nearly half a century, until it was aroused from its masterly inactivity, throttled the demon of rebellion, and asserted its potency.

We heard in the course of this debate those diatribes which were so familiar to the ear of the country in times past, the declamation of which contributed in no ordinary degree toward fermenting that bitter sectional spirit which culminated in conflict and bloodshed. The condition of the colored race reminds me forcibly of what is said of Mohammed's coffin, which is affirmed to be oscillating between heaven and earth. The passage of this bill, the purpose of which is to accord equal civil rights to my race, who have felt and are still feeling the sad necessity for the same, will go further to allay the restive public sentiment in this regard and define more definitely the status of us, the new-born citizens, than any statutory enactment that has yet taken place.

It was declared, sir, that if we were enfranchised it would provoke conflict and create strife; that if we were placed in the jury-box it would create a similar result. We have been in the jury-box; we have sat upon cases involving the interests of our fellow-citizens and have rendered verdicts, and I can say with confidence and pride that in my own State our action in this respect has been recognized and accepted even by the democratic lawyers, who frequently select colored jurors. We have also had the pleasure of voting; and the only trouble to-day is that the colored man is so loyal to the Government and true to the party that has given him such rights as he has, that he cannot be prevailed upon to enter the ranks of the opposition. That is the reason why gentlemen on the other side are fighting so strenuously against our advancement. But I will say to them that we intend to continue to vote so long as the Government gives us the right and the necessary protection; and I know that right accorded to us now will never be withheld in the future if left to the republican party. The sooner those opposed to us will understand and concede the fact the better it will be for the tranquillity, prosperity, and happiness of the whole country.

I say to the gentleman from Virginia, I do not doubt that here are privileges accorded to the colored people in his State; that they are allowed to live quietly and without moles- tation; but I ask why? The answer is, since the election of Governor Walker in that State colored men have been com- pelled, to a great degree, to vote as the democracy dictated or else not vote at all, without detriment to their business. Whenever the democrats get control of a State, they say "Everything is lovely, and the negroes are happy and pros- perous"; but just as soon as the republicans obtain control, then the cry is made loudly that anarchy, ruin, and general destruction are upon the people; that they are oppressed nigh unto death by burdensome taxation, and that the Government is a failure.

Sir, in the State of South Carolina, where we have a republican form of government indeed, where the colored people are in a majority, we are endeavoring with a fair prospect of success, to demonstrate that the reconstruction policy is not a failure. You may overrule us in Virginia, North Carolina, and Georgia; but we will hold our own in South Carolina; and when her government passes out of the hands of republicans our flag shall yet be flying.

It may be true that in Virginia they have some regard for the colored people; but I can mention a circumstance from my personal observation which does not show regard for the dead and little for the living. When in Richmond some two or three years ago I was taken to the outskirts of the city where there was a burial-ground in which the slaves had formerly been buried. To my astonishment I found that grave- yard cut through for the purpose of opening a street, and the city carts hauling away the dust of those poor dead slaves and strewing the same about the streets to fill up the low places and mudholes. I saw this with my own eyes, and therefore can testify before God and man as to the fact. Does not this statement show that with some people there is no re- gard for the poor negro, living or dead? Think of it! The sacred dust of the dead in a civilized community used to fill up mud-holes and low places!

Yet you talk about humanity; your kindly feeling for the colored race. Gracious Heaven! If you have no feelings for the ashes of the dead; if you have no regard for the dust of the dead slave who served you all the days of his life faith- fully, honestly, well, we may have apprehensions as to the manner in which we will be treated, now that we are free

and struggling for equal rights, unless we are protected by
the strong arm of the law.

We do not intend to be driven to the frontier as you
have driven the Indian.   Our purpose is to remain in your
midst an integral part of the body-politic.   We are training
our children to take our places when we are gone.   We desire this bill that we may train them intelligently and re-
spectably, that they may thus be qualified to be useful citizens in their day and time.   We ask you, then, to give us
every facility, that we may educate our sons and our daughters as they should be.   Deprive us of no rights belonging to
us as citizens; give us an equal opportunity in life, then if
we fail we will be content if driven to the wall.

But, Mr. Speaker, the subject under consideration is
one in which I naturally feel a deep and almost inexpressible
interest, not on account of any personal aggrandizement or
exclusive individual benefit which I hope to enjoy, but for
reasons far more patriotic, lofty, and disinterested in their
conception.   I speak in behalf of my race and people, who
have long endured hardship, degradation, and proscription to
subserve the pernicious and diabolical ends of slavery.

I speak in behalf of that people which was found ready
and willing when they were needed and an opportunity was
afforded to show their fealty to the Government and their
readiness with strong arms and willing hearts to contribute
toward our country's cause.   Are such men to be hooted at
and treated contemptuously because of their color?   Would
you have their loyal aspirations crushed out beneath the heel
of tyranny or tramp of prejudice?   And yet these very men,
or their offsprings, are told that they cannot receive "full
and equal enjoyment of any accommodation, advantage, facility, or privilege furnished by innkeepers; by common carriers, whether by land or water; by licensed owners, managers, or lessees of theaters, or other places of public
amusement; by trustees, commissioners, superintendents,
teachers, and other officers of common schools and public
institutions of learning. " Is not such action calculated to
damp their ardor and fill them with cold indifference and dis-
may?

Sir, it is not within the scope of reason to expect that
any people will continue to be loyal and faithful to a government that disregards their rights and treats with indifference
their earnest appeal for the accordment of those privileges

and immunities enjoyed by other citizens within its confines;
but more especially is this true when they are aware that the
only ground upon which these privileges and immunities are
withheld is because of complexional differences. Sir, there
may exist this difference between the hue of our skins and
that of other citizens; but that does not deprive us of principle and such sterling elements of character as would be desirable and befit any class of people and make the man. This
may be denied by some and questioned by others. To such
I reply, lay aside your prejudices, and doubt will give place
to conviction.

          Much apprehension and fear have been exhibited on
account of the social aspect of this subject. A few words on
that point will not be out of place. This fear and apprehension are unwarranted; there is no social precedent for this
alarm. It is merely conjectural, or, in other words, it is
nothing more than the result engendered by a diseased and
prejudiced mind. Every impartial thinker is aware that no
law is supposed possible to regulate the social customs of
any people. What is social equality? Is it the undisturbed
right to enter public places of amusement, and receive the
same accommodations as are offered others at like cost?
Surely that cannot be, for it is obvious that suspicious
characters are frequently the occupants of first-class seats
among the spectators; so if this settles the question we may
well tremble for the purity and reputation of good society.
Is it the unrestricted right to be entertained at public inns or
restaurants and be respectfully treated? That cannot be, for
we have daily instances before us where thieves and others
of questionable repute enjoy these advantages without, I hope,
being considered social equals of other guests. Is it the
right of franchise, of being accommodated by common carriers, whether by land or water, and treated as other first-
class passengers are? I think not. It is therefore a waste
of argument to insist upon it. Social equality consists in
congeniality of feeling, a reciprocity of sentiment, and
mutual, social recognition among men, which is graded according to desire and taste, and not by any known or possible
law. Men as a rule are always careful never to introduce
into the sancity of their family circles those who would abuse
the privilege, or who are not recognized as social equals.
This is a right that cannot be disputed, neither can it be invaded by any law or statutory enactment.

          Reference has been made, for the purpose of arousing
public opposition and resentment upon the ground that it would

signalize the overthrow of opposing barriers, to unrestrained
association between the races and thus inaugurate intermarri-
age of whites and blacks.   Such argument shows the weakness
of this supposed salient point adduced by the opposition.   It
is a mere subterfuge, and unworthy of those who announce it.
If their arguments are of any value and force, it reflects un-
favorably upon those whose cause they are supposed to defend.   Need 1 say it is unknown to the spirit of our Constitutions, Federal or State; the possible enactment of any compulsory law forcing alliance between parties having no affinities whatever?

The superiority of the Anglo-Saxon race--which has
been flaunted in our faces during this discussion--is enough
to lead one to believe that there is no occasion whatever for
this dread of indiscriminate association, inasmuch as this
much talked of superiority would be of sufficient security and
a safeguard of itself to defy all assaults, intrusions, or intrigues.

Surely there is no constraining power in one class over
another to compel or induce that intimate relationship which
custom has declared can only be brought about by desirable
and mutual agreement.   This is not only an acknowledged
social right, but one guaranteed by the Constitution, which
says, "No State shall make or enforce any law which shall
abridge the privileges or immunities of citizens of the United
States."

If the future may be judged from the results of the
past, it will require much effort upon the part of the colored
race to preserve the purity of their own households from the
intrusions of those who have hitherto violated and are now
violating with ruthless impunity those precious and inestimable
rights which should be the undisturbed heritage of all good
society.

We are grateful, however, that the day has come when
no slave mother will lament in plaintive strains the parting
of herself and daughters thus:

> Gone, gone--sold and gone
> To the rice-swamp, dank and lone--
> Toiling through the weary day,
> And at night the spoiler's prey.
> O, that they had earlier died,
> Sleeping calmly, side by side,

Where the tyrants power is o'er
And the fetter galls no more!
Gone, gone--sold and gone
To the rice-swamp, dank and lone,
From Virginia's hills and waters--
Woe is me, my stolen daughter!

I venture to assert to my white fellow-citizens that
we, the colored people, are not in quest of social equality.
For one I do not ask to be introduced into your family circles if you are not disposed to receive me there. Among
my own race we have as much respectability, intelligence,
virtue, and refinement possible to expect from any class cir-
cumstanced as we have been. This being so, why should I
cast imputation upon my people by saying to them, "I do not
want your society; I prefer to associate with the whites"?
Why should I be ashamed of them with their blood flowing in
my veins? Such is not the prompting of my heart nor of my
colored colleagues on this floor. We are not naturally more
disposed to immorality than others. Under the new order of
things we are hopeful, however, that a higher order of
morality will be established in the South than existed there in
antebellum days; for the time has come when it is admitted
that the negroes have rights that white men are bound to respect.

Among my race I am free to confess that we have
some immoral men and women, but our consolation is that
such regretful examples are not confined to any race or
people. It might be said, however, in extenuation of this
condition of affairs, that many of them have been kept bowed
down in the fetid trenches of slavery for so long a time that
their senses have become blunted beyond a keen conception
of their own rights and interests, which has led many to believe that they are contented with such privileges as they now
enjoy, without desiring further legislation in their behalf.
The misfortunes of this class are not chargeable to any but
those who delighted to degrade us in the past and desire to
continue the same treatment in the present. It is to be
hoped, therefore, that they will not be considered as reflect-
ing the opinions or wishes of the more intelligent in this regard.

The earnest desire for the passage of this bill as a
measure of justice and equity becomes more evident from
the stubborn opposition made to it. There has been no measure passed by Congress having for its avowed object the

benefit of the negro race in any way but what has met the
same contention that has been so apparent in this instance.

Much has been said about the Constitution and its
bearing upon the passage of this bill, and the ultimate result
of such an event.   Time will not permit me to refer to them
all.   I will say, by way of general reply, that those who
read the Constitution with partial and selfish motives in view
fail to see the interests of the colored race apart from what
is implied in the three last amendments thereto, and frequently with a narrow conception of those.   We claim equal
rights and interests with other citizens who are embraced
within the limits of all its provisions.   If this should not be
admitted, the people would soon lose appreciation for that instrument, and clamor for a change that would afford them
more general and better protection.   Believing it to be adequate for the ample security of all, the people are content
with it.

Article 4, section 2, of the Constitution reads thus:

> The citizens of each State shall be entitled to all
> privileges and immunities of citizens in the several
> States.

According to this provision it is unconstitutional to
deny any privilege or immunity to colored citizens in either
Virginia, Georgia, Kentucky, or any other State that is
guaranteed to other citizens.   It must be remembered that
we are not dealing with the past, but with the immediate present and for the future.

In this connection reference may be properly made to
the public schools.   All the objections that have been urged
against the general commingling of white and colored children
in these schools have been stated and successfully refuted in
the past.   There was great dissatisfaction shown at the inauguration of this system in those States where it has been
in successful operation for years.   It is gratifying to state
that the satisfactory results of its working has dispelled all
doubts in regard to its practicability, quieted apprehension,
and contributed largely to remove fears and annihilate that
prejudice which has been declared upon this floor should be
fostered and respected.   It is with the aim of making more
complete the destruction of this uncharitable sentiment and
proscription that the opening of the public schools to all is
so much to be desired.   Surely the children are not better

than their parents, who now sit with us in the jury box, the legislative hall, and are daily to be seen in the same public conveyances. Therefore I can see no reason why the white and colored children cannot attend the same public school.

What we desire, Mr. Speaker, is to have the cloud of proscription removed from our horizon, that we may clearly see our way to intellectual and moral advancement. This is nothing more than what all good citizens desire to enjoy and ought to have. I therefore favor the passage of the Senate bill now on your table.

This being done, complaints will cease, for we can then justly say, let "caps, hands, and tongues applaud it to the clouds"; the republican party has been just and true to its pledges.

BIBLIOGRAPHY

1. Biographical Directory of the American Congress 1774-1971. Washington, D.C.: United States Government Printing Office, 1971.

2. U.S. Congress. House. Defense of Fourteenth Amendment. 42nd Congress, 1st session, 1871.

3. U.S Congress. House. A Plea for National Education. 42nd Congress, 2nd session, 1872.

4. U.S Congress. House. Civil Rights. 42nd Congress, 2nd session, 1872.

5. U.S. Congress. House. Removal of Personal Disabilities. 42nd Congress, 2nd session, 1872.

6. U.S. Congress. House. Civil Rights. 43rd Congress, 1st session, 1873.

7. U.S. Congress. House. Establishment of A National Monument. 43rd Congress, 1st session, 1874.

8. U.S. Congress. House. Civil Rights. 43rd Congress, 2nd session, 1875.

XIII.   ALONZO JACOB RANSIER

Ransier, Alonzo Jacob, a Representative from South Carolina; born in Charleston, South Carolina, January 3, 1834; was of the Negro race; received a limited schooling; employed as shipping clerk in 1850; member of a convention of the friends of Equal Rights at Charleston in 1865 and was persuaded to present the memorial there framed to Congress; member of the State constitutional convention in 1868 and 1869; presidential elector on the Republican ticket of Grant and Colfax in 1868; Lieutenant Governor of South Carolina in 1870; president of the Southern States Convention at Columbia in 1871; delegate to the Republican National Convention at Philadelphia in 1872; elected as a Republican to the Forty-third Congress (March 4, 1873-March 3, 1875); United States internal-revenue collector for the second district of South Carolina in 1875 and 1876; died in Charleston, South Carolina, on August 17, 1882.   (1:1586)

CIVIL RIGHTS

The Negro desires harmonious relationship with all other races.... It will increase his opportunities for learning and make him a more intelligent and independent voter, and make him feel a deeper interest in those questions affecting his material welfare and that of the community in which he lives. He will then have no animosities to feed or nourish, or at least no occasion for any, and as he advances in the scale of intelligence and usefulness, and acquires wealth through the unobstructed avenues to the school-house and to the industrial marts, and finds his undisputed way to the witness-box, the jury-box, and the ballot-box, which is his right, then the prejudices against him will melt as does the snow under a burning sun. (2:1311-1314)

Mr. RANSIER. Mr. Speaker, but for some remarks made by the gentleman from Georgia (Mr. HARRIS), the gentleman from North Carolina (Mr. ROBBINS), and the gentleman from New York, our learned and genial friend (Mr. COX), during the protracted debate on civil rights, made before and subsequent to the recommittal of the bill on the subject to the Judiciary Committee, which in my judgment call for a specific reply, I would not again ask the attention and indulgence of the House for myself.

Statements have been made by one or all of these gentlemen, and others who oppose such a bill as many of us think ought to pass, that ought not to go to the country uncontradicted, and a condition of affairs pictured by them as likely to follow its enactment into law which if true or likely to occur ought to go far toward the defeat of such a measure. If, on the other hand, these statements are shown to be untrue and to rest upon no foundation in point of fact, and that the enactment of such a law by Congress will be of benefit to all classes of our people and promotive of the ends of justice, of concord, and harmonious relationships, as we think

we can show, then we cannot pass this measure a day too
soon.

Mr. Speaker, this measure has been presented to us
in masterly efforts in its constitutional aspects, and we are
asked to consider it now in the light of practical statesmanship. We are asked to consider what would be the effect of
its operation as to our school system and upon the relationships between the races. To these inquiries I propose to
address myself as briefly as possible, and to this end I ask
the indulgence of the House.

Before proceeding I desire to express my regret that
anything should have occurred calculated to create ill-feeling
between members of this House during this debate, and which
the press of the country has characterized as contravening
the legitimate limits of parliamentary courtesy.

It were far better if grave questions such as are involved in the consideration of a measure like this could be
discussed in a spirit of fairness, and without passion or indulgence in such allusions as are calculated to give offense
to members personally. Each of the friends of the measure,
however, can say truthfully, "Thou canst not say, I did it:
never shake thy gory locks at me. "

Mr. Speaker, the honorable gentleman from Georgia
(Mr. HARRIS), in his speech on the bill, said:

> I am satisfied, Mr. Speaker, that a very large
> majority of the republican members of this House
> do not understand the true condition of affairs in
> the South. For if they did, and are sincere in
> their avowals of solicitude for the welfare of the
> country, and especially for the prosperity and ad-
> vancement of the colored race, I am very sure
> that they would indicate it in some better way than
> the adoption of legislative enactments which in my
> judgment, when tried, will not only prove unac-
> ceptable to the masses of colored people at the
> South, but alike destructive of the harmony and
> great interests of both races.

Now, sir, I am sure that a very large majority of the
republican members of this House do know the true condition
of affairs in the South, hence the desire on their part for the
passage of such a measure. As to the remark that such en-

actments, "when tried, will not only prove unacceptable to the
masses of colored people at the South, but alike destructive
of the harmony and great interests of both races, " he evidently misunderstands the situation himself. He is not the
only member who has said during this debate that the colored
people, the masses of them, are not asking for the passage
of such a bill. The gentleman from Texas suggested the
same thing.

THE COLORED PEOPLE A UNIT FOR CIVIL RIGHTS

Mr. Speaker, there are organizations in nearly every
State in the Union the object of which, in part at least, is to
endeavor to secure for the colored people of the country their
equal rights. They have been asking this of the country,
through individuals with delegated authority to act, through
State and county organizations, and through national conventions assembled for the purpose. In this connection I quote
from the journal of the proceedings of the convention of
colored men held at Columbia, South Carolina, October 18,
1871; which convention was composed of regularly elected delegates from nearly every Southern State:

To the People of the United States of America:

FELLOW-CITIZENS: The colored people of the
States of Alabama, Arkansas, Delaware, Florida,
Georgia, Kentucky, Louisiana, Maryland, Mississippi, North Carolina, South Carolina, Tennessee,
Texas, and the District of Columbia, have delegated to us, their representatives, assembled in
convention, authority to give expression to their
purposes, desires, and feelings, in view of the
relation they sustain to the Government and people
of the United States, under the course of events
that has arisen since, and as a consequence of,
the war of rebellion.
We owe to Almighty God and the spirit of liberty and humanity that animates the great body of
the people of this country the personal liberty and
the rights of citizenship that we enjoy, and shall,
under the promptings of duty, labor for the perm-
anence and perfection of the institutions that have
served as the great instrument of consummating
this act of justice.
In seeking more perfect recognition as members

of the great political family to which the interests
of humanity have been peculiarly committed, we
desire to recognize our obligations and responsibilities as members of this great family, and to
assure the American people that we stand among
them inbued with a national spirit, with confidence
in and devotion to the principles of representative
popular government, and with ideas of policy that
embrace every individual and interest of our common country.

We ask of you that you will give to the Government the fullest measure of moral support, to enable it to complete that which is so auspiciously
begun, and that minor differences of sentiment
and policy may be hushed while the nation is gath-
ering up its strength to purge the land of the
foulest crimes by the sword of justice. When the
nation was threatened with division, political differences yielded to the necessity of maintaining its
territorial integrity. Now, that it is again threatened from the vortex of passion and crime affili-
ated, let the same devotion to right and justice
induce equal efforts to preserve its moral integrity.

While there remains anything to be accomplished, in order to secure for ourselves the full
enjoyment of civil and political rights, we shall
have class interests calling for the united efforts
of persons of color. The moment these ends are
secured, the motives for separate action will
cease, and, in common with all other citizens,
we can take our places wherever the interest of
the Government, industry, or humanity may appoint, recognizing only one standard of duty, interest, or policy for all citizens.

We do not ask the Government or people of the
United States to treat us with peculiar favor, but
that, in the policy of the laws, our interest may
be grouped with those that receive the consideration of our legislative bodies, and that, in the administration of the laws, no invidious distinctions
be made to our prejudice.

We affirm that the colored people of the States
represented by us have no desire to strike out a
line of policy for their action involving interests
not common to the whole people.

While we have, as a body, contributed our
labor in the past to enhance the wealth and pro-

mote the welfare of the community, we have, as
a class, been deprived of one of the chief benefits
to be derived from industry, namely, the acquisi-
tion of education and experience, the return that
civilization makes for the labor of the individual.
Our want, in this respect, not only extends to
general education and experience, such as fits the
man to adorn the society of his fellows, but that
special education and experience required to enable us to enter successfully the departments of a
diversified industry.

The growth of this nation has shown that its
institutions are capable of blending into a harmonious brotherhood all nationalities and all interests
and industries. In all other instances than that of
the accession of our race, to citizenship, the ac-
cretion of the elements of its population has been
gradual, giving time to complete the process of
assimilation. In our case we are well aware that
there was much to alarm the apprehensions of
those careful statesmen who hesitated to speculate
as to the strength of our institutions much beyond
what was demonstrated by the precedents in parallel cases in Europe and in our own country. The
instantaneous embodiment of four million citizens
who had for years looked upon the Government as
not only denying them citizenship, but as preventing them from acquiring that capacity under any
other national existence, was, it must be admitted, a startling political fact.

But we are happy to point to the proof of the
wisdom of those who regarded that course the
safest that was indicated by the demands of justice. We are proud to be able to point to the
history of our people since their admission to citizenship as proof that they understand what is due
from the citizen to the Government owing him protection. Although they have suffered much at the
hands of those who would deprive them of their
rights, they have appreciated the difficulties and
embarrassments that necessarily surrounded the
attempts of the Government to vindicate their
rights, and have waited uncomplainingly until relief could be afforded; although many times they
could have found instantaneous relief by imitating
their oppressors and taking the law into their own
hands.

A convention subsequently held at New Orleans, Louisiana, which was composed of delegates from all parts of the
country, issued a similar address as did the one recently
held in this city. I have similar papers from meetings held
all over this country to the same import. I will call attention to the following, which has been adopted by the Leglisla-
ture of my own State; and be it known that in that Legislature
there are about thrity-five democrats. The News and Courier
newspaper, published in the city of Charleston, where I live,
one of the leading democratic organs of the South, commenting upon the adoption of these resolutions, says that the democratic members, with a single exception, in both houses,
voted for them. The following are the resolutions:

SUMNER AND CIVIL RIGHTS

The following preamble and resolutions were
adopted almost unanimously, only one vote being
in the negative:
Whereas the recent introduction of the civil-
rights bill in the Senate of the United States, by
Hon. CHARLES SUMNER, Senator from Massachusetts, shows that he is determined to crown a
series of inestimable services to the cause of
freedom and equal rights in America by removing
the last vestige of the late barbarism, and placing the capstone of equal civil rights on the dome
of the reconstructed Union; and whereas the State
of South Carolina, ever mindful of the rights of
all her citizens, and watchful for their privileges,
has placed on her statute-book a bill to protect
them in their civil rights within her domain; but
is aware of its inadequacy to protect them when
outside her limits; and whereas both by a common
line of policy and by the solemn pledges of the
Philadelphia convention, by the noble words of the
last inaugural, and by the sentiments of our dominant party, the national and State republicans,
and the honored Chief Magistrate, have placed
themselves on record as favoring the passage of
such a bill; and whereas a large party of the loyal
citizens of this State and of the nation, irrespective of their intelligence, wealth, or position,
whether they are private citizens or public officials, are discriminated against, in public travel
and in places of general entertainment, to the degradation of their manhood and the violation of

their rights as human beings: Therefore be it
Resolved, That we instruct our Senators and
request our Representatives in Congress assembled
to sustain, by their influence and by their votes,
the bill introduced by Senator SUMNER to attain
the equality of civil rights before the law.

Resolved, That we sympathize with the movement on the part of the large class of citizens
whose rights are thus willfully and persistently
outraged to unite in a convention on the 9th of
December, 1873, to memorialize Congress on this
subject; and in view of the near approach of the
meeting aforesaid, we, representing the people of
the State of South Carolina, authorize those of our
Representatives who may be identified with the
class whose rights are thus daily violated to attend the said convention and represent our State.

Resolved, That copies of these resolutions be
engrossed and forwarded to Hon. CHARLES SUM-
NER, his excellency the President of the United
States, and to our Representatives in Congress,
and to the president of the equal rights convention.

I call the attention also to the following, a copy of
which has just been presented in another body:

ATLANTA, GEORGIA, January 26, 1874

Whereas Hon. A. H. STEPHENS, in his speech
before Congress January 5, 1874, said that colored
people of the State of Georgia did not desire the
passage of the civil-rights bill; and whereas the
Georgia Legislature has also adopted resolutions
informing the Congress of the United States that
the colored people of Georgia do not desire the
passage of said civil-rights bill; and whereas the
allegations of Mr. STEPHENS and the Georgia
Legislature are without foundation in fact: Therefore,

Resolved, That we, a portion of the colored
citizens of Georgia, do most solemnly deny both
the speech of A. H. STEPHENS and said resolutions of the Georgia Legislature, so far as they
relate to the colored citizens of this State being
adverse to the passage of said civil-rights bill.

Resolved, That some arrangement be made by

this meeting to deny the fact of the said assertions
of Mr. STEPHENS and the Georgia Legislature.

Resolved, That we, the citizens of the city of
Atlanta, Georgia, immediately inform the Congress
of the United States that we desire a speedy passage of the civil-rights bill, and that we claim it
as a right they owe us as members of the republican party, and more particularly as citizens of
the United States.

Resolved, That we most heartily congratulate
and thank Mr. ELLIOTT for his able and pointed
speech, January 6, 1874, in the House of Representatives of the United States, in behalf of the
passage of the civil-rights bill, and in vindicating
the ability and patriotism of the colored citizens
of the country.

J. B. FULLER,
Chairman.
J. W. WIMBISH,
W. D. MOORE,
Secretaries.

Therefore, we, a committee appointed at a
mass-meeting of the colored citizens of the city
of Atlanta, Georgia, held on the 26th day of January, 1874, with power to forward the above expression of 11, 000 of the colored citizens of this
city, do make this petition:

To the honorable Senate and House of Representatives:

We, the undersigned committee, do hereby respectfully petition your honorable bodies to speedily pass the civil-rights bill, now under consideration in Congress, as the earnest request of the
above-stated citizens, with the further request
that your honorable bodies will, in view of the unjust manner in which we are now treated by the
Legislature and judicial tribunals in this State,
enact such laws as, in your wisdom, are necessary to secure each citizen in the United States,
without regard to race, color, or previous condition of servitude, equal civil and political rights,
privileges, and immunities before the law.

And we your petitioners will ever pray.

H. E. BAULDIN,
ROMULUS MOORE,
C. WIMBISH,
C. H. MORGAN,
JAS. A. TATE,
Committee.

I affirm, Mr. Speaker, that so far from the masses of the colored people not desiring civil-rights, no man could, having made known his object, obtain without intimidation or coercion in some form the signatures or assent of one hundred colored men in any State of the Union against the passage of a full and complete civil-rights bill by Congress, or to indicate a disapproval of it "when tried. "

The gentleman from Georgia (Mr. HARRIS) suggests that such a measure "will not only prove unacceptable to the masses of the colored people at the South, but alike destructive of the harmony and great interests of both races. " Just here he thinks, and very properly so, is a wide field for practical statesmanship.

Mr. Speaker, not only since the rebellion, passing through some terrible scenes during and since reconstruction (if indeed that work is completed), and during the terrible four years when the country groaned amid the throes of rebellion, but during the entire two hundred and fifty years, whether as slave or freeman, has the blackman in our country exhibited a patience under long suffering, a forbearance under most provoking citcumstances, and a forgiving and friendly disposition, that make him at once a good and peaceable citizen and perhaps a study.

He is taunted for his conduct during the war by the honorable gentleman from North Carolina (Mr. ROBBINS), because he did not lay in ashes the home of his master and murder the women and children while he (the master) was engaged in that which the gentleman seems to glorify.   He says:

Look at one more fact.   Nearly three years before the war ended the four million negroes of the South knew that its result involved the question of their liberty.   Yet while the continent shook with the earthquake of war, and nobody was

at home but old men and boys to keep them in
order, those negroes seized no weapon and struck
no blow. I do not mention it as a reproach to
them. It merits rather the thanks of southern
men. I mention it only to show that the negro is
not like the white man. What race of white men
would have remained quiet under the same circumstances? When the proclamation of emancipation was issued the peculiar patrons of the negro
in the North expected him to rise and throw off
the yoke and butcher our wives and children; and
in the abundance of their philanthropy and humanity
they hoped so, too.

Mr. Speaker, I have nothing to say in reply to those
remarks as to the conduct of the colored people during the
rebellion. Upon this and some other points he has been
answered by my colleague (Mr. CAIN), except that if (and I
say this in the kindliest spirit), those with whom the gentleman acts politically had shown during the years of the agitation of the question of slavery in this country, especially in
the past fifteen years or so, that patience, Christian spirit,
and I might add good sense, exhibited by the negro during the
rebellion, the country would not have been called upon to
mourn the loss of three hundred thousand of her sons, cut
off by the casualties of war, and to groan today under a debt
of over $2, 000, 000, 000.

Nor is this all. The gentleman from North Carolina
uses language that is calculated to keep alive whatever of
sectional feeling there may be existing between the people of
the North and the people of the South, which it is the business of the statesmanship of to-day to allay and to bury in
the oblivion of the past, if possible, in the interest of both
sections and of all classes and colors. This language I shall
not repeat; it is found in the concluding sentence of the extract of his speech just quoted.

Mr. Speaker, when I plead for the passage of a full
and complete civil-rights bill that shall seek to prevent and
punish discriminations against the citizens, I know that I
speak for five million people, and ask for that which is a
necessity to them; and when I say that these five million
people desire to live on terms of amity with their white fellow-citizens, I know that I correctly represent them. The
negro desires to forget the wrongs of the past, and has imposed no disabilities upon those who held him as a slave,

when and where he has been in a position to do so; and he
rejoices to-day, both from motives of patriotism and self-in-
terest, that the bitter feeling against him in the South, especially on the part of those who were his owners, which
found expression in acts of violence and butchery, is fast
dying out; that a better state of feeling exists, which must increase as he becomes educated, and, therefore, better acquainted with his duties and responsibilities as a citizen,
and as the other unlearns some of the teachings of the past.

THE NEGRO DESIRES HARMONIOUS RELATIONSHIP
WITH ALL OTHER RACES

Mr. Speaker, if I believed with the gentleman from
Georgia (Mr. HARRIS) that such a measure as the bill we
are now discussing would be "destructive of the harmony and
great interest of both races," I, for one, would not insist
upon its passage. I insist upon it, sir, not only because it
is right in the abstract, but also because I feel that it will
remove from the field of politics that which goes far to array
one class against the other, in the South especially--I mean
those class and caste distinctions--and would go far to disarm the mere political demagogue who is ever on the alert
to use the colored vote, indifferent as to the ultimate results,
so long as their selfish purpose can be best served thereby.
It will increase his opportunities for learning and make him
a more intelligent and independent voter, and make him feel
a deeper interest in those questions affecting his material
welfare and that of the community in which he lives. He will
then have no animosities to feel or nourish, or at least no
occasion for any, and as he advances in the scale of intelligence and usefulness, and acquires wealth through the unobstructed avenues to the school-house and to the industrial
marts, and finds his undisputed way to the witness-box, the
jury-box, and the ballot-box, which is his right, then the
prejudices against him will melt as does the snow under a
burning sun. Then, and not until then, will a more harmonious relationship be brought about between him and his more
favored brother, the Caucasian, to whose interest it is, especially in the South, that this desirable result should be
brought about. Sir, permit me to say we want peace and
good-fellowship in the South, and throughout the country; we
want race lines and sectional feelings blotted out and buried
forever. We want new life and vigor infused into the arteries
of our industries in the South; we want assistance in the direction of developing our vast and hidden material resources,

and to rebuild our waste places, and to this end I ask, in the
name of the black man and in the name of the white man of
the South alike, the generous aid and encouragement of the
powerful North, the great and liberal East, and the sturdy
and growing West.

VINDICATION OF THE COLORED MAN AS A SOLDIER
DURING THE WAR OF THE REBELLION

Mr. Speaker, the honorable gentleman from North
Carolina (Mr. ROBBINS) said in his speech the other day, in
which he compared the colored man to somebody's "merry-
andrew, " referring to the dissimilarity of the races, that
"this is a question which has puzzled the brains of scientists
for centuries, " and that--

>If we were in a lyceum discussing ethnology, I
>would enlarge upon and fortify it. Here I merely
>throw out the hint, to be laughed at by fools, but
>to be pondered by those who realize the mystery
>and (as Carlyle says) 'the deep tragedy of human
>life. '

Now, Mr. Speaker, I doubt not that if that gentleman
undertook to discuss that subject, "which has puzzled the
brains of scientists for centuries, " in a lyceum, he would
find as many fools, judged by his standard, among his audi-
ence as he must have noticed here when he made this modest
exhibition of his prodigious attainments in the direction indicated.

I desire to call attention to another remark he made
in the speech referred to. The honorable gentleman said:

>Despite all that we have heard on that subject, the
>negro is no fighter. To prove that he is, we are
>pointed to the records of the recent war between
>the States. Yes; infuriated with whisky, he was
>brought to the scratch a few times, only to be
>sacrificed without result.

He said also:

>Even here on this floor (and I mean no disrespect
>to any fellow-member by this remark) he does
>nothing, he says nothing, except as he is prompted

by his managers; even here he obeys the bidding
of his new white masters, who move him like a
puppet on the chess-board.

As to this remark, Mr. Speaker, I beg to refer the
honorable gentleman to the fifth chapter of the Acts of the
Apostles, and to call his attention to the terrible fate of the
persons therein spoken of (Ananias and Sapphira). The gentleman is indeed fortunate in having escaped a similar fate
while uttering the words just quoted from his speech.

As to the other remark, that the negro is no fighter,
in proof of which he says that only fifteen hundred of them
were killed in action during the rebellion, I have a word to
say.

I cannot, Mr. Speaker, within anything like the time
allowed, read over or quote the opinions of those who have
made this very question raised by the gentleman a matter of
study at any considerable length. I quote the following, however, from a book entitled Military Services of General David
Hunter, United States Army, during the War of the Rebellion,
pages 18 and 19, which, while it is complimentary to the
colored soldier, also shows the animus underlying such statements as those made by this impartial "scientist" and others
like him:

EXECUTIVE MANSION, Washington, April 1, 1863.

MY DEAR SIR: I am glad to see the accounts of
your colored force at Jacksonville, Florida. I
see the enemy are driving at them fiercely, as is
to be expected. It is important to the enemy that
such force shall not take shape, and grow, and
thrive in the South; and in precisely the same
proportion it is important to us that is shall; hence
the utmost caution and vigilance is necessary on
our part. The enemy will make extra efforts to
destroy them and we should do the same to preserve and increase them.
                    Yours, truly,

                                           A. LINCOLN
Major-General HUNTER.

I also quote from the same book, pages 26 and 27,
being in part reply by General Hunter (who first employed
colored men in the South as soldiers during the rebellion) to

resolutions of the United States Senate inquiring as to the authority for so employing these people.

The general says:

> The experiment of arming the blacks, so far as I have made it, has been a complete and marvelous success. They are sober, docile, attentive, and enthusiastic, displaying great natural capacities in acquiring the duties of the soldier. They are now eager beyond all things to take the field and be led into action, and it is the unanimous opinion of the officers who have had charge of them that, in the peculiarities of this climate and country, they will prove incalculable auxiliaries, fully equal to the similar regiments so long and successfully used by the British.

Nor was the conviction that the colored men could be employed to advantage as soldiers during the rebellion confined to the officers of the Union Army. The confederate government passed an act, approved March 30, 1865, authorizing the employment of negroes as soldiers. A copy of this act is printed in the report of the Secretary of War, first session Thirty-ninth Congress, pages 139 and 140. It reads as follows:

> An act to increase the military forces
> of the Confederate States, &c.

> That if under the previous sections of this act the president shall not be able to raise a sufficient number of troops to prosecute the war successfully and maintain the sovereignty of the States and the independence of the Confederate States, then he is hereby authorized to call on each State, whenever he thinks it expedient, for her quota of three hundred thousand troops in addition to those subject to military service under existing laws, or so many thereof as the president may deem necessary for the purposes therein mentioned, to be raised from such of the population, irrespective of color, in each State, as the proper authorities thereof may determine.

This law was never put in force, the rebellion having collapsed before colored men were mustered in that service vi et armis.

This action is the one remarkable instance where the southern people were perhaps a unit in favor of the doctrince of no discrimination on account of race, color, or previous condition of servitude.

A study of the opinions expressed by one hundred and fifteen surgeons engaged in the examination of both black and white recruits and substitutes goes to substantiate an idea which is common among ethnological authorities, namely, that no race is equally adapted to all circimstances of life; that mankind obey the same general laws that govern the distribution of florae and faunae upon the earth; and that the isotherms between which are limited the health and development of the negro do not comprehend less space upon its surface than those within which the others are confined.

It may be confidently affirmed that the statistics of the Medical Bureau, which refer principally to physico-geographical influences and to the effects of the intermixture of blood upon the negro, when taken in connection with those parts of the Surgeon-General's forthcoming report in which he is regarded as amenable to the vicissitudes of war, will form a more complete and reliable physical history of this race than exists at this time.

It would not be in accordance with the plan of this report to enter upon a discussion of the comparative aptitude for military service exhibited by the two types of mankind of which I have been speaking without the accompanying tables as evidence of the data upon which my opinions were based.

It appears, however, that of the surgeons of boards of enrollment five have given their opinion that the negro recruits and substitutes examined by them were physically a better class of men than the whites; nineteen that they were equal; two that they were inferior. A favorable opinion as to their fitness for the Army is expressed by seventeen; a doubtful one, because of insufficient data on which to ground the decision, by forty-three; an unfavorable opinion by nine; and by twenty a statement of not having come to any conclusion upon this subject. The question of the prevalence of disease among the negro inhabitants of different sections of the country is one upon which, at present, no specific opinion can be expressed. As in the case of the white race it may be shown hereafter that their maladies conform to those general principles which have been heretofore established. The discussion of the physical characteristics of the negro, as involving

the propriety of his use in war, only belongs to this department.   It is difficult and, in the present state of science,
most uncertain to erect upon any general characteristics of
organization anything but the most general rules concerning
the effect of that structure upon the moral and intellectual
nature.   It may be said, however, that there are not more
instances of disqualifying causes of this nature among the
negroes in proportion to the numbers examined than are to
be found in the records of exemption among the white race.

Again, Mr. Speaker, the total number of white troops,
regulars and volunteers, in service during the rebellion in
the Union Army is put down at 2, 041, 154.   Of this number
42, 724 are reported killed in action, 1-1/2 percent.

The total number of colored troops in service during
the rebellion was 180, 000.   Of that number 1, 514 are put
down as killed in action; to which number are added 896 reported missing by competent authority, who were evidently
killed, making 2, 410 or about 1-1/8 percent, showing on the
whole a difference of about 1/6 of one percent.   When it is
considered that the colored soldier participated in no battle,
because he was not admitted into the service, until some of
our heaviest battles were fought, is it not fair to strike off
this difference of 1/6 of one percent?   This done, would it
not be fair to say that the white and the colored troops in
the Union Army during the rebellion, in the direction indicated by the gentleman from North Carolina, stand upon about
the same footing?

But, Mr. Speaker, enough of this.   All of us might
read the following lines, which are found in the works of
CHARLES SUMNER, volume 2, page 34, to advantage.   It
appears that they were written by Edmund Waller:

> Earth praises conquerors for shedding blood:
> Heaven, those that love their foes and do 'em good.
> It is terrestrial honor to be crowned
> For strewing men, like rushes, on the ground:
> True glory 'tis to rise above them all,
> Without the advantage taken by their fall.
> He that in fight diminishes mankind
> Does no addition to his stature find;
> But he that does a noble nature show,
> Obliging others, still does higher grow:
> For virtue practiced such an habit gives
> That among men he like an angel lives;

Humbly he doth and without envy dwell,
Loved and admired by those he does excel.

Mr. Speaker, that which seems to be most objectionable to many gentlemen, some of whom are in favor of the
bill in other respects, is the provision prohibiting discriminations in the public schools on account of color or race. It
is feared, and so said by some gentlemen who favor the bill,
that to incorporate this feature in the bill, and to attempt to
enforce it, will destroy the school systems in the South especially, and operate as a check upon the education of the
children of both races.

Mr. Speaker, it does not seem to me that these fears
are well founded. About the same line of argument was
urged by many good people as to the abolition of slavery and
clothing the colored man with the elective franchise, and at
every step in the grand march toward freedom. Yet, sir, in
nearly every instance these objections and apprehensions
vanished, and were in a great part lost sight of upon trial.
Then, too, sir, the principle upon which you concede, if you
please, the right of the colored man to the privileges of the
car, the inn, the theater, the witness and the jury box, apply
in this case as well.

Sir, the learned gentleman from New York (Mr. COX),
whose speeches are always to be read with interest and profit, well said in a speech delivered here recently:

Is it not irrefragable that if the right to the inn,
railroad, theater, and cemetery be conceded to
the black (as provided in the civil-rights bill) to
the same extent as to the white to enjoy them
(though the enjoyment of the grave-yard is perhaps
a melancholy hilarity), that the same right should
be extended to them as to the schools? The
colored members are correct in their reasoning,
assuming these premises. Indeed, all the amis
de noirs who have spoken, if right at all, are
right in demanding equality alike in school and
inn, in cemetery and car. When you debar them
from the school you as much keep up the bar sin-
ister as by keeping them from the play-house.
Would it not be a craven logic, unworthy of the
struggling blacks and their admirers, to insist on
the one and not the other?

NON-PROSCRIPTIVE SCHOOLS PROMOTIVE OF HARMONY

Sir, as to the practical working of non-proscriptive schools, or, in other words, schools where black and white are taught in the North and East as well as in the South, it does not appear that either race is injured, or that the cause of general education suffers. At Yale, Harvard, Wilberforce, Cornell, Oberlin, the testimony is that both races get along well together. Nor is the South without such schools. In Madison, Kentucky, there is the Berea College, a notice of which I read from The American Missionary, for November 1873, pages 243 and 244. It reads as follows:

> Less than thirteen years ago sixty-five armed men drew themselves up in line before Professor Roger's house, close to the spot where now stands this new building, and notified the professors and trustees that they must leave the State within ten days. Less than six years ago half the whites left the school because black men were admitted to its privileges; but the white students came back in time and some of those who participated in mobs are not ashamed now to be recognized as friends.... Here are gathered from twelve to fifteen hundred people from the mountains and from the Blue Grass country, literate and illiterate, rich and poor, white and colored, farmers, mechanics, and professional men; a very mingled crowd, but a very attentive and orderly audience.

> It is an interesting sight, that large number under the green roof, listening eagerly through the morning and evening. But the fact that southern-born whites and blacks, in nearly equal proportion and in large numbers, have, for the past six years, recited together and in perfect harmony, makes this institution typical of what may be accomplished throughout the nation, and makes it of more than local importance. It requires no argument to show how much the colored people will be benefited by such an education. There is nothing like just such a school as this to teach mutual respect and forbearance, to dignify labor, to enforce a regard for the person and property of all classes, and to take away some of the arrogant superciliousness of caste and race.

I also call attention to the following from the New
York Independent, January 22, 1874, headed "Civil Rights
and Yale College:"

Where the principles of impartiality have been
brought to bear, whether in reference to schools,
cars, churches, or hotels, there has always been
first a huge outcry from the whole herd of white
tyrants; then, upon the first trial, an ostentatious
repugnance on the one hand, and a visible sensitiveness on the other, but finally both repugnance
and sensitiveness forgotten in general acquiescence
and oblivion. If Mr. HARRIS has forgotten it,
will he please listen to a chapter in the history
of Yale College!

In the year 1831 there was an effort put forth
to secure a college for colored youth. At that
time even the crumbs which fell from the mental
boards of the various colleges were denied these
people. It was proposed to locate this college in
the city of New Haven. But when this plan became known a violent opposition at once arose.
The officers of the city called a public meeting.
The city-hall was densely packed, and the whole
afternoon was given to the consideration of the
matter. The following is the public record of the
result:

'At a city meeting, duly warned and held in
the city-hall, in the city of New Haven, on Satur-
day, September 10, 1831, to take into consideration a project for the establishment in this city of
a college for the education of colored youth, the
following preamble and resolutions were by said
meeting adapted, namely:
'Whereas, in the opinion of this meeting, Yale
College, the institutions for the education of females, and the other schools already existing in
this city, are important to the community and the
general interest of science, and as such have been
deservedly patronized by the public; and the establishment of a college in the same place, to educate the colored population, is incompatible with
the prosperity, if not the existence of the present
institutions of learning, and will be destructive of
the best interests of the city: Therefore
'Resolved, by the mayor, aldermen, common

council and freemen of the city of New Haven in
city meeting assembled. That we will resist the
establishment of the proposed college in this place
by every lawful means.
                     'DENNIS KIMBERLY, Mayor.
'ELISHA MONSON, Clerk. '

It is needless to add that the danger was
averted by this prompt and imposing array of
force, and Yale College was saved to New Haven,
and Connecticut, and the country. In 1831 the
delicate nerves of Yale College could not endure
the shock of seeing black boys educated a mile
away; now she takes them to her own arms, and
bids them call her alma mater, and to our notion
she looks quite as fair and buxom as ever. We
are not a bit surprised to hear Mr. HARRIS, of
Virginia, talk in the same wild strain as did
Mayor Kimberly in 1831; for we knew him to be
forty-three years behind the times.

Again, the following from Old and New for February,
1874, a respectable monthly published in Boston, Massachusetts, and written by C. G. Fairchild, a writer not unknown to fame, will be read with interest by all thoughtful
persons. It is headed 'Non-proscriptive Schools in the
South. " The writer says:

The question of non-proscriptive schools at the
South takes us at once to the fountain head of a
formative influence, to that which in itself begets
force, which is noiseless and imperceptible, but
which is as pervasive as sunlight, and as powerful to build up that against which tempests may
waste their energies in vain. 'Whatever you
would have appear in a nation's life that you must
put into its schools, ' was long since a Prussian
motto. Powerful as Prussia has proved this
subtle work of strengthening or allaying social
prejudices. Are non-proscriptive schools, therefore, desirable; and can they be secured?
Few can understand, without careful and extended personal observation how essentially different was the construction of society in the South
from that in the North. It recognized two distinct classes--the laboring class and the cultured
class; classes as distinct as the roots and the

fruitage of a tree. The one class needed only the
shelter of the hut, as the horse has his stable;
for the other, no mansion within the reach of
their means could be too spacious or elegant.
Theoretically all labor was to be performed by
slaves; while the fruits of labor were to raise to
the highest culture and perfection the ruling class.
Such a society had no place for an industrious,
self-respecting middle class. Slave labor placed
its own badge of servile degradation upon all labor.
The white man whose hands were roughened in the
strife for his daily bread was despised even by
the negro slave. No southern conception was
more natural than that northern society was composed of 'mud-sills.' Universal labor meant
nothing else to them.

How, then, shall this exploded idea of civilization be overcome: In time past the negro race
has been the exponent of labor at the South; and
it is, for many years to come to be closely asso-
ciated with it. If, therefore, this race is to be
separated from all others in the public schools,
and even the youngest children are made to feel
that the race is set apart for its special mission,
and destiny in society, how can we hope to make
labor respectable? The old badge of servile degradation will attach to it not only for the black
man but for the white man. To place blacks and
whites in the same school is not to say that the
races are equal or unequal. It is to animate to
all the individuals with a common purpose, with
reference to which color or nationality has nothing
to do. If color or nationality has anything to do
with social affinities, non-proscriptive schools
will not affect their natural and healthy influence.
But color and nationality have nothing to do with
labor. That is a matter of capacity and necessity.
This fact a truly common-school system will impress constantly and effectively upon society, and
thus relieve labor from a most unnatural and
damning stigma put upon it by slavery.

The class distinctions perpetuated and taught by
class schools infuse a detrimental influence into
politics. Black men, no less than white men,
should differ on public questions. But such differences cannot show itself in political action to
any great extent as long as there is perpetuated

a distinction so fundamental between the white man
and the black as that the children of the latter
cannot go to school with those of the former. In
such a case class interests will predominate over
those interests which are more general and less
personal.

The same writer, in noticing an institution at Marys-
ville, Tennessee, where black and white children and youths
are taught, says:

If all the facts bearing upon this point could be
collated, not only the enemies but the friends of
non-proscriptive schools would be astonished.

Let the doors of the public-school house be thrown
open to us alike, sir, if you mean to give these people equal
rights at all, or to protect them in the exercise of the rights
and privileges attaching to all freemen and citizens of our
country.

THE COLORED VOTE

It is true, sir, that these people, the colored of our
country, compose a very small minority of the American
people, yet they contribute largely toward its industrial interests and at times play an important part in political affairs. For instance, President Grant's popular majority in
the last presidential election was 762, 991. The total colored
vote is put down at 900, 000. Now, allowing 10, 000 of this
vote to have been cast for Mr. Greeley, and 50, 000 of these
voters as not voting at all, which I am satisfied is in excess
of the number of this class not voting, making 60, 000, then
deduct the 60, 000 from the 900, 000, and the result will show
a colored vote polled of 840, 000 for General Grant; yet the
popular majority of General Grant as taken from the Tribune
Almanac for 1873 was not more than 762, 991, as already
stated.

To the curious in such matters, and to those who
seriously consider our institutions in this respect, this might
be considered as not unworthy of a passing notice.

BIBLIOGRAPHY

1. Biographical Directory of the American Congress 1774-
    1971. Washington, D. C. : United States Government
    Printing Office, 1971.

2. U. S. Congress. House. Civil Rights. 43rd Congress,
    1st session, 1874.

XIV. JAMES THOMAS RAPIER

Rapier, James Thomas, a Representative from Alabama; born in Florence, Lauderdale County, Alabama, November 13, 1837; was of the Negro race; educated by private tutors in Alabama and studied in Canada; studied law and was admitted to the bar; taught school; returned to the South and traveled as a correspondent for a Northern newspaper; became a cotton planter in Alabama in 1865; appointed a notary public by the Governor of Alabama in 1866; member of the first Republican Convention held in Alabama and was one of the committee that framed the platform; member of the State Constitutional Convention at Montgomery in 1857; unsuccessful candidate for secretary of state in 1870; appointed assessor of internal revenue in 1871; appointed State Commissioner to the Vienna Exposition by the Governor of Alabama in 1873; Commissioner on the part of the United States to the World's Fair in Paris; elected as a Republican to the 43rd Congress (March 4, 1873-March 3, 1875); unsuccessful candidate for reelection in 1874 to the 44th Congress; appointed collector of internal revenue for the 2nd district of Alabama on August 8, 1878, and served until his death in Montgomery, Alabama, May 31, 1883. (1:1587)

JAMES THOMAS RAPIER

James Thomas Rapier--"Rapier was ... tall, dark with a gleam of fun in his eyes, and with an expression of internal satisfaction. " (Moseley, p. 36)

CIVIL RIGHTS (June 9, 1874)

I wish to say in justice to myself that no one regrets more than I do the necessity that compels
one to the manner born to come in these Halls
with hat in hand (so to speak) to ask at the hands
of his political peers the same public rights they
enjoy. And I shall feel ashamed for my country
if there be any foreigners present, who have been
lured to our shores by the popular but untruthful
declaration that this land is the asylum of the oppressed, to hear a member of the highest legislative body in the world declare from his place,
upon his responsibility as a Representative, that
notwithstanding his political position he has no
civil rights that another class is bound to respect.... Nothing short of complete acknowledge-
ment of my manhood will satisfy me. I have no
compromise to make and shall unwillingly accept
any. (2:4782-4786)

Mr. RAPIER   Mr. Speaker, I had hoped there would
be no protracted discussion on the civil-rights bill. It has
been debated all over the country for the last seven years;
twice it has done duty in our national political campaigns; and
in every minor election during that time it has been pressed
into service for the purpose of intimidating the weak white
men who are inclined to support the republican ticket. I was
certain until now that most persons were acquainted with its
provisions, that they understood its meaning; therefore it was
no longer to them the monster it had been depicted, that was
to break down all social barriers, and compel one man to
recognize another socially, whether agreeable to him or not.

I must confess it is somewhat embarrassing for a
colored man to urge the passage of this bill, because if he
exhibit an earnestness in the matter and express a desire
for its immediate passage, straight-way he is charged with a
desire for social equality, as explained by the demagogue and
understood by the ignorant white man. But then it is just as

259

embarrassing for him not to do so, for, if he remain silent
while the struggle is being carried on around, and for him,
he is liable to be charged with a want of interest in a matter
that concerns him more than any one else, which is enough
to make his friends desert his cause.   So in steering away
from Scylla I may run upon Charybdis.   But the anomalous,
and I may add the supremely ridiculous, position of the
negro at this time, in this country, compel me to say something.   Here his condition is without a comparison, parallel
alone to itself.   Just think that the law recognizes my right
upon this floor as a law-maker, but that there is no law to
secure to me any accommodations whatever while traveling
here to discharge my duties as a Representative of a large
and wealthy constituency.   Here I am the peer of the proud-
est, but on a steamboat or car I am not equal to the most
degraded.   Is not this most anomalous and ridiculous?

What little I shall say will be more in the way of
stating the case than otherwise, for I am certain I can add
nothing to the arguments already made in behalf of the bill.
If in the course of my remarks I should use language that
may be considered inelegant, I have only to say that it shall
be as elegant as that used by the opposition in discussing
this measure; if undignified, it shall not be more so than my
subject; if ridiculous, I enter the plea that the example has
been set by the democratic side of the House, which claims
the right to set examples.   I wish to say in justice to myself that no one regrets more than I do the necessity that
compels one to the manner born to come in these Halls with
hat in hand (so to speak) to ask at the hands of his political
peers the same public rights they enjoy.   And I shall feel
ashamed for my country if there be any foreigners present,
who have been lured to our shores by the popular but untruthful declaration that this land is the asylum of the oppressed, to hear a member of the highest legislative body in
the world declare from his place, upon his responsibility as
a Representative, that notwithstanding his political position he
has no civil rights that another class is bound to respect.
Here a foreigner can learn what he cannot learn in any other
country, that it is possible for a man to be half free and
half slave, or, in other words, he will see that it is possible
for a man to enjoy political rights while he is denied civil
ones; here he will see a man legislating for a free people,
while his own chains of civil slavery hang about him, and
are far more galling than any the foreigner left behind him;
here he will see what is not to be seen elsewhere, that position is no mantle of protection in our "land of the free and

home of the brave"; for I am subjected to far more outrages
and indignities in coming to and going from this capital in
discharge of my public duties than any criminal in the country
providing he be white.   Instead of my position shielding me
from insult, it too often invites it.

   Let me cite a case.   Not many months ago Mr. Car-
doza, treasurer of the State of South Carolina, was on his
way home from the West.   His route lay through Atlanta.
There he made request for a sleeping-berth.   Not only was
he refused this, but was denied a seat in a first-class carriage, and the parties went so far as to threaten to take his
life because he insisted upon his rights as a traveler.   He
was compelled, a most elegant and accomplished gentleman,
to take a seat in a dirty smoking-car, along with the traveling rabble, or else be left, to the detriment of his public
duties.

   I affirm, without the fear of contradiction, that any
white ex-convict (I care not what may have been his crime,
nor whether the hair on the shaven side of his head has had
time to grow out or not) may start with me to-day to Montgomery, that all the way down he will be treated as a gentleman, while I will be treated as the convict.   He will be
allowed a berth in a sleeping-car with all its comforts, while
I will be forced into a dirty, rough box with the drunkards,
apple-sellers, railroad hands, and next to any dead that may
be in transit, regardless of how far decomposition may have
progressed.   Sentinels are placed at the doors of the better
coaches, with positive instructions to keep persons of color
out; and I must do them the justice to say that they guard
these sacred portals with a vigilance that would have done
credit to the flaming swords at the gates of Eden.   Tender,
pure, intelligent young ladies are forced to travel in this way
if they are guilty of the crime of color, the only unpardonable sin known in our Christian and Bible lands, where sinning against the Holy Ghost (whatever that may be) sinks into
insignificance when compared with the sin of color.   If from
any cause we are compelled to lay over, the best bed in the
hotel is his if he can pay for it, while I am invariably
turned away, hungry and cold, to stand around the railway
station until the departure of the next train, it matters not
how long, thereby endangering my health, while my life and
property are at the mercy of any highwayman who may wish
to murder and rob me.

   And I state without the fear of being gainsaid, the

statement of the gentleman from Tennessee to the contrary
notwithstanding, that there is not an inn between Washington
and Montgomery, a distance of more than a thousand miles,
that will accommodate me to a bed or meal. Now, then, is
there a man upon this floor who is so heartless, whose
breast is so void of the better feelings, as to say that this
brutal custom needs no regulation? I hold that it does and
that Congress is the body to regulate it. Authority for its
action is found not only in the fourteenth amendment to the
Constitution, but by virtue of that amendment (which makes
all persons born here citizens), authority is found in article
4, section 2 of the Federal Constitution, which declares in
positive language "that the citizens of each State shall have
the same rights as the citizens of the several States." Let
me read Mr. Brightly's comment upon this clause; he is
considered good authority, I believe. In describing the several rights he says they may be all comprehended under the
following general heads: "Protection by the Government; the
enjoyment of life and liberty, with the right to acquire and
possess property of every kind, and to pursue and obtain
happiness and safety; the right of a citizen of one State to
pass through or to reside in any other State for purposes of
trade, agriculture, professional pursuits, or otherwise. "

    It is very clear that the right of locomotion without
hindrance and everything pertaining thereto is embraced in
this clause; and every lawyer knows if any white man in ante
bellum times had been refused first-class passage in a steamboat or car, who was free from any contagious disease, and
was compelled to go on deck of a boat or into a baggage-car,
and any accident had happened to him while he occupied that
place, a lawsuit would have followed and damages would have
been given by any jury to the plaintiff; and whether any accident had happened or not in the case I have referred to, a
suit would have been brought for a denial of rights, and no
one doubts what would have been the verdict. White men had
rights then that common carriers were compelled to respect,
and I demand the same for the colored men now.

    Mr. Speaker, whether this deduction from the clause
of the Constitution just read was applicable to the negro prior
to the adoption of the several late amendments to our organic
law is not now a question, but that it does apply to him in
his new relations no intelligent man will dispute. Therefore
I come to the national, instead of going to the local Legislatures for relief, as has been suggested, because the griev-
ance is national and not local; because Congress is the law-

making power of the General Government, whose duty it is to
see that there be no unjust and odious discriminations made
between its citizens. I look to the Government in the place
of the several States, because it claims my first allegiance,
exacts at my hands strict obedience to its laws, and because
it promises in the implied contract between every citizen and
the Government to protect my life and property. I have fulfilled my part of the contract to the extent I have been called
upon, and I demand that the Government, through Congress
do likewise. Every day of my life and property are exposed,
are left to the mercy of others, and will be so as long as
every hotel-keeper, railroad conductor, and steamboat captain
can refuse me with impunity the accommodations common to
other travelers. I hold further, if the Government cannot
secure to a citizen his guaranteed rights it ought not to call
upon him to perform the same duties that are performed by
another class of citizens who are in the free and full enjoyment of every civil and political right.

    Sir, I submit that I am degraded as long as I am
denied the public privileges common to other men, and that
the members of this House are correspondingly degraded by
recognizing my political equality while I occupy such a humiliating position. What a singular attitude for law-makers of
this great nation to assume: rather come down to me than
allow me to go up to them. Sir, did you ever reflect that
this is the only Christian country where poor, finite man is
held responsible for the crimes of the infinite God whom you
profess to worship? But it is; I am held to answer for the
crime of color, when I was not consulted in the matter. Had
I been consulted, and my future fully described, I think I
should have objected to being born in this gospel land. The
excuse offered for all this inhuman treatment is that they
consider the negro inferior to the white man, intellectually
and morally. This reason might have been offered and
probably accepted as truth some years ago, but no one now
believes him incapable of a high order of culture, except
someone who is himself below the average of mankind in
natural endowments. This is not the reason, as I shall show
before I have done.

    Sir, there is a cowardly propensity in the human heart
that delights in oppressing somebody else, and in the gratification of this base desire we always select a victim that
can be outraged with safety. As a general thing the Jew has
been the subject in most parts of the world; but here the
negro is the most available for this purpose; for this reason

in part he was seized upon, and not because he is naturally
inferior to anyone else. Instead of his enemies believing him
to be incapable of a high order of mental culture, they have
shown that they believe the reverse to be true, by taking the
most elaborate pains to prevent his development. And the
smaller the caliber of the white man the more frantically has
he fought to prevent the intellectual and moral progress of
the negro, for the simple but good reason that he has most
to fear from such a result. He does not wish to see the
negro approach the high moral standard of a man and gentleman.

        Let me call your attention to a case in point. Some
time since a well-dressed colored man was traveling from
Augusta to Montgomery. The train on which he was stopped
at a dinner-house. The crowd around the depot, seeing him
well dressed, fine-looking, and polite, concluded he must be
a gentleman (which was more than their righteous souls could
stand), and straightway they commenced to abuse him. And,
sir, he had to go into the baggage-car, open his trunks,
show his cards, faro-bank, dice, etc., before they would
give him any peace; or, in other words, he was forced to
give satisfactory evidence that he was not a man who was
working to elevate the moral and intellectual standard of the
negro before they would respect him. I have always found
more prejudice existing in the breasts of men who have feeble
minds and are conscious of it, than in the breasts of those
who have towering intellects and are aware of it. Henry
Ward Beecher reflected the feelings of the latter class when
on a certain occasion he said: "Turn the negro loose; I am
not afraid to run the race of life with him. " He could
afford to say this, all white men cannot; but what does the
other class say? "Build a Chinese wall between the negro
and the school-house, discourage in him pride of character
and honest ambition, cut him off from every avenue that
leads to the higher grounds of intelligence and usefulness,
and then challenge him to a contest upon the highway of life
to decide the question of superiority of race. " By their
acts, not by their words, the civilized world can and will
judge how honest my opponents are in their declarations that
I am naturally inferior to them. No one is surprised that
this class opposes the passage of the civil-rights bill, for if
the negro were allowed the same opportunities, the same
rights of locomotion, the same rights to comfort in travel,
how could they prove themselves better than the negro?

        Mr. Speaker, it was said, I believe by the gentleman

from Kentucky (Mr. Beck), that the people of the South, particularly his State, were willing to accord the colored man
all the rights they believe him guaranteed by the Constitution.
No one doubts this assertion. But the difficulty is they do
not acknowledge that I am entitled to any rights under the
organic law. I am forced to this conclusion by reading the
platforms of the democratic party in the several States.
Which one declares that that party believes in the constitutionality of the Reconstruction Acts or the several amendments? But upon the other hand, they question the constitutionality of every measure that is advanced to ameliorate the
condition of the colored man; and so skeptical have the democracy become respecting the Constitution, brought about by
their unsuccessful efforts to find constitutional objections to
every step that is taken to elevate the negro, that now they
begin to doubt the constitutionality of the Constitution itself.
The most they have agreed to do, is to obey present laws
bearing on manhood suffrage until they are repealed by Congress or decided to be unconstitutional by the Supreme Court.

Let me read what the platform of the democratic party
in Alabama has to say on this point:

> The democratic and conservative party of the
> State of Alabama, in entering upon the contest
> for the redemption of the State government from
> the radical usurpers who now control it, adopt
> and declare as their platform---1. That we stand
> ready to obey the Constitution of the United States
> and the laws passed in pursuance thereof, and the
> constitution and laws of the State of Alabama, so
> long as they remain in force and unrepealed.

I will, however, take the gentleman at his word; but
must be allowed to ask if so why was it, even after the
several amendments had been officially announced to be part
of the Federal Constitution, that his State and others refused
to allow the negro to testify in their courts against a white
man? If they believed he should be educated (and surely this
is a right) why was it that his school-houses were burned
down, and the teachers who had gone down on errands of
mercy to carry light into dark places driven off, and in some
places killed? If they believe the negro should vote (another
right, as I understand the Constitution), why was it that Ku-
Klux Klans were organized to prevent him from exercising
the right of an American citizen, namely, casting the ballot
--the very thing they said he had a right to do?

The professed belief and practice are sadly at variance, and must be intelligently harmonized before I can be made to believe that they are willing to acknowledge that I have any rights under the Constitution or elsewhere. He boasts of the magnanimity of Kentucky in allowing the negro to vote without qualification, while to enjoy the same privilege in Massachusetts he is required to read the constitution of that State. He was very unhappy in this comparison. Why, sir, his State does not allow the negro to vote at all. When was the constitution of Kentucky amended so as to grant him the elective franchise? They vote there by virtue of the fifteenth amendment alone, independent of the laws and constitution of that Commonwealth; and they would to-day disfranchise him if it could be done without affecting her white population. The Old Bay State waited for no "act of Congress" to force her to do justice to all of her citizens, but in ante bellum days provided in her constitution that all male persons who could read and write should be entitled to suffrage. That was a case of equality before the law, and who had a right to complain? There is nothing now in the amended Federal Constitution to prevent Kentucky from adopting the same kind of clause in her constitution, when the convention meets to revise the organic law of that State, I venture the assertion that you will never hear a word about it; but it will not be out of any regard for her colored citizens, but the respect for that army of fifty-thousand ignorant white men she has within her borders, many of whom I see every time I pass through that State, standing around the several depots continually harping on the stereotyped phrase, "The damned negro won't work."

I would not be surprised though if she should do better in the future. I remember when a foreigner was just as unpopular in Kentucky as the negro is now; when the majority of the people of that State were opposed to according the foreigner the same rights they claimed for themselves; when that class of people were mobbed in the streets of her principal cities on account of their political faith, just as they have done the negro for the last seven years. But what do you see to-day? One of that then proscribed class is Kentucky's chief Representative upon this floor. Is not this an evidence of a returning sense of justice? If so, would it not be reasonable to predict that she will in the near future send one of her now proscribed class to aid him in representing her interests upon this floor?

Mr. Speaker, there is another member of this body who has opposed the passage of this bill very earnestly,

whose position in the country and peculiar relations to the
Government compel me to refer to him before I conclude. I
allude to the gentleman from Georgia (Mr. Stephens). He
returns to this House after an absence of many years with
the same old ideas respecting State-rights that he carried
away with him. He has not advanced a step; but unfortunately
for him the American people have, and no longer consider
him a fit expounder of our organic law. Following to its
legitimate conclusion the doctrine of State-rights (which of itself is secession), he deserted the flag of his country, followed his State out of the Union, and a long and bloody war
followed. With its results most men are acquainted and
recognize; but he, Bourbon-like, comes back saying the very
same things he used to say, and swearing by the same gods
he swore by in other days. He seems not to know that the
ideas which he so ably advanced for so many years were by
the war swept away, along with that system of slavery which
he intended should be the chief corner-stone, precious and
elect, of the transitory kingdom over which he was second
ruler.

Sir, the most of us have seen the play of Rip Van
Winkle, who was said to have slept twenty years in the
Katskill Mountains. On his return he found that the small
trees had grown up to be large ones; the village of Falling
Waters had improved beyond his recollection; the little
children that used to play around his knees and ride into the
village upon his back had grown up to be men and women
and assumed the responsibilities of life; most of his friends,
including Nick Vedder, had gone to that bourn whence no
traveler returns; but, saddest of all, his child, "Mene,"
could not remember him. No one can see him in his efforts
to recall the scenes of other days without being moved almost to tears. This, however, is fiction. The life and
actions of the gentleman from Georgia most happily illustrate
this character. This is a case where truth is stranger than
fiction; and when he comes into these Halls advocating the
same old ideas after an absence of so many years, during
which time we have had a conflict of arms such as the world
never saw, that revolutionized the entire body-politic, he
stamps himself a living "Rip Van Winkle."

I reiterate, that the principles of "State-rights," for
the recognition of which, he now contends, are the ones that
were in controversy during our late civil strife. The arguments pro and con were heard in the roar of battle, amid
the shrieks of the wounded, and the groans of the dying; and

the decision was rendered amid shouts of victory by the Union
soldiers. With it all appear to be familiar except him, and
for his information I will state that upon this question an
appeal was taken from the forum to the sword, the highest
tribunal known to man, that it was then and there decided
that National rights are paramount to State-rights, and that
liberty and equality before the law should be coextensive with
the jurisdiction of the Stars and Stripes. And I will further
inform him that the bill now pending is simply to give practical effect to that decision.

I sympathize with him in his inability to understand
this great change. When he left here the negro was a chat-
tel, exposed for sale in the market places within a stone's
throw of the Capitol; so near that the shadow of the Goddess
of Liberty reflected by the rising sun would fall within the
slave-pen as a forcible reminder that there was no hopeful
day, nothing bright in the future, for the poor slave. Then
no negro was allowed to enter these Halls and hear discussions on subjects that most interested him. The words of
lofty cheer that fell from the lips of Wade, Giddings, Julian,
and others were not allowed to fall upon his ear. Then, not
more than three negroes were allowed to assemble at any
place in the capital of the nation without special permission
from the city authorities. But on his return he finds that
the slave-pens have been torn down, and upon their ruins
temples of learning have been erected; he finds that the Goddess of Liberty is no longer compelled to cover her radiant
face while she weeps for our national shame, but looks with
pride and satisfaction upon a free and regenerated land; he
finds that the laws and regulations respecting the assembling
of negroes are no longer in force, but on the contrary he
can see on any public holiday the Butler Zouaves, a fine-
looking company of colored men, on parade.

Imagine, if you can, what would have been the effect
of such a sight in this city twelve years ago. Then one
negro soldier would have caused utter consternation. Congress would have adjourned; the Cabinet would have sought
protection elsewhere; the President would have declared mar-
tial law; troops and marines would have been ordered out;
and I cannot tell all that would have happened; but now such
a sight does not excite a ripple on the current of affairs; but
over all, and worse to him than all, he finds the negro here,
not only a listener but a participant in debate. While I sympathize with him in his inability to comprehend this marvelous
change, I must say in all earnestness that one who cannot

understand and adjust himself to the new order of things is
poorly qualified to teach this nation the meaning of our
amended Constitution. The tenacity with which he sticks to
his purpose through all the vicissitudes of life is commendable, though his views he objectionable.

While the chief of the late confederacy is away in
Europe fleeing the wrath to come in the shape of Joe Johns-
ton's history of the war, his lieutenant, with a boldness that
must challenge the admiration of the most impudent, comes
into these Halls and seeks to commit the nation through Congress to the doctrine of State-rights, and thus save it from
the general wreck that followed the collapse of the rebellion.
He had no other business here. Read his speech on the
pending bill; his argument was cunning, far more ingenious
than ingenuous. He does not deny the need or justness of
the measure, but claims that the several States have exclusive
jurisdiction of the same. I am not so willing as some others
to believe in the sincerity of his assertions concerning the
rights of the colored man. If he were honest in this matter,
why is it he never recommended such a measure to the
Georgia Legislature? If the several States had secured to
all classes within their borders the rights contemplated in
this bill, we would have had no need to come here; but they
having failed to do their duty, after having had ample opportunity, the General Government is called upon to exercise its
right in the matter.

Mr. Speaker, time will not allow me to review the
history of the American negro, but I must pause here long
enough to say that he has not been properly treated by this
nation; he has purchased and paid for all, and for more,
than he has yet received. Whatever liberty he enjoys has
been paid for over and over again by more than two hundred
years of forced toil; and for such citizenship as is allowed
him he paid the full measure of blood, the dearest price required at the hands of any citizen. In every contest, from
the beginning of the revolutionary struggle down to the war
between the States, has he been prominent. But we all remember in our late war when the Government was so hard
pressed for troops to sustain the cause of the Union, when
it was so difficult to fill up the ranks that had been so fearfully decimated by disease and the bullet; when every train
that carried to the front a number of fresh soldiers brought
back a corresponding number of wounded and sick ones; when
grave doubts as to the success of the Union arms had seized
upon the minds of some of the most sanguine friends of the

Government; when strong men took counsel of their fears;
when those who had all their lives received the fostering care
of the nation were hesitating as to their duty in that trying
hour, and others questioning if it were not better to allow
the star of this Republic to go down and thus be blotted out
from the great map of nations than to continue the bloodshed;
when gloom and despair were widespread; when the last ray
of hope had nearly sunk below our political horizon, how the
negro then came forward and offered himself as a sacrifice
in the place of the nation, made bare his breast to the steel,
and in it received the thrusts of the bayonet that were aimed
at the life of the nation by the soldiers of that government in
which the gentleman from Georgia figured as second officer.

Sir, the valor of the colored soldier was tested on
many a battlefield, and to-day his bones lie bleaching beside
every hill and in every valley from the Potomac to the Gulf;
whose mute eloquence in behalf of equal rights for all before
the law, is and ought to be far more persuasive than any
poor language I can command.

Mr. Speaker, nothing short of a complete acknowledg-
ment of my manhood will satisfy me. I have no compromises
to make, and shall unwillingly accept any. If I were to say
that I would be content with less than any other member upon
this floor I would forfeit whatever respect anyone here might
entertain for me, and would thereby furnish the best possible
evidence that I do not and cannot appreciate the rights of a
freeman.   Just what I am charged with by my political enemies. I cannot willingly accept anything less than my full
measure of rights as a man, because I am unwilling to present myself as a candidate for the brand of inferiority, which
will be as plain and lasting as the mark of Cain. If I am
to be thus branded, the country must do it against my solemn
protest.

Sir, in order that I might know something of the feelings of a freeman, a privilege denied me in the land of my
birth, I left home last year and traveled six months in
foreign lands, and the moment I put my foot upon the deck
of a ship that unfurled a foreign flag from its mast-head,
distinctions on account of my color ceased. I am not aware
that my presence on board the steamer put her off her
course. I believe we made the trip in the usual time. It
was in other countries than my own that I was not a stranger,
that I could approach a hotel without the fear that the door
would be slammed in my face. Sir, I feel this humiliation

very keenly; it dwarfs my manhood, and certainly it impairs
my usefulness as a citizen.

	The other day when the centennial bill was under dis-
cussion I would have been glad to say a word in its favor,
but how could I?   How would I appear at the centennial cele-
bration of our national freedom, with my own galling chains
of slavery hanging about me?   I could no more rejoice on
that occasion in my present condition than the Jews could sing
in their wonted style as they sat as captives beside the Bab-
ylonish streams; but I look forward to the day when I shall
be in the full enjoyment of the rights of a freeman, with the
same hope they indulged, that they would again return to their
native land.   I can no more forget my manhood than they
could forget Jerusalem.

	After all, this question resolves itself to this: either
I am a man or I am not a man.   If one, I am entitled to all
the rights, privileges, and immunities common to any other
class in this country; if not a man, I have no right to vote,
no right to a seat here; if no right to vote, then 20 percent
of the members on this floor have no right here, but, on the
contrary, hold their seats in violation of law.   If the negro
has no right to vote, then one-eighth of your Senate consists
of members who have no shadow of a claim to the places
they occupy; and if no right to a vote, a half-dozen governors
in the South figure as usurpers.

	This is the legitimate conclusion of the argument, that
the negro is not a man and is not entitled to all the public
rights common to other men, and you cannot escape it.   But
when I press my claims I am asked, "Is it good policy?"
My answer is, "Policy is out of the question; it has nothing
to do with it; that you can have no policy in dealing with your
citizens; that there must be one law for all; that in this case
justice is the only standard to be used, and you can no more
divide justice than you can divide Deity."   On the other hand,
I am told that I must respect the prejudices of others.   Now,
sir, no one respects reasonable and intelligent prejudices
more than I.   I respect religious prejudices, for example;
these I can comprehend.   But how can I have respect for the
prejudices that prompt a man to turn up his nose at the
males of a certain race, while at the same time he has a
fondness for the females of the same race to the extent of
cohabitation?   Out of four poor unfortunate colored women
who from poverty were forced to go to the lying-in branch of
the Freedmen's Hospital here in the District last year three

gave birth to children whose fathers were white men, and I
venture to say that if they were members of this body, would
vote against the civil-rights bill. Do you, can you wonder at
my want of respect for this kind of prejudice? To make me
feel uncomfortable appears to be the highest ambition of many
white men. It is to them a positive luxury, which they seek
to indulge at every opportunity.

        I have never sought to compel anyone, white or black,
to associate with me, and never shall; nor do I wish to be
compelled to associate with anyone. If a man do not wish to
ride with me in the street-car I shall not object to his hiring
a private conveyance; if he do not wish to ride with me from
here to Baltimore, who shall complain if he charter a special
train? For a man to carry out his prejudices in this way
would be manly, and would leave no cause for complaint, but
to crowd me out of the usual conveyance into an uncomfortable place with persons for whose manners I have a dislike,
whose language is not fit for ears polite, is decidedly un-
manly and cannot be submitted to tamely by any one who has
a particle of self-respect.

        Sir, this whole thing grows out of a desire to establish
a system of "caste, " an anti-republican principle, in our free
country. In Europe they have princes, dukes, lords, etc.,
in contradistinction to the middle classes and peasants.
Further East they have the brahmans or priests, who rank
above the sudras or laborers. In those countries distinctions
are based upon blood and position. Every one there under-
stands the custom and no one complains. They, poor innocent creatures, pity our condition, look down upon us with a
kind of royal compassion, because they think we have no
tangible lines of distinction, and therefore speak of our society as being vulgar. But let not our friends beyond the
seas lay the flattering unction to their souls that we are without distinctive lines; that we have no nobility; for we are
blessed with both. Our distinction is color (which would
necessarily exclude the brahmans), and our lines are much
broader than anything they know of. Here a drunken white
man is not only equal to a drunken negro (as would be the
case anywhere else), but superior to the most sober and
orderly one; here an ignorant white man is not only the equal
of an unlettered negro, but is superior to the most cultivated;
here our nobility cohabit with our female peasants, and then
throw up their hands in holy horror when a male of the same
class enters a restaurant to get a meal, and if he insist upon
being accommodated our scion of royalty will leave and go to

the arms of his colored mistress and there pour out his
soul's complaint, tell her of the impudence of the "damned
nigger" incoming to a table where a white man was sitting.

What poor, simple-minded creatures these foreigners
are. They labor under the delusion that they monopolize the
knowledge of the courtesies due from one gentleman to another. How I rejoice to know that it is a delusion. Sir, I
wish some of them could have been present to hear the representative of the F. F. V. 's upon this floor (and I am told
that that is the highest degree that society has yet reached
in this country) address one of his peers, who dared asked
him a question, in this style: 'I am talking to white men. "
Suppose Mr. Gladstone--who knows no man but by merit--
who in violation of our custom entertained the colored jubilee
singers at his home last summer, or the Duke de Broglie,
had been present and heard this eloquent remark drop from
the lips of this classical and knightly member, would they
not have hung their heads in shame at their ignorance of po-
liteness, and would they not have returned home, repaired to
their libraries, and betaken themselves to the study of Ches-
terfield on manners? With all these absurdities staring them
in the face, who can wonder that foreigners laugh at our ideas
of distinction?

Mr. Speaker, though there is not a line in this bill
the democracy approve of, yet they made the most noise
about the school clause. Dispatches are freely sent over the
wires as to what will be done with the common-school system in the several Southern States in the event this bill becomes a law. I am not surprised at this, but, on the other
hand, I looked for it. Now what is the force of that school
clause? It simply provides that all the children in every
State where there is a school system supported in whole or
in part by general taxation shall have equal advantages of
school privileges. So that if perfect and ample accommodations are not made convenient for all the children, then any
child has the right to go to any school where they do exist.
And that is all there is in this school clause. I want someone to tell me of any measure that was intended to benefit
the negro that they have approved of. Of which one did they
fail to predict evil? They declared if the negroes were
emancipated that the country would be laid waste, and that in
the end he would starve, because he could not take care of
himself. But this was a mistake. When the reconstruction
acts were passed and the colored men in my State were
called upon to express through the ballot whether Alabama

should return to the Union or not, white men threw up their
hands in holy horror and declared if the negro voted that
never again would they deposit another ballot.   But how does
the matter stand now?   Some of those very men are in the
republican ranks, and I have known them to grow hoarse in
shouting for our platforms and candidates.   They hurrah for
our principles with all the enthusiasm of a new-born soul,
and sir, so zealous have they become that in looking at them
I am amazed, and am often led to doubt my own faith and
feel ashamed for my lukewarmness.   And those who have not
joined our party are doing their utmost to have the negro vote
with them.   I have met them in the cabins night and day
where they were imploring him for the sake of old times to
come up and vote with them.

I submit, Mr. Speaker, that political prejudices prompt
the democracy to oppose this bill as much as anything else.
In the campaign of 1868 Joe Williams, an uncouth and rather
notorious colored man, was employed as a general democratic
canvasser in the South.   He was invited to Montgomery to
enlighten us, and while there he stopped at one of the best
hotels in the city, one that would not dare entertain me.   He
was introduced at the meeting by the chairman of the democratic executive committee as a learned and elegant, as well
as eloquent gentleman.   In North Alabama he was invited to
speak at the Seymour and Blair barbecue, and did address
one of the largest audiences, composed largely of ladies, that
ever assembled in that part of the State.   This I can prove
by my simon-pure democratic colleague, Mr. SLOSS, for he
was chairman of the committee of arrangements on that occasion, and I never saw him so radiant with good humor in
all my life as when he had the honor of introducing 'his
friend, " Mr. Williams.   In that case they were extending
their courtesies to a coarse, vulgar stranger, because he
was a democrat, while at the same time they were hunting
me down as the partridge on the mount, night and day, with
their Ku-Klux Klan, simply because I was a republican and
refused to bow at the foot of their Baal.   I might enumerate
many instances of this kind, but I forbear.   But to come
down to a later period, the Greeley campaign.   The colored
men who were employed to canvass North Carolina in the interest of the democratic party were received at all the hotels
as other men and treated I am informed with marked distinction.   And in the State of Louisiana a very prominent colored
gentleman saw proper to espouse the Greeley cause, and when
the fight was over and the McEnery government saw fit to
send on a committee to Washington to present their case to

the President, this colored gentleman was selected as one of
that committee. On arriving in the city of New Orleans prior
to his departure he was taken to the Saint Charles, the most
aristocratic hotel in the South. When they started he occupied a berth in the sleeping-car; at every eating-house he
was treated like the rest of them, no distinction whatever.
And when they arrived at Montgomery I was at the depot, just
starting for New York. Not only did the conductor refuse to
allow me a berth in the sleeping-car, but I was also denied
a seat in the first-class carriage. Now, what was the difference between us? Nothing but our political faith. To prove
this I have only to say that just a few months before this
happened, he, along with Frederick Douglass and others, was
denied the same privileges he enjoyed in coming here. And
now that he has returned to the right party again I can tell
him that never more will he ride in another sleeping-car in
the South unless this bill become law. There never was a
truer saying than that circumstances alter cases.

Mr. Speaker, to call this land the asylum of the oppressed is a misnomer, for upon all sides I am treated as
a pariah. I hold that the solution of this whole matter is to
enact such laws and prescribe such penalties for their violation as will prevent any person from discriminating against
another in public places on account of color. No one asks,
no one seeks the passage of a law that will interfere with
anyone's private affairs. But I do ask the enactment of a
law to secure me in the enjoyment of public privileges. But
when I ask this I am told that I must wait for public opinion;
that it is a matter that cannot be forced by law. While I
admit that public opinion is a power, and in many cases is a
law of itself, yet I cannot lose sight of the fact that both
statute law and the law of necessity manufacture public opinion.
I remember, it was unpopular to enlist negro soldiers in our
late war, and after they enlisted it was equally unpopular to
have them fight in the same battles; but when it became a
necessity in both cases public opinion soon came around to
that point. No white father objected to the negro's becoming
food for powder if thereby his son would be saved. No white
woman objected to the negro marching in the same ranks and
fighting in the same battles if by that her husband could escape burial in our savannas and return to her and her little
ones.

Suppose there had been no reconstruction acts nor
amendments to the Constitution, when would public opinion in
the South have suggested the propriety of giving me the ballot?

Unaided by law when would public opinion have prompted the Administration to appoint members of my race to represent this Government at foreign courts? It is said by some well-meaning men that the colored man has now every right under the common law; in reply I wish to say that that kind of law commands very little respect when applied to the rights of colored men in my portion of the country; the only law that we have any regard for is uncommon law of the most positive character. And I repeat, if you will place upon your statute-books laws that will protect me in my rights, that public opinion will speedily follow.

Mr. Speaker, I trust this bill will become law, because it is a necessity, and because it will put an end to all legislation on this subject. It does not and cannot contemplate any such idea as social equality; nor is there any man upon this floor so silly as to believe that there can be any law enacted or enforced that would compel one man to recognize another as his equal socially; if there be, he ought not to be here, and I have only to say that they have sent him to the wrong public building. I would oppose such a bill as earnestly as the gentleman from North Carolina, whose associations and cultivations have been of such a nature as to lead him to select the crow as his standard of grandeur and excellence in the place of the eagle, the hero of all birds and our national emblem of pride and power. I will tell him that I have seen many of his race to whose level I should object to being dragged.

Sir, it matters not how much men may differ upon the question of State and national rights; there is one class of rights, however, that we all agree upon, namely, individual rights, which includes the right of every man to select associates for himself and family, and to say who shall and who shall not visit at his house. This right is God-given and custom-sanctioned, and there is, and there can be no power overruling your decision in this matter. Let this bill become law and not only will it do much toward giving rest to this weary country on this subject, completing the manhood of my race and perfecting his citizenship, but it will take him from the political arena as a topic of discussion where he has done duty for the last fifty years, and thus freed from anxiety respecting his political standing, hundreds of us will abandon the political fields who are there from necessity and not from choice, and enter other and more pleasant ones; and thus relieved, it will be the aim of the colored man as well as his duty and interest, to become a good citizen, and to do all in his power to advance the interests of a common country.

CIVIL RIGHTS (n. d., 1875)

I have no compromise to offer on this subject; I
shall not willingly accept any. After all, this
question resolves itself into this; either I am a
man or I am not a man. If I am a man, I am
entitled to all the right and privileges and immunities that any other American citizen is entitled to. If I am not a man, then I have no
right to vote, I have no right to be here upon
this floor; or if I am tolerated here, it is in violation of the Constitution of our country. If the
Negro is not a man, and has no right to vote,
then there are many occupying seats here in violation of law. (3:1001)

Mr. RAPIER. That I deny, Mr. Speaker. The last
time the colored people in Alabama were heard from upon
this subject they expressed their opinions in a platform one
clause of which I ask the Clerk to read.

The Clerk read as follows:

As citizens of the United States and of the State
of Alabama, we claim all the civil and political
rights, privileges, and immunities secured to
every citizen by the Constitution of The United
States and of the State of Alabama; and we will
be satisfied with nothing less.

Mr. RAPIER. That class of people commissioned me
to speak for them upon this subject in this House. If any
man in the State of Alabama is acquainted with the colored
people, I hold that I am the man. And when my colleague
(Mr. WHITE) says that the "colored people of Alabama" in-
structed him to offer such a bill as that, I have only to say
that he has placed them in a very false position.

The platform which he had read from the Clerk's desk

277

yesterday, and which he said was the platform of the republican party in the State of Alabama, was never framed or adopted by them.   They never read that platform and never saw it until it was read in the republican convention of the State of Alabama, and there were not more than eighteen colored men in the convention at the time when that platform was adopted.   The reason why the colored men there did not oppose that platform was that the republicans in the northern part of Alabama said that unless such a platform was put forth they were afraid they could not secure the white vote of that portion of the State.   Therefore we allowed them to have their platform; and that platform was sent forth to the people of Alabama, and they repudiated it.   I am unqualifiedly opposed to the White substitute, but favor the Senate bill as it stands.

I have no compromise to offer on this subject, I shall not willingly accept any.   After all, this question resolves itself into this: either I am a man or I am not a man.   If I am a man, I am entitled to all the right and privileges and immunities that any other American citizen is entitled to.   If I am not a man, then I have no right to vote, I have no right to be here upon this floor; or if I am tolerated here, it is in violation of the Constitution of our country.   If the negro is not a man, and has no right to vote, then there are many occupying seats here in violation of law.

Sir, if any man is entitled to the protection of the laws of his country, I hold that the colored man is that man. When he had no particular reason for liking this Government; when your Government was threatened with destruction, when those who had always been fostered and cared for by the Government hesitated as to what they should do, when this great Republic was in the act of going down, then it was that the negro came forward, made bare his breast and in it received the thrusts of the bayonets aimed at the life of the nation.   And now you hesitate to say whether I shall be regarded as a man or not in this country, being a representative of that race.

(Here the hammer fell.)

Mr. RAPIER.   In the name of my constituents I demand the passage of the Senate bill.

BIBLIOGRAPHY

1. Biographical Directory of the American Congress 1774-
    1971. Washington, D. C. : United States Government
    Printing Office, 1971.

2. U. S. Congress. House. Civil Rights. 43rd Congress,
    1st session, 1874.

3. U. S. Congress. House. Civil Rights. 43rd Congress,
    2nd session, 1875.

Hiram Revels--"Revels was tall and portly, with a benevolent expression and a pleasant impressive voice. He spoke
with distinctiveness and conviction. " (Moseley, p. 11)

XV. HIRAM REVELS

Revels, Hiram Rhodes, a Senator from Mississippi; born in
Fayetteville, Cumberland County, North Carolina, September
27, 1827; was of the Negro race; attended the Quaker Sem-
inary, Union County, Indiana, and Drake County (Ohio) Sem-
inary; was graduated from Knox College, Bloomington, Illinois, was ordained a minister in the African Methodist
Episopal Church at Baltimore, Maryland, in 1845; lectured
among his people in the states of Indiana, Illinois, Kansas,
Kentucky, Tennessee, and Missouri; taught school in St.
Louis, Missouri; accepted a pastorate in Baltimore, Maryland, 1860; at the outbreak of the Civil War assisted in the
organization of the first two colored regiments in Maryland;
served Vicksburg, Mississippi, as Chaplain of a colored
regiment in 1864; settled in Natchez, Mississippi, in 1866;
was alderman in that city in 1868; member of the State
Senate of Mississippi in 1870; upon the readmission of Mississippi to representation was elected as a Republican to the
United States Senate and served from February 23, 1870 to
March 3, 1871; Secretary of State ad interim of Mississippi
in 1873; President of the Alcorn Agriculture College, Rodney,
Mississippi, 1876-1882; moved to Holly Springs, Marshall
County, Mississippi, and became District Superintendent in
the AME Church; died in Aberdeen, Mississippi, January 16,
1901.   (1:1599)

READMISSION OF GEORGIA

And now, sir, I protest in the name of truth and
human rights against any and every attempt to
fetter the hands of one hundred thousand white
and colored citizens of the state of Georgia. Sir,
... I wish my last words upon the great issues
involved in the bill before us to be my solemn
and earnest demand for full and prompt protection
for the helpless loyal people of Georgia. (2:1986-
1989)

Mr. REVELS. Mr. President, I rise at this particular juncture in the discussion of the Georgia bill with feelings which perhaps never before entered into the experience
of any member of this body. I rise, too, with misgivings as
to the propriety of lifting my voice at this early period after
my admission into the Senate. Perhaps it were wiser for
me, so inexperienced in the details of senatorial duties, to
have remained a passive listener in the progress of this debate; but when I remember that my term is short, and that
the issues with which this bill is fraught are momentous in
their present and future influence upon the well-being of my
race, I would seem indifferent to the importance of the hour
and recreant to the high trust imposed upon me if I hesitated
to lend my voice on behalf of the loyal people of the South.
I therefore waive all thoughts as to the propriety of taking a
part in this discussion. When questions arise which bear
upon the safety and protection of the loyal white and colored
population of those States lately in rebellion I cannot allow
any thought as to mere propriety to enter into my consideration of duty. The responsibilites of being the exponent of
such a constituency as I have the honor to represent are
fully appreciated by me. I bear about me daily the keenest
sense of their weight, and that feeling prompts me now to
lift my voice for the first time in this Council Chamber of
the nation; and, sir, I stand to-day on this floor to appeal
for protection from the strong arm of the Government for her
loyal children, irrespective of color and race, who are citizens of the southern States, and particularly of the State of
Georgia.

I am well aware, sir, that the idea is abroad that an
antagonism exists between the whites and blacks, that that
race which the nation raised from the degradation of slavery,
and endowed with the full and unqualified rights and privileges
of citizenship, are intent upon power, at whatever price it
can be gained.   It has been the well-considered purpose and
aim of a class not confined to the South to spread this charge
over the land, and their efforts are as vigorous to-day to
educate the people of this nation into that belief as they were
at the close of the war.   It was not uncommon to find this
same class, even during the rebellion, prognosticating a
servile war.   It may have been that "the wish was father to
the thought. "   And, sir, as the recognized representative of
my downtrodden people, I deny the charge, and hurl it back
into the teeth of those who make it, and who, I believe, have
not a true and conscientious desire to further the interests
of the whole South.   Certainly no one possessing any personal
knowledge of the colored population of my own or other States
need be reminded of the noble conduct of that people under
the most trying circumstances in the history of the late war,
when they were beyond the protection of the Federal forces.
While the confederate army pressed into its ranks every white
male capable of bearing arms, the mothers, wives, daughters,
and sisters of the southern soldiers were left defenseless and
in the power of the blacks, upon whom the chains of slavery
were still riveted; and to bind those chains the closer was
the real issue for which so much life and property was sac-
rificed.

And now, sir, I ask, how did that race act?   Did they
in those days of confederate weakness and impotence evince
the malignity of which we hear so much?   Granting, for the
sake of argument, that they were ignorant and besotted,
which I do not believe, yet with all their supposed ignorance
and credulity they in their way understood as fully as you or
I the awful import of the contest.   They knew if the gallant
corps of national soldiers were beaten back and their flag
trailed in the dust that it was the presage of still heavier
bondage.   They longed, too, as their fathers did before them,
for the advent of that epoch over which was shed the hallowed
light of inspiration itself.   They desired, too, with their
fathers, to welcome the feet of the stranger shod with the
peaceful preparation of good news.   Weary years of bondage
had told their tale of sorrow to the court of Heaven.   In the
councils of the great Father of all they knew the adjudication
of their case, albeit, delayed for years, in which patient
suffering had nearly exhausted itself, would in the end bring

to them the boon for which they sighed--God's most blessed
gift to His creatures--the inestimable boon of liberty. They
waited, and they waited patiently. In the absence of their
masters they protected the virtue and chastity of defenseless
women. Think, sir, for a moment, what the condition of
this land would be to-day if the slave population had risen in
servile insurrection against those who month by month were
fighting to perpetuate that institution which brought to them
all the evils of which they complained. Where would have
been the security for property, female chastity, and child-
hood's innocence? The bloody counterpart of such a story of
cruelty and wrong would have been paralleled only in those
chapters of Jewish history as recorded by Josephus, or in
the still later atrocities of that reign of terror which sent
the unfortunate Louis XVI and Marie Antoinette to the scaf-
fold. Nay, the deeds in that drama of cold-blooded butchery
would have out-Heroded the most diabolical acts of Herod
himself.

Mr. President, I maintain that the past record of my
race is a true index of the fellings which to-day animate
them. They bear toward their former masters no revenge-
ful thoughts, no hatreds, no animosities. They aim not to
elevate themselves by sacrificing one single interest of their
white fellow-citizens. They ask but the rights which are
theirs by God's universal law, and which are the natural out-
growth, the logical sequence of the condition in which the
legislative enactments of this nation have placed them. They
appeal to you and to me to see that they receive that protection which alone will enable them to pursue their daily avoca-
tions with success and enjoy the liberties of citizenship on
the same footing with their white neighbors and friends. I
do not desire simply to defend my own race from unjust and
unmerited charges, but I also desire to place upon record an
expression of my full and entire confidence in the integrity
of purpose with which I believe the President, Congress, and
the Republican party will meet these questions so prolific of
weal or woe, not only to my own people, but to the whole
South. They have been, so far as I can read the history of
the times, influenced by no spirit of petty tyranny. The poet
has well said that--

It is excellent
To have a giant's strength; but it is tyrannous
To use it like a giant.

And how have they used that power lodged in them by

the people? In acts of cruelty and oppression toward those
who sought to rend in twain this goodly fabric of our fathers,
the priceless heritage of so much hardship and endurance in
revolutionary times? Let the reconstruction enactments
answer the interrogation. No poor words of mine are needed
to defend the wise and beneficent legislation which has been
extended alike to white and colored citizens. The Republican
party is not inflamed, as some would fain have the country
believe, against the white population of the South. Its borders are wide enough for all truly loyal men to find within
them peace and repose from the din and discord of angry
faction. And be that loyal man white or black, that great
party of our Republic will, if consistent with the record it
has already made for posterity, throw around him the same
impartial security in his pursuit of liberty and happiness. If
a certain class at the South had accepted in good faith the
benevolent overtures which were offered to them with no nig-
gard hand, to-day would not find our land still harassed with
feuds and contentions.

I remarked, Mr. President, that I rose to plead for
protection for the defenseless race who now send their dele-
gation to the seat of Government to sue for that which this
Congress alone can secure to them. And here let me say
further, that the people of the North owe to the colored race
a deep obligation which it is no easy matter to fulfill. When
the Federal armies were thinned by death and disaster, and
somber clouds overhung the length and breadth of the Republic, and the very air was pregnant with the rumors of foreign
interference--in those dark days of defeat, whose memories
even yet haunt us as an ugly dream, from what source did
our nation in its seeming death throes gain additional and
new-found power? It was the sable sons of the South that
valiantly rushed to the rescue, and but for their intrepidity
and ardent daring many a northern fireside would miss to-day
paternal counsels or a brother's love.

Sir, I repeat the fact that the colored race saved to
the noble women of New England and the middle States men
on whom they lean to-day for security and safety. Many of
my race, the representatives of those men on the field of
battle, sleep in the countless graves of the South. If those
quiet resting-places of our honored dead could speak to-day
what a mighty voice, like to the rushing of a mighty wind,
would come up from those sepulchral homes! Could we resist the eloquent pleadings of their appeal? Ah, sir, I think
that this question of immediate and ample protection for the

loyal people of Georgia would lose its legal technicalities,
and we would cease to hesitate in our provisions for their
instant relief.   Again, I regret this delay on other grounds.
The taunt is frequently flung at us that a Nemesis more terrible than the Greek personation of the anger of the gods
awaits her hour of direful retribution.   We are told that at
no distant day a great uprising of the American people will
demand that the reconstruction acts of Congress be undone
and blotted forever from the annals of legislative enactment.
I inquire, sir, if this delay in affording protection to the
loyalists of the State of Georgia does not lend an uncomfortable significancy to this boasting sneer with which we so often
meet?   Delay is perilous, at best; for it is as true in legislation as in physic, that the longer we procrastinate to apply
the proper remedies the more chronic becomes the malady
that we seek to heal.

> The land wants such
> As dare with rigor execute the laws.
> Her festered members must be lanced and tented.
> He's a bad surgeon that for pity spares
> The part corrupted till the gangrene spread
> And all the body perish.   He that's merciful
> Unto the bad is cruel to the good.

Mr. President, I favor the motion to strike out so
much of the bill under debate as tends to abridge the term
of the existing Legislature of Georgia.   Let me, then, as
briefly as possible, review the history of the case which so
urgently claims our prompt action.   In the month of November, 1867, an election was held by the authority of the reconstruction policy of this Congress in the State of Georgia.
Its object was to settle by the ballot of her whole people,
white and colored, whether it was expedient to summon a convention which should frame a constitution for civil government
in that State.   A certain class of the population declined to
take any part in the election.   The vote cast at that election
represented thirty thousand white and eighty thousand colored
citizens of the State.   It was a majority, too, of the registered vote, and in consequence a convention was called.   A
number of the delegates who formed that convention were
colored.   By its authority a constitution was framed just and
equitable in all its provisions.   Race, color, or former condition of servitude found no barrier in any of its ample enactments, and it extended to those lately in armed rebellion
all the privileges of its impartial requirements.   This constitution was submitted to the people of the State for ratifi-

cation.   Every effort which human ingenuity could call into
requisition to defeat its adoption was resorted to.   The loyal
population of the State was victorious; and notwithstanding the
determination of some to defeat the constitution that same
class sought under its provisions to procure the nomination
for all the offices within the gift of the people.   A number
were declared elected as county officers and members of the
General Assembly.

Under the authority given by the act of Congress of
June 25, 1868, the Legislature thus elected convened on the
4th of July of the same year in Atlanta.   The act of Congress
to which I refer reaffirmed certain qualifications which were
demanded from all persons who were to hold office in the reconstructed States.   After some delay a resolution was adopted by the Legislature of Georgia declaring that that body was
duly qualified, and thus began the civil government in the
State.   Peace and harmony seemed at last to have met together, truth and justice to have kissed each other.   But
their reign was of short duration.   By and by the reconstruction acts of Congress began to be questioned, and it was alleged that they were unconstitutional; and the Legislature
which was elected under the constitution framed and supported
by colored men declared that a man having more than an
eighth of African blood in his veins was ineligible to office
or a seat in the Legislature of the State of Georgia.   These
very men, to whom the Republican party extended all the
rights and privileges of citizenship, whom they were em-
powered, if deemed expedient, to cut off forever from such
beneficent grants, were the men to deny political equality to
a large majority of their fellow-citizens.   In the month of
September, 1868, twenty-eight members of the Legislature
were expelled from that body, and upon the assumption of the
strange and startling hypothesis just mentioned they continued
to legislate in open violation of the constitution.   That constitution required by its provisions the establishment of a
system of free schools.   Such provisions were wholly abor-
tive, indeed a dead letter, for none were established.   The
courts of law, at least so far as colored men were regarded,
were a shameless mockery of justice.   And here an illustration, perhaps will the better give point to my last remark.
A case in which was involved the question whether or not a
colored man was eligible to one of the county offices was
taken before the superior court, and the judge upon the bench
rendered as his judicial opinion that a man of color was not
entitled to hold office.   I am told, sir, that the colored man
in question is a graduate of Oberlin, Ohio, and served with

honor as a commissioned officer in the Union Army during
the late war. Is any comment needed in this body upon such
a condition of affairs in the State of Georgia? Sir, I trust
not.

Then, again, these facts were presented for the calm
consideration of Congress in the following December, and the
results of their deliberation may be seen in the report of the
Committee on the Judiciary toward the close of January of
last year. Congress took no action to remedy this state of
affairs and aid the people of Georgia in obtaining the rights
clearly guaranteed to them by the provisions of their State
constitution.

In December last, at the earnest recommendation of
the President, the act of the 22d of that month was adopted.
It provided for the reassembling of the parties declared to
have been elected by the general commanding that district,
the restoration of the expelled persons of the Legislature,
and the rejection of disqualified persons by that body. The
present Legislature of Georgia has adopted the fourteenth and
fifteenth amendments to the Constitution of the United States
and the fundamental conditions required by the act of June 25,
1868. The reconstructed State of Georgia now offers herself,
through the constitutionally elected Senators, as meet and fit
for the recognition and admission by this Congress.

I have thus rapidly gone over the history of the events
which have transpired in the State of Georgia till I have come
to the legislation of the present time. The Committee on
Reconstruction in the other House prepared and presented a
bill providing for the admission of the State on similar
grounds to those on which my own State and Virginia were
allowed to take their places in the Union. An amendment
however, was proposed in the House and adopted, the aim
and purport of which is to legalize the organization of 1868,
and declare that the terms of the members of the Legislature,
who have so recently qualified for a fair and just recognition
by Congress, shall expire before they have completed their
full term of two years under the constitution. Again, this
amendment seeks to retain in office, whether approved by the
Legislature of the State or not, the judges who have declared,
in opposition to the constitution and the law, that in the State
of Georgia at least there exists a distinction as to race and
color, so far as civil and political rights are concerned. If
there be any meaning to the words of the constitution of that
State no such class distinction as this exists; and, sir, I am

at a loss to determine upon what grounds we are called upon
to hedge in by congressional enactment any public servant
who may still give utterance to such doctrines, which are
part and parcel of the effete civilization of our Republic. If
the Legislature of Georgia thinks it right and proper to place
in positions of trust and responsibility men of this school of
political thought, certainly I shall not offer one objection.
But let that Legislature assume the risk, as it is its true
province, and let it also bear the consequence.

I do not believe that it can be proved that the State of
Georgia has ever been beyond the control of Congress, nor
that she has ever become fully admitted into the Union or entitled to representation since her impotent efforts to promote
rebellion; and that therefore, when the act now under consideration and properly amended shall have been adopted, the
government of that State and the Legislature of that State will
enter upon the terms of office, will assume the powers for
good and right and justice which are prescribed in the constitution of that State, and that under the circumstances the
Senate will not deny to the loyal men of Georgia the recognition of their recent victory.

And now, sir, I protest in the name of truth and human rights against any and every attempt to fetter the hands
of one hundred thousand white and colored citizens of the
State of Georgia.   Sir, I now leave this question to the consideration of this body, and I wish my last words upon the
great issues involved in the bill before us to be my solemn
and earnest demand for full and prompt protection for the
helpless loyal people of Georgia.

I appeal to the legislative enactments of this Congress,
and ask if now, in the hour when a reconstructed State most
needs support, this Senate, which hitherto has done so nobly,
will not give it such legislation as it needs.

REMOVAL OF DISABILITIES FROM MISSISSIPPI

> I am in favor of removing the disabilities of those
> upon whom they are imposed in the South just as
> fast as they give evidence of having become loyal
> and of being loyal. If you can find one man in
> the South who gives evidence that he is a loyal
> man, and gives that evidence in the fact that he
> has ceased to denounce the laws of Congress as
> unconstitutional, has ceased to oppose them, and
> respects them and favors the carrying of them
> out, I am in favor of removing his disabilities;
> and if you can find one hundred men that the same
> is true of I am in favor of removing their dis-
> abilities. If you can find a whole State that that
> is true of I am in favor of removing the disabili-
> ties of all its people. (3:3520)

Mr. REVELS. Mr. President, I did not intend to take
any part in this discussion. It was not my desire to do so.
I do not rise now for the purpose of doing so, but merely to
explain my position and that of the State which I in part represent, in regard to the question of general amnesty. I have
been referred to by quite a number of honorable Senators
who have already addressed the Senate on this subject, and
at last I have been called upon by one to define my position
and that of my State.

First allow me to speak of my own position, and then
I will speak of that of the Republican party in the State that
I represent.

I am in favor of removing the disabilities of those
upon whom they are imposed in the South just as fast as they
give evidence of having become loyal and of being loyal. If
you can find one man in the South who gives evidence that he
is a loyal man, and gives that evidence in the fact that he
has ceased to denounce the laws of Congress as unconstitutional, has ceased to oppose them, and respects them and
favors the carrying of them out, I am in favor of removing

his disabilities; and if you can find one hundred men that the same is true of I am in favor of removing their disabilities. If you can find a whole State that that is true of I am in favor of removing the disabilities of all its people.

Now, my position is fully understood. Often I receive petitions from citizens of my State asking Congress to remove their disabilities; and how much I regret that it is not in our power to take that class of persons and put them by themselves and remove the disabilities of all of them at once. I would be glad to see this done, but we can only do it by the process adopted by Congress.

In regard to the State of Mississippi I have this to say: the Republican party, now dominant there, pledged itself to universal amnesty. That was in their platform; the speakers pledged themselves to it; and the Legislature redeemed that pledge by unanimously adopting a resolution asking Congress to remove the political disabilities of all the citizens of Mississippi, which resolution they placed in my hands, and made it my duty to present here, and which I have presented.

Now, I can say more, I believe, for the State of Mississippi than I can say for any of the other lately insurrectionary States. I do not know of one State that is altogether as well reconstructed as Mississippi. We have reports from a great many other States of lawlessness and of violence, and from parts of States we have well-authenticated reports to this effect; but while this is the case, do you hear one report of any more lawlessness or violence in the State of Mississippi? No; the people now I believe are getting along as quietly, pleasantly, harmoniously, and prosperously as the people are in any of the formerly free States. I think this is the case. I do not think my statement exaggerated anything at all. Now, sir, I hope that I am understood. I am in favor of amnesty in Mississippi. We pledged ourselves to it. The State is fit for it.

CONSTRUCTION OF LEVEES IN MISSISSIPPI

Sir, there is no staple, I believe, that forms a
more prominent and important element in the commercial industry of the nation at large, and of the
South particularly, than the cotton interest. By
common consent, as it were, this great medium
of national wealth once assumed so extraordinary
a place in our political economy as to be regarded
in point of commercial power as king of the industrial pursuits of the nation....
If the State of Mississippi is to take her share
in building up this great commercial industry
which, on the principles of a just and well attested political economy, affects the interests of
both North and South, she can do it only in the
way her legislative body has marked out; that is,
by an appeal for aid from the Federal Government. The building of the levees on the Mississippi is a national work, and, as such, her citizens look for such appropriations and grants as
the magnitude and importance of the undertaking
demand. (4:425-426)

Mr. REVELS. I move that the Senate proceed to the
consideration of the bill (S. No. 1136) to aid in the repairs
and construction of levees in the State of Mississippi.

The motion was agreed to; and the Senate, as in Committee of the Whole, proceeded to consider the bill.

Mr. REVELS. Mr. President, a few days prior to
the recess of Congress I presented the resolutions passed by
the Legislature of Mississippi during its last session, praying for an appropriation of $2,000,000 from the public Trea-
sury and a grant of land of five million acres from the public
domain for the rebuilding of the levees of the Mississippi
river. At or about the same time I introduced, for the ac-

292

complishment of that purpose, the bill which is now before
the Senate, and I then gave notice that at an early day I
would call up the bill and briefly state the claims on which
the action of Mississippi is founded.

Sir, there is no staple, I believe, that forms a more
prominent and important element in the commercial industry
of the nation at large, and of the South particularly, than the
cotton interest. By common consent, as it were, this great
medium of national wealth once assumed so extraordinary a
place in our political economy as to be regarded in point of
commercial power as king of the industrial pursuits of the
nation. In this restricted sense, may not the phrase "king
cotton" still speak of the magnitude and importance of the
cotton-growing interest of the whole country? Let me, in
view of the unlimited weight which the culture and production
of cotton give to the scales of the nation's wealth, refer to
some facts which are familiar perhaps to those who have
given any attention to the cotton markets of the world.

But three countries may be said to possess sufficient
power to enter into competition with us in the product of cotton, and if the question of labor adjusts itself in the other
southern cotton-producing States as it has done in Mississippi
I do not hesitate to hazard the opinion that this land will again
win back its supremacy in the cotton markets of the world,
and will wield, other things being equal, an undivided commercial power for all time to come.

Egypt, Brazil, and India, taking advantage of the disastrous results which our long internecine struggle afforded,
have developed their resources to their fullest capacity, and
although during the blockade English manufacturing rivals controlled the cotton market, I cannot but believe that the mastery of this great element in the commerce of the world is
within our grasp if the South, in her impoverished condition,
is granted the aid from the nation's Treasury which she now
seeks.

Every phase of the cotton question points out the magnificent advantages which this nation holds for maintaining its
place as master in the markets of the world; and this supremacy it must control at all risks if the industry of the
South be a subject of watchful care with those who shape the
legislation upon which, indeed, in a large measure the whole
industrial interests of that section of our land depend.

Among the cotton-producing countries of the world
which bear their share in the race of competition, the smallest, perhaps, is Egypt.

Previous to the war the South hardly looked with jeal-
ous eyes upon the part which Egypt was capable of taking in
the rivalry of cotton exportation to England; but at this day
she is altogether the most insignificant of our rivals, and but
for the combination of European manufacturers against the
southern cotton interest I would not waste words in dwelling,
even for a moment, on the facilities, such as they are,
which Egypt may seem to possess.

Again, I mention them only to exhibit by comparison
the superiority of the South over every other country for the
production of cotton.

First, then, Egypt has only about five hundred miles
of arable land along the Nile which can be made at all pro-
ductive of cotton, and its productiveness is in the main due
to artificial aids rather than to suitable soil or climate. The
irrigation which nature has given the entire South in the vast
system of arteries fed by the rivers which wind themselves
from one side of our continent to the other is almost wholly
wanting in Egypt. What nature does for the culture of cotton
with us is performed in Egypt by manual toil; water being
carried from the Nile in order to supply defects almost insuperable in the irrigation of the soil.

Despite such barriers in the way of cotton-growing,
Egypt exported to England in 1863-64, 257,102 bales, but two
years later a decline began, for the exportation amounted to
167,000.

Never in the history of the cotton interests of Egypt
am I able to find the number of bales exported so large, and
since the close of the late war, and as the people of the
South again turned their attention to the pursuits of peace,
the decline of exportation of cotton from Egypt to England is
patent and significant.

Brazil stands next as affecting our cotton interest, and
here the cultivators of the plant are met with natural ob-
stacles as in Egypt. South America is proverbial for the
myriads of insects of endless variety and description which
impregnate the atmosphere, so to speak, along her coasts,
in the dense woods, and over the arable fields of the interior

of the country.   To use the language of a noted English writer,
Mrs. Somerville--

> The quantity of insects is so great in the woods
> that their noise is often heard in a ship anchored
> some distance from the shore.

The same author, in speaking of the invasion of lo-
custs, describes it as--

> Under the guidance of a leader, in a mass so
> dense that it forms a cloud in the air, and the
> sound of their wings is like the murmur of the
> distant sea.   -- Physical Geography, English
> edition, page 398.

On the destructive effects to the cotton plant of these
teeming millions of insects and worms, some of which are
scarcely visible to the naked eye, I need place no special
emphasis, as it must be apparent to all.   In addition to the
fearful havoc at times made by the infinitesimal inhabitants
of the air, a no less formidable enemy to the growth of cotton is found in the very elements themselves.   Crossing
South America, as tho trade winds do, they bear in their
bosom such a volume of water that when it falls the rain is
not only of long duration and of excessive quantity, but often
surcharges itself at that very season which proves most disastrous to the cotton crop.

In view of such unconquerable disadvantages for the
cultivation of the cotton plant in Brazil, it is surprising that
in 1864 about 212, 192 bales were exported to England, and
in 1867 upward of 400, 000 bales, each bale weighing probably
one hundred and seventy-odd pounds.   Such, then, are the
results that even Brazil can boast, laboring, as I have shown,
under natural influences which, if they existed but a tithe in
extent in the cotton growing States of the South, would discourage all but the righ capitalists of the country from ven-
tures at best doubtful and precarious.   Certainly the poor men
and the freedmen would hesitate in grappling with such difficulties and encountering such risks.

From South America I turn to India, known for many
centuries as the richest cotton-growing country, excepting,
perhaps, our own, of the world.   Here, at a period of time
which goes back beyond the veritable records of history into
the dim and uncertain realm of tradition, cotton was cultivated

and manufactured into such articles of clothing as the climate
and the exigencies of its inhabitants required. And even in
our day a respectable authority on all questions appertaining
to the culture of cotton in India, Mr. J. A. B. Money, a resident of Calcutta, remarks that the population of India is
about one hundred and eighty millions, and that each inhab-
itant averages the consumption of nearly twenty pounds of
every cotton crop for his own domestic use. If this statement be true, and I see no good reason to doubt it, one can
realize in a moment the enormous crops which India yearly
yields, making it, too, the great supplier of the factories of
Great Britain. India is, beyond the shadow of all cavil and
conjecture, the great cotton rival of the South, and against
the dominant influence of England in India over the cotton
trade, and the power that she exercises in the cotton markets
of the world, the cotton planters of the United States must
meet in competition.

I maintain that in this competition the South is made
for the mastery, for, be the production of cotton in India as
great as Mr. Money's statement makes it, there are even in
India impediments in the way of the culture of the plant which
do not exist in the cotton-growing States of the South. Although India is not wanting in a large volume of water for
purposes of irrigation, for the Ganges and Indus supply all in
this respect which the character of its soil, aside from cotton culture, may require, yet the distribution is not so general and not so admirably fitted for the safety and security
of the growth of cotton as in the southern States. Aside from
this, too, at the South we have incomparable advantages as to
climate, ours being far less capricious than that of India; and
again, we are free from the continuous tropical rains which
so often damage the cotton crop. Like Egypt, India has to
resort to artifical means of irrigation, and the estimates for
the same in 1868-69 in the India budget of 1867-68 are
827, 000 pounds, or $4, 135, 000.

If I demand it necessary I might dwell at some length
on the differences as to quality produced on a fixed number
of acres in India compared with an equal number in the South.
So, too, I could refer to the greater labor in preparing India
cotton for manufacture, and the more expensive care attending it in the mills, such as machinery, etc. But I may remark that upon all these questions I believe the cotton producers of the United States have by all odds undisputed advantages, and I base my opinion upon the following figures:

The exportations of cotton to England from India in 1862 were 1,168,390 bales; in 1866, 1,848,000 bales, being a gain in four years of 678,610 bales. And Mr. President, this gain must be viewed in the light which the history of our country for this period affords. The greater part of this time the nation at home was struggling under the gigantic weight of a war which taxed the resources of the country almost beyond calculation, while our commerce on the seas was crippled and very nearly restricted to the products of the North. Our cotton interests were prostrate, and India, profiting by our calamities, had every opportunity to test her soil to the utmost, and put into operation every conceivable element to win for itself an unchallenged supremacy in the cotton markets of the world. And yet, with all these advantages in her favor, her exportations to England were augmented only to the extent just mentioned.

The two chief subjects which enter into the consideration of cotton culture are soil and climate; and in these respects I regard the South as unequaled by any country of the globe. The prodigal hand of nature has done all for the South in this regard that her most enthusiastic planter could desire, and her cotton product surpasses that of any other cotton-growing land. One thousand pounds of seed cotton generally yield about five hundred pounds of clean cotton, and the average product to the acre is about five hundred and thirty pounds of unclean cotton. And if we take into account the large extent of land which can be made serviceable to the cotton interests of the country, I think the fact will bear with it prima facie evidence that the South, if developed, will reign supreme as the ruler and master of the cotton markets of the world. For instance, Texas has ten million acres, Alabama and Mississippi fully six millions, and Georgia three millions. Where, I ask, are there to be found such a wealth of territory, such an admirable soil, and such an equable climate for the production of cotton?

If the state of Mississippi is to take her share in building up this great commercial industry which, on the principles of a just and well attested political economy, affects the interests of both North and South, she can do it only in the way her legislative body has marked out; that is, by an appeal for aid from the Federal Government. The building of the levees on the Mississippi is a national work, and, as such, her citizens look for such appropriations and grants as the magnitude and importance of the undertaking demand.

It is needless for me to press upon the attention of
the Senate the impoverished condition of my State. The ruin
and devastation that follow the march of great armies are too
well known.

Of the reconstruction of Mississippi on enduring and
substantial grounds I can speak with no uncertainty. Every
element in the policy of the State seems to argue continuance
of prosperity. In our land after years of frightful carnage
the sword is sheathed, and may it never again be drawn from
its scabbard. In its stead there is a more fitting symbol,
and now that the smoke of battle has passed away and the sky
is again clear and serene may its lesson to civilization be
learned anew over the length and breadth of the land.

On the walls of the Rotunda of this Capitol hangs a
historical representation of the planting of that symbol on the
banks of the father of waters, the great Mississippi. Three
centuries ago De Soto felled a gigantic tree and hewed it into
a cross, under whose outstretched arms his followers chanted
their glorious Te Deum, and as that symbol now portrays the
pursuits of well-established peace within the borders of the
State of Mississippi, is it not a just ground upon which to
ask from the General Government such aid as will enable its
citizens to pursue their labors with profit to themselves and
benefit to the nation?

I will read a part of the resolution of the Legislature
of the State, which will afford a basis upon which an intelligent opinion may be formed of the fertility of the land included in what is known as the Delta, between the Mississippi
and Yazoo rivers. This delta--

> contains an immense body of land unsurpassed in
> richness; and because of these further considera-
> tions namely, that those lands lie at the very
> heart of the American cotton zone; that, while the
> richest of the cotton uplands do not yield an aver-
> age of half a bale to the acre, the lands lying be-
> tween the Mississippi and the Yazoo yield an aver-
> age per acre of a full bale; that, with the excep-
> tion of some tracts found scattered through it at a
> level above ordinary floods, the agricultural in-
> dustry of the country had been excluded from that
> luxuriant waste by inundations of the Mississippi;
> that to such an extent had all the places available
> for settlement under that state of the case been

settled before 1850 that the five river counties,
which produced forty-two thousand bales of cotton
in that year, had produced even ten years previ-
ously so many as thirty-nine thousand bales; that
the Government of the United States, seeking to
convert the immense areas of rich lands which
had remained thus useless, into an element of
wealth, granted them to the State of Mississippi
in trust for the reclamation by levees; that the
following statement will show the results of that
grant on the production of five counties already
referred to:

	Bales
In 1840, before the grant, the counties being unleveed	39,000
In 1850, before the grant, the counties being still unleveed	42,000
In 1860, after the grant, the counties having been leveed	156,000

And now, sir, I can do little else than urge upon this
body prompt and generous action relative to the bill before
us. I conclude with the earnest and logical words of Governor Alcorn:

The scepter is about to depart from us in the
commerce of the world if we do not break down
at once the rivalry that is being developed by a
combination of the great Powers of Europe under
the opportunity of high prices; and while we enter
on this battle, which can only be won by us in the
future, as it has been won by us in the past, by
driving our rivals from the field before the force
of cheap production, we stand confronted with the
embarrassment of a labor system in transition,
and a system of capital in but imperfect organization. But inasmuch as our upland protection yields
but one third or one half of a bale to the acre,
while our production in the Mississippi-Yazoo delta
yields a bale to the acre, the plainest suggestion
of policy demands that, whatever disadvantages
may be in the case, we must fix the field of battle
with the European combination against us on cotton
culture in the invincible stronghold of productiveness in such rich soils as those of the delta of the
Yazoo. And thus it is that the construction of the
levees of the Mississippi, as a means of keeping

our cotton power at a height which gives strength
to our diplomacy, volume to our commerce, and
gold tribute to our treasury, constitutes a work
which rises to the very highest dimensions of the
national.

Give a substantial protection to the magnificent
waste lands between the Mississippi and the Yazoo,
and you throw open to immediate settlement between three and four million acres of the finest
cotton lands on the face of the earth.   When Italy
builds railways, constructs macadamized roads,
makes elaborate surveys, and offers large gifts
for settlement of a less extent of soil, inferior in
yield, in order to crush the power of the United
States in the cotton markets of the world, shall
the United States hesitate to reassert that power
at a small outlay, which will enable her to bid defiance as a cotton producer to the whole world
combined, from the unequaled yield of the cotton
soils of the Mississippi-Yazoo?

I now move, Mr. President, that the bill be taken
from the table and referred to the select committee on the
subject of the levees of the Mississippi river.

ABOLISHMENT OF SEPARATE SCHOOLS

By some it is contended that if we establish mixed
schools here a great insult will be given to the
white citizens, and that the white schools will be
seriously damaged.... [in] the New England States
where they have mixed schools ... there they will
find schools in as prosperous and flourishing a
condition as any to be found in any part of the
world. They will find such schools there; and
they will find between the white and colored citizens friendship, peace, and harmony. (5:1059-
1060)

Mr. REVELS. Mr. President, I rise to express a
few thoughts on this subject. It is not often that I ask the
attention of the Senate on any subject, but this is one on
which I feel it to be my duty to make a few brief remarks.

In regard to the wishes of the colored people of this
city I will simply say that the trustees of colored schools
and some of the most intelligent colored men of this place
have said to me that they would have before asked for a bill
abolishing the separate colored schools and putting all children
on an equality in the common schools if they had thought
they could obtain it. They feared they could not; and this is
the only reason why they did not ask for it before.

I find that the prejudice in this country to color is
very great, and I sometimes fear that it is on the increase.
For example, let me remark that it matters not how colored
people act, it matters not how well they behave themselves,
how well they deport themselves, how intelligent they may be,
how refined they may be--for there are some colored persons
who are persons of refinement; this must be admitted--the
prejudice against them is equally as great as it is against
the most low and degraded colored man you can find in the
streets of this city or in any other place.

This, Mr. President, I do seriously regret. And is

this prejudice right? Have the colored people done anyting to justify the prejudice against them that does exist in the hearts of so many white persons, and generally of one great political party in this country? Have they done anything to justify it? No, sir. Can any reason be given why this prejudice should be fostered in so many hearts against them, simply because they are not white? I make these remarks in all kindness, and from no bitterness of feeling at all.

Mr. President, if this prejudice has no cause to justify it, then we must admit that it is wicked, we must admit that it is wrong; we must admit that it has not the approval of Heaven. Therefore I hold it to be the duty of this nation to discourage it, simply because it is wicked, because it is wrong, because it is not approved of by Heaven. If the nation should take a step for the encouragement of this prejudice against the colored race, can they have any ground upon which to predicate a hope that Heaven will smile upon them and prosper them? It is evident that it is the belief of Christian people in this country and in all other enlightened portions of the world that as a nation we have passed through a severe ordeal, that severe judgments have been poured out upon us on account of the manner in which a poor, oppressed race was treated in this country.

Sir, this prejudice should be resisted. Steps should be taken by which to discourage it. Shall we do so by taking a step in this direction, if the amendment now proposed to the bill before us is adopted? Not at all. That step will rather encourage, will rather increase this prejudice; and this is one reason why I am opposed to the adoption of the amendment.

Mr. President, let me here remark that if this amendment is rejected, so that the schools will be left open for all children to be entered into them, irrespective of race, color, or previous condition, I do not believe the colored people will act imprudently. I know that in one or two of the late insurrectionary States the Legislatures passed laws establishing mixed schools, and the colored people did not hurriedly shove their children into those schools; they were very slow about it. In some localities where there was but little prejudice or opposition to it they entered them immediately; in others they did not do so. I do not believe that it is in the colored people to act rashly and unwisely in a matter of this kind.

But, sir, let me say that it is the wish of the colored

people of this District, and of the colored people over this land, that this Congress shall not do anything which will increase that prejudice which is now fearfully great against them. If this amendment be adopted you will encourage that prejudice; you will increase that prejudice; and, perhaps, after the encouragement thus given, the next step may be to ask Congress to prevent them from riding in the street cars, or something like that. I repeat, let no encouragement be given to a prejudice against those who have done nothing to justify it, who are poor and perfectly innocent, as innocent as infants. Let nothing be done to encourage that prejudice. I say the adoption of this amendment will do so.

Mr. President, I desire to say here that the white race has no better friend than I. The southern people know this. It is known over the length and breadth of this land. I am true to my own race. I wish to see all done that can be done for their encouragement, to assist them in acquiring property, in becoming intelligent, enlightened, useful, valuable citizens. I wish to see this much done for them; but, at the same time, I would not have anything done which would harm the white race.

Sir, during the canvass in the State of Mississippi I traveled into different parts of that State, and this is the doctrine that I everywhere uttered: that while I was in favor of building up the colored race I was not in favor of tearing down the white race. Sir, the white race need not be harmed in order to build up the colored race. The colored race can be built up and assisted, as I before remarked, in acquiring property, in becoming intelligent, valuable, useful citizens, without one hair upon the head of any white man being harmed.

Let me ask, will establishing such schools as I am now advocating in this District harm our white friends? Let us consider this question for a few minutes. By some it is contended that if we establish mixed schools here a great insult will be given to the white citizens, and that the white schools will be seriously damaged. All that I ask those who assume this position to do is to go with me to Massachusetts, to go with me to some other New England States where they have mixed schools, and there they will find schools in as prosperous and flourishing a condition as any to be found in any part of the world. They will find such schools there; and they will find between the white and colored citizens friendship, peace, and harmony.

When I was on a lecturing tour in the State of Ohio, I
went to a town, the name of which I forget. The question
whether it would be proper or not to establish mixed schools
had been raised there. One of the leading gentlemen connected with the schools in that town came to see me and con-
versed with me on the subject. He asked me, "Have you
been to New England, where they have mixed schools?" I
replied, "I have, sir." "Well," said he, "please tell me
this: does not social equality result from mixed schools?"
"No, sir; very far from it," I responded. "Why," said he,
"how can it be otherwise?" I replied, "I will tell you how it
can be otherwise, and how it is otherwise. Go to the schools
and you see there white children and colored children seated
side by side, studying their lessons, standing side by side,
and reciting their lessons, and perhaps, in walking to school,
they may walk along together; but that is the last of it. The
white children go to their homes; the colored children go to
theirs; and on the Lord's day you will see those colored
children in colored churches, and the white children in white
churches; and if an entertainment is given by a white family,
you will see the white children there, and the colored children
at entertainments given by persons of their own color." I
aver, sir, that mixed schools are very far from bringing
about social equality.

Then, Mr. President, I hold that establishing mixed
schools will not harm the white race. I am their friend. I
said in Mississippi, and I say here, and I say everywhere,
that I would abandon the Republican party if it went into any
measures of legislation really damaging to any portion of the
white race; but it is not in the Republican party to do that.

In the next place, I desire to say that school boards,
and school trustees, and railroad companies, and steamboat
companies are to blame for the prejudice that exists against
the colored race, or to their disadvantage in those respects.
Go to the depot here, now, and what will you see? A well-
dressed colored lady, with her little children by her side,
whom she has brought up intelligently and with refinement, as
much so as white children, comes to the cars; and where is
she shown to? Into the smoking car, where men are cursing,
swearing, spitting on the floor; where she is miserable, and
where her little children have to listen to language not fitting
for children who are brought up as she has endeavored to
bring them up, to listen to.

Now, sir, let me ask, why is this? Is it because the

white passengers in a decent, respectable car are unwilling
for her to be seated there? No, sir; not as a general thing.
It is a rule that the company has established, that she shall
not go there.

Let me give you a proof of this. Some years ago I
was in the State of Kansas and wanted to go on a train of
cars that ran from the town where I was to St. Louis, and
this rule prevailed there, that colored people should go into
the smoking car. I had my wife and children with me, and
was trying to bring up my children properly, and I did not
wish to take them into the smoking car. So I went to see
the superintendent who lived in that town, and I addressed
him thus: "Sir, I propose to start for St. Louis to-morrow
on your road, and wish to take my family along; and I do not
desire to go into the smoking car. It is all that I can do to
stand it myself, and I do not wish my wife and children to
be there and listen to such language as is uttered there by
men talking, smoking, spitting, and rendering the car very
foul; and I want to ask you now if I cannot obtain permission
to take my family into a first-class car, as I have a first-
class ticket?" Said he: "Sir, you can do so; I will see the
conductor and instruct him to admit you." And he did admit
me, and not a white passenger objected to it, not a white
passenger gave any evidence of being displeased because I
and my family were there.

Let me give you another instance. In New Orleans,
and also in Baltimore, cities that I love and whose citizens
I love, some trouble was raised some time ago because
colored people were not allowed to ride in the street cars.
The question was taken to the courts; and what was the decision? That the companies should make provision for colored passengers to go inside of the cars. At first they had a
car with a certain mark, signifying that colored people should
enter. I think the words were, in Baltimore, "Colored
people admitted into this car"; and in New Orleans they had
a star upon the car. They commenced running. There
would be a number of white ladies and white gentlemen who
wanted to go in the direction that this car was going, and
did not want to wait for another; and notwithstanding there
was a number of colored persons in the car, they went in
and seated themselves just as if there had not been a colored
person there. The other day, in Baltimore, I saw one of
these cars passing along with the words, "Colored persons
admitted into this car." The car stopped, and I saw a number of white ladies and gentlemen getting in, and not one

colored person there.   It was the same way in New Orleans.
Let me tell you how it worked in New Orleans.   The company
finally came to the conclusion that if white persons were willing to go into a car appropriated to colored persons and ride
with them without a word of complaint, they could not con-
sistently complain of colored persons going into cars that
were intended for white persons; and so they repealed their
rule and opened the cars for all to enter.   And ever since
that time all have been riding together in New Orleans, and
there has not been a word of complaint.   So it will be I believe in regard to the schools.   Let lawmakers cease to make
the difference, let school trustees and school boards cease to
make the difference, and the people will soon forget it.

Mr. President, I have nothing more to say.   What I
have said I have said in kindness, and I hope it will be received in that spirit.

BIBLIOGRAPHY

1.   Biographical Directory of the American Congress 1774-
        1971.   Washington, D. C. :   United States Government
        Printing Office, 1971.

2.   U. S. Congress.   Senate.   The Readmission of Georgia.
        41st Congress, 2nd session, 1870.

3.   U. S. Congress.   Senate.   Removal of Disabilities From
        the State of Mississippi.   41st Congress, 2nd session,
        1870.

4.   U. S. Congress.   Senate.   Construction of Levees in the
        State of Mississippi.   41st Congress, 3rd session,
        1871.

5.   U. S. Congress.   Senate.   Abolishment of Separate
        Schools.   41st Congress, 3rd session, 1871.

XVI. ROBERT SMALLS

Smalls, Robert, a Representative from South Carolina; born
in Beaufort, South Carolina, April 5, 1839; was of the Negro
race; moved to Charleston, South Carolina, in 1851; appointed
pilot in the United States Navy and served in that capacity on
the Monitor Keokuk in the attack on Fort Sumter; also served
as pilot in the quartermaster's department; promoted to the
rank of captain for gallant and meritorious conduct, December 1, 1863; placed in command of the Planter and served
until that vessel was placed out of commission in 1866;
member of the State constitutional convention in 1868; served
in the State house of representatives in 1868; member of the
State Senate, 1870-1872; delegate to the Republican National
Convention at Philadelphia in 1872 and at Cincinnati in 1876;
elected as a Republican to the Forty-fourth and Forty-fifth
Congresses (March 1, 1875-March 3, 1879); unsuccessful candidate for reelection in 1878 to the Forty-sixth Congress;
successfully contested the election of George D. Tillman to
the Forth-seventh Congress and served from July 19, 1882
to March 3, 1883; unsuccessful candidate for reelection in
1882; elected to the Forty-eighth Congress to fill the vacancy
caused by the death of Edmund W. M. Mackey; reelected to
the Forty-ninth Congress and served from March 18, 1884 to
March 3, 1887; unsuccessful for reelection in 1886 to the
Fiftieth Congress; collector of the Port of Beaufort, South
Carolina, 1897-1913; died in Beaufort, South Carolina, February 22, 1915. (1:1708)

BIBLIOGRAPHY

1. Biographical Directory of the American Congress 1774-
     1971. Washington, D. C. : United States Government
     Printing Office, 1971.

ROBERT SMALLS

XVII.   BENJAMIN STERLING TURNER

Turner, Benjamin Sterling (1825-1894), member from Alabama of the House of Representatives in the 42nd Congress;
was born a slave in Halifax, North Carolina.   His master
moved his establishment to Alabama in 1830, and the boy
obtained a passable education by studying secretly.   After
the War, Turner, developing a prosperous business in Dallas
County, was elected tax collector of the area in 1867.   He
became a responsible citizen and leader through service on
many local committees.   He was elected a member of the
Selma city council in 1869.

Nominated by the Republican Party for the 42nd Congress in
1870, Turner was elected; but he failed to be re-elected in
the power structure of the Republican Party in Alabama,
which at this time forced most of the Negro politicians into
retirement.   After his defeat, Turner confined himself to his
business and to local affairs.   (1:132)

BENJAMIN STERLING TURNER

BUILDING PUBLIC BUILDINGS IN ALABAMA

> In the year 1865 two-thirds of the City of Selma
> was reduced to ashes by the United States
> Army.... From 1865 until quite recently that
> city lay prostrate in the dust. I now ask Con-
> gress, in behalf of the people of that ruined city,
> to be as bountiful toward them in mercy as the
> Army was vigorous and ambitious in reducing
> them to subjugation. (2:appendix)

Mr. TURNER. Mr. Speaker, in April last I had the
honor to introduce a bill in this House providing for the
erection of public buildings in the city of Selma, Alabama,
suitable for the pressing demands of business and commerce
in that growing city. That bill has been referred to the Committee on Public Buildings and Grounds, and without knowing
what their report may be, I desire to offer some reasons to
this House why the bill should pass at once. And before
proceeding farther, let me say to the members of the House
that I am earnest and pressing for the passage of this bill,
and I shall not relinquish one foot of ground until I shall have
succeeded in my efforts. The people of Selma have been
magnanimous toward me; they have buried in the tomb of
oblivion many of those animosities upon which we hear so
many eloquent appeals in this Chamber; and I intend to stand
by and labor for them in their need and desolation. In doing
this I repay personal kindness, resent wrong by upholding
right, and at the same time advocate a measure of necessity
to the Government of my country.

In the year 1865 two-thirds of the city of Selma was
reduced to ashes by the United States Army. Churches,
school-houses, manufactories, stores, workshops, public
buildings, barns, stock pens, and a thousand or more private
residences were swept away by the destroying flames. In
short, nearly the whole city was burned. The Government
made a display in that unfortunate city of its mighty power
and conquered a gallant and high-toned people. They may
have sinned wonderfully, but they suffered terribly. War was

311

once the glory of her sons, but they paid the penalty of their offense, and for one, I have no coals of fiery reproach to heap upon them now. Rather would I extend the olive branch of peace, and say to them, let the past be forgotten and let us all, from every sun and every clime, of every hue and every shade, go to work peacefully to build up the shattered temples of this great and glorious Republic.

But to proceed. From 1865 until quite recently that city lay prostrate in the dust. I now ask Congress, in behalf of the people of that ruined city, to be as bountiful toward them in mercy as the Army was vigorous and ambitious in reducing them to subjugation. I introduced the bill asking Congress to appropriate $200,000 for the erection of public buildings in that city--

First, because there is a great and absolute need for these buildings for Government use;

Second, because the erection of the buildings will give work to many who need and deserve it, and who, without sinning, have suffered from the sins of others; and

Third, because this is a growing city, and if aided in this manner by the Government will soon become flourishing and an honor to the commercial growth of our country.

Already the city has a population of over ten thousand inhabitants. Nine railroads radiate from its center, manufactories, stores, and private residences are springing up everywhere, the result of private enterprise. The city is situated upon the Alabama river, where steamboats and other water craft can reach it at all seasons of the year with safety. It is within three miles of the center of the State, and is in the midst of the largest and most prosperous cotton-growing region in the whole United States. More cotton and property were destroyed in this city than in any other place in the reconstructed States. The future of the city is brilliant, and I do hope that Congress will see the necessity of making this appropriation. All that is required to make this place the "queen city" of the South is for "Uncle Sam" to wield the scepter of "peace and plenty" around her with the same determination and vigor as he did the fiery sword in time of war. The passage of this bill will convince my people that you mean forgetfulness of the bloody past, and only want harmony and peace with the proffers of your aid.

And now, in conclusion, Mr. Speaker, let me say that when Chicago, the proud city of the West, was swept away and her noble people left in penury and want, this same little city of which I have spoken, destitute and impoverished as she was, was among the first in the South to respond to the call of humanity and send her heartfelt tribute to her fallen sister of the West. The people of the city claim nothing for this act of kindness; but they do ask, that while with lavish hands you rear your magnificent edifices in other places, you will not quite forget them who need so much, and for whose honesty and sincerity in their attachment to the Government I am proud to boast.

REFUNDING THE COTTON TAX

... the cotton tax falling upon a special section
of the country and upon a certain class of citizens
is unconstitutional; because, in the first place, it
is detrimental to one section of the country and
beneficial to another; next, it is a tax upon industry in that part of the country where cotton is
made. And, sir, instead of paying the people a
premium for their industry it is a direct prohibition of cotton making.... Cotton, therefore, being an indispensable article of dress, and an absolute necessity to protect us from the many
changes of weather, should not be placed in the
same category with tobacco and whisky [sic],
recognized and acknowledged poisonous luxuries
of life. (3:appendix)

Mr. TURNER. Mr. Speaker, I had the honor on the
20th day of February last to present a petition and memorial
to Congress praying Congress and the country to refund the
cotton tax. Sir, the understanding of the people is that this
tax fell upon a certain section and class. It did not fall
upon the owner of the land, nor upon the merchant, nor upon
the consumer, but directly upon the laborer who tilled the
soil and gathered the cotton with his blood-stained fingers
from the pods. The seventh section of the Constitution of
the United States authorizes Congress to levy a uniform tax.
Our understanding of uniformity is that every State in the
Union shall pay a tax in proportion to its population and
wealth; hence we claim that the cotton tax falling upon a
special section of the country and upon a certain class of
citizens is unconstitutional; because, in the first place, it is
detrimental to one section of the country and beneficial to
another; next, it is a direct tax upon industry in that part of
the country where cotton is made. And, sir, instead of paying the people a premium for their industry it is a direct
prohibition of cotton making.

In 1866, 1867, and 1868 there was a cotton tax levied

amounting to $70, 000, 000. We claim that this tax was un-
just, inequitable, and unconstitutional. This law was the
creature of Congress, for it was not supported by the people
in any section of the country; and we hold now that Congress
has the same power to refund this tax as it had to collect it.
This tax wrought a more serious influence and destructive
consequence than seems to be understood by Congress and
the people in general.

The war through which we have passed stopped cotton
making for a time, and thus caused cotton to be scarce and
high in other markets of the world. Other nations, looking
upon cotton as one of the chief necessities of life, went into
cotton making in self-defense, and continued so to do till the
war was over in the United States.

During the war cotton went up as high as eighty cents
per pound; and as soon as the war ended and cotton was
shipped from the United States it began to go down and was
as low as forty-three cents in 1866. This was no dobut
caused by other nations taking the idea that American cotton
was coming into the markets of the world, and could be purchased for less than they could make it at their homes.

But when Congress imposed the prohibitory tax in
1866, it caused the people of the world to believe as before,
that it would be impossible to purchase cotton from the United
States at any reasonable price; therefore, they again made an
effort to defend themselves by going into cotton making and
bringing their cotton in competition with that of the United
States.

These nations, by their energy, industry, and success,
glutted the markets of the world with cotton, so much so that
it reduced the cotton of the United States from forty-three
cents in 1866 to thirty-one cents in 1867, and to seventeen
cents in 1868.

And when the cotton tax was repealed in 1868, the
outside influence began to decrease and the price of our cotton to increase, and has been getting higher and higher ever
since.

Mr. Speaker, a fair calculation will show that if there
had been no tax upon cotton the minimum value would never
have gone below thirty-five cents per pound.

And, sir, as I have said before, the Government collected $70, 000, 000 upon cotton, thereby bringing about the influence of which I have spoken before, namely, increasing competition, glutting the markets and reducing the price of our cotton to an additional amount of $250, 000, 000, besides the $70, 000, 000 paid on cotton. This $250, 000, 000 fell into the hands of other nations by the prohibitory influence of our own Government, consequently the whole loss to the cotton making section of the country by the direct tax and its indirect influence amounts to $320, 000, 000.

To prove my argument to be true, I will refer to other products of industry than cotton. For instance, take away the tariff from iron and place a prohibitory tax of three cents per pound for making iron. What would be the effect? I am satisfied, sir, that such would be the effect that iron-masters from all parts of the world would be bringing iron to the United States, while the iron-masters in our country would have to abandon their business or starve. This I know, Mr. Speaker, will not be disputed by the tariff men of Pennsylvania upon this floor.

Mr. Speaker, I will place any other article in the same situation that cotton has been placed. Salt, for instance. Take away the tariff and impose a tax of one cent per pound, and the effect will be the same as upon cotton. Or take sugar, and impose the prohibitory tax of three cents per pound upon it, and the effect upon it will be the same as that upon cotton.

According to the Constitution, I deny that this tax is uniform, since it would have been as fair to tax either of the just-named articles as it was to tax cotton, for custom and the present status of civilization recognize these articles to be the necessity according to custom, decency, civilization, and under rules and regulations of society. There are no rules nor regulations laid down by law, neither constitutional, statute, common, nor municipal law, that compels any man to eat or drink; but, on the other hand, municipal law, moral customs, and influences of every civilized community, compel every man to properly clothe himself, making it a penal offense for him to appear in the street unless his nakedness is thoroughly concealed; nor does custom stop with a mere concealing of nakedness, but even a superfluity of clothing is necessary, so as to add to his personal appearance. Cotton, therefore, being an indispensable article of dress, and an absolute necessity to protect us from the many changes of

weather, should not be placed in the same category with tobacco and whisky, recognized and acknowledged poisonous
luxuries of life.

Again I refer to the class of people who make cotton.
The statistics will show that twenty-nine bales of cotton out
of every thirty made in the United States are made directly
by the negroes in the southern States, and to them, Mr.
Speaker, this tax is due. I will say for them, when they
were set free, found themselves without homes, without
clothes, and without bread, with all their means of subsis-
tence in the North and northwestern States, thousands of
miles from them, slandered and abused, said to be too lazy
to make cotton unless a will superior to their own were
placed over them to control, they united themselves and determined to make cotton under their own direction in order
that they might refute the base slanders which had been
heaped upon them. And but for this tax which I have mentioned they would have been able to purchase one-eighth of
the land upon which this cotton was made. Further, this
three percent per pound came directly from the labor of the
man who made the cotton. In addition to this tax, he pays
large freights upon all substances, meat, bread, and other
articles, such as are shipped to him from the great distances
above mentioned. He must pay the freights on cotton to and
from the New England mills, also the manufacturer's per-
centage and the merchant's profit.

Now, Mr. Speaker, I plead in behalf of the poor people
of the South, regardless of caste or color, because this tax
had its blighting influence. It cut the jugular vein of our
financial system, bled it near unto death, and wrought a destructive influence upon every line of business. It so crippled every trade and industry that our suffering has been
greater under its influence than under that of the war. That
tax took away all the income and left us no profit and very
little of the circulating medium. I therefore beg Congress
to correct the error and refund the cotton tax to that class
of people from whom it was taken and for whom I plead in
my imperfect way.

And further, I had the honor to introduce bill No.
2277, which cannot be reached in the regular order of business during this session of Congress, and I therefore ask the
indulgence of members for a few minutes, while I make some
remarks in relation to this bill.

The bill purports to authorize the United States Land
Commissioners to bid for large tracts of private land, when
sold at public auction, with the right to secure titles to these
lands in the name of the United States, in the same manner
as they are secured by private individuals; and to subdivide
these tracts into small tracts containing not more than one
hundred and sixty acres, and as much less as suits the con-
venience of the purchaser. The latter shall have the right to
receive from the Land Commissioner a certificate of entry,
and shall pay to the United States, at the time of purchase,
ten percent on the cost, and shall continue to pay annually
ten percent on cost until the whole is paid. When the final
payment has been made the Land Commissioner shall be required to give to the purchaser a warrantee title to the land
purchased.

Mr. Speaker, I ask Congress to make this appropriation, and I ask it in behalf of the landless and poor people of
our country. In that section of country which I have the
honor in part to represent upon this floor the people are ex-
tremely poor, having been emancipated from slavery after
hundreds of years of disappointment and privation. These
people have struggled longer and labored harder, and have
made more of the raw material than any people in the world.
Notwithstanding the fact that they have labored long, hard,
and faithfully, they live on little clothing, the poorest food,
and in miserable huts. Since they have been free they have
not slackened their industry, but have materially improved
their economy. While their labor has rewarded the nation
with larger revenue, they have consumed less of the substance
of the country than any other class of people. If dressing
less, eating little, and hard and continued labor means economy, these people are the most economical in the world.
And, sir, it is a universal understanding among themselves
that they are not to live in any extravagant way so far as
eating and dressing is concerned. They are laboring and
making every effort to secure land and houses. It is next to
an impossibility in this generation to accomplish it without
such aid as I now ask from the Government.

Mr. Speaker, I am frequently met on the floor with
the argument that the Government should be just before it is
generous. Then, I call the attention of the gentlemen of the
House to the fact that we should look to our own interests before we care for those of our neighbors. What has been the
result of our legislation? We have subsidized for the people
of China; we have subsidized for the people of Japan; we have

subsidized to feed the wild Indians, roaming over the do-
mains of the West, pillaging, robbing, and murdering our
citizens. These subsidies are sucking vampires upon our
people, for not one of those who are benefitted by them pay
to the United States a single dollar of taxes, while the people
in whose behalf I plead pay annually $70, 000, 000 taxes to the
United States Government.

While we pay gratuitously to Chinese, Japanese, and
Indians, millions of dollars annually, we hesitate to even lend
to the landless but peaceable and industrious citizens of the
South $1, 000, 000 annually to help them aid themselves and at
the same time greatly develop the resources of the country.
Nor can this loan be attended with the least risk to the Government, for it is secured by the best of security placing a
small portion of the surplus money of the Treasury to profit-
able use, at the same time paying the Government large interests.

I thank the gentlemen for their attention, and again
beg them to give us a united vote on the bill to refund this
cotton tax.

BIBLIOGRAPHY

1.   Robinson, Wilhelmena S. International Library of Negro
       Life and History: Historical Negro Biographies.   New
       York: Publishers, Inc., 1967,

2.   U. S. Congress. House.   Building Public Buildings in
       Alabama. 42nd Congress, 2nd session, 1872.

3.   U. S Congress. House.   Refunding the Cotton Tax.
       42nd Congress, 2nd session, 1872.

JOSIAH T. WALLS

XVIII. JOSIAH THOMAS WALLS

Walls, Josiah Thomas, a Representative from Florida; born
in Winchester, Frederick County, Virginia, December 30,
1842; was of the Negro race; received a limited schooling;
engaged in truck farming; moved to Florida; delegate to the
State Constitutional Convention in 1868; served in the State
senate, 1869-1872; presented credentials as a member-elect
to the Forty-second Congress and served from March 4, 1871
to January 29, 1873, when he was succeeded by Silas L.
Niblack, who contested his election; elected as a Republican
to the Forty-third Congress (March 4, 1873-March 3, 1875);
presented credentials as a member-elect to the Forty-fourth
Congress and served from March 4, 1875 to April 19, 1876,
when he was succeeded by Jesse J. Finley, who contested his
election; resumed his occupation as truck farmer; died in
Tallahassee, Florida, May 5, 1905. (1:1874)

ESTABLISHMENT OF A NATIONAL SYSTEM OF EDUCATION

> I am in favor, Mr. Speaker, of not only this bill, but of a national system of education, because I believe that the national Government is the guardian of the liberties of all its subjects. And having within a few years incorporated into the body-politic a class of uneducated people, the majority of whom, I am sorry to say, are colored, the question for solution and the problems to be solved, then, are: can these people protect their liberties without education; and can they be educated under the present condition of society in the states where they were when freed? ... I think we should lend all our aid to the establishment of a national educational fund. (2:808-809)

Mr. WALLS. Mr. Speaker, my remarks will be principally directed as in answer to the remarks made by the gentleman from Georgia (Mr. MCINTYRE), who it appears was in opposition to the bill establishing a national education fund as proposed by the Committee on Education and Labor.

The gentleman from Georgia, in his effort in opposition to this bill, said that it was objectionable because it interfered with State rights. I quote him:

> The details of the original bill are objectionable and ought to be objectionable to every man who feels any interest in his State government.

He then proceeded to tell us why the bill is objectionable. I again quote him:

> Why do I say so? Simply from the fact that by the Constitution of the United States the powers of legislation have been distributed. How distributed? All those which the people of the country desired the Congress of the United States to exercise have

been ascertained and defined by the terms of the
Constitution, while all those powers which the
people desired should be prohibited to the States
have also been defined and set forth in the same
instrument. By the Constitution, all those powers
which have not been delegated to the Congress of
the United States, nor prohibited to the States,
are reserved to the States themselves. Now, sir,
since the organization of the General Government
under which we are legislating to-day it has always been understood that the power of regulating
the common schools belonged exclusively to the
States; and I am unwilling that Congress should
take from the States any of their reserved rights.
The provisions of the pending bill seek to vest the
entire control of this fund in the General Government without regard to the will of the respective
States.

If we did not understand those who keep up this great
clamor for State rights, we might be constrained to believe
as the gentleman from Georgia, that no one had any interest
in their respective State governments but those who duly
warn us against the infringements upon the rights of the
States. But we understand them. We know what the cry
about State rights means, and more especially when we hear
it produced as an argument against the establishment of a
fund for the education of the people.

Judging from the past, I must confess that I am somewhat suspicious of such rights, knowing, as I do, that the
Democratic party in Georgia, as well as in all of the other
southern States, have been opposed to the education of the
negro and poor white children. And I can, without doing that
party any wrong, safely and truthfully state that the Democratic party to-day in Georgia, as well as in Florida, are
opposed to the education of all classes. We know that the
Democratic party used to argue that to educate the negro was
to set him free, and that to deprive him of all the advantages necessary to enable him to acquire an education was to
perpetuate his enslavement. Their argument against educating the poor whites was that the negro more directly asso-
ciated with the poor whites than with that class who controlled
the destinies of slavery. Why, sir, so fearful were they that
the negro would become educated, either through his own
efforts or by the aid of some poor white person, they enacted laws prohibiting him from being educated even by his

own master; and if a poor white person was caught teaching
a negro, he was whipped, or in some States sold or compelled to leave the State; and if by chance a negro did learn
to read, and it was found out, he was whipped every time he
was caught with a book, and as many times between as his
master pleased. We must remember that this state of affairs
existed only about six years ago, and this being the case, is
it unreasonable for us to suppose that the Deomocratic party
of Georgia is opposed to the negro being included in the bill
that proposes to establish an educational fund, and his being
educated out of the public money? I think not.

The gentleman from Georgia also tells us that he is
in favor of seeing the schools of the country promoted, and
we believe he is, but he wishes to promote them under the
old system, which has so far been a failure in the South, and
every fair-minded and unprejudiced man will admit it.

Mr. McINTYRE. I should like to make a correction
there. It would seem that he seeks to produce the impression upon the House that I am opposed to education, which,
of course, I am not.

Mr. WALLS. The gentleman will be answered in the
course of my remarks. I must ask him not to interrupt me
now, as I did not interrupt him when he addressed the House.

The gentleman informs us also that the Georgia Legislature has within the last twenty days appropriated $300,000
for the purpose of education, and that the educational system
is not confined to the whites alone. He says that--

> Within the last twenty days the Legislature of
> Georgia has appropriated $300,000 for the purpose
> of education; and that educational system is not
> confined to the whites alone.

He then informs us that the "colored people of his
State are entitled under the law to the same rights that the
whites will enjoy." Mark his words--entitled to the same
rights that the whites will enjoy. This, Mr. Speaker, is very
true; but will the colored people have an opportunity, or be
permitted to enjoy the same rights that the whites enjoy?
This is the question. The echo of the past answers no! Not
while the Ku Klux Democracy are permitted to burn the
school-houses and churches belonging to the colored people of
Georgia; not while they shut the doors of the school-houses

against the colored children, will the colored people of Georgia enjoy the same educational advantages that the whites enjoy.

We find that in July, 1783, the Georgia Legislature appropriated one thousand acres of land to each county for the support of free schools. In 1784 the General Assembly appropriated forty thousand acres of land for the endowment of a college or university. In 1792 an act was passed by the Legislature appropriating one thousand acres of land for the endowment of each of the country academies; $250,000 were appropriated in 1817 for the support of poor schools. Now, sir, we see that the Georgia Legislature prior to 1868 appropriated thousands of acres of land for the support of colleges, county academies, and free schools, but did Georgia have a free-school system in operation prior to 1870?

Again, we see that the Georgia Legislature appropriated $250,000 for the support of what they called "poor schools." If this appropriation was applied to the establishment of schools, did the poor white and colored children get an equal benefit of it? We are informed by Colonel J. R. Lewis that Georgia had indeed a very "poor school" system prior to 1870, and no free schools in operation at all; Savannah and Columbus were the only places where they had any schools worthy of the name. I now quote from the report of the Commissioner of Education, who says:

> The latest communication to this office, from a leading educator in Georgia, gives an encouraging account of the prospect that an excellent school law will soon go into operation in that State, which has just passed the Legislature. At present Savannah and Columbus are the only cities in the State that have school systems worthy of the name."

The gentleman from Georgia also calls our attention to what he thinks of the patriotism existing in Georgia. He says:

> I feel safe in expressing my belief that there is intelligence and patriotism enough in the State of Georgia to-day to manage its proportion of this fund properly if it is turned over to the State.

I suppose he refers to that patriotism existing among

the colored people, or that which the whites have inculcated
since May, 1865. Now, Mr. Speaker, if we judge of the patriotism existing among the Democratic party in Georgia to-
day from the course that party has pursued in that State relative to free schools and the education of the negro, our conclusion will be that Georgia is now opposed to free schools,
and the education of the negro and poor white children, as
heretofore.

It is useless to talk about patriotism existing in those
States in connection with free schools under Democratic system, and in connection with those who now and always have
believed that it was wrong to educate the negro, and that such
offenses should be punishable by death or the lash. Away with
the patriotism that advocates and prefers ignorance to intelligence!

Let us look into the patriotism of Florida's sister
State, Georgia. My State has been very retrogressive in
connection with free schools, but she is still ahead of Georgia
in this respect. I am indeed sorry I cannot say as much for
the patriotism of the Democratic party of my State as the
gentleman has about Georgia, when I know that in 1845 the
General Government donated to Florida, while under Democratic rule, 908, 503 acres of the public domain of that State
for common-school purposes. And what did they do with it?
Why, sir, they enacted a common-school law which did not
mean anything, which was enacted only to obtain the possession of the lands donated. In this same law they created a
common-school fund, and under the operation of this bogus
law they obtained fraudulent possession of the lands, sold
them, and applied the proceeds to everything else except that
for which they were donated. Is this the kind of patriotism
to which the gentleman alluded in his remarks?

I am in favor, Mr. Speaker, of not only this bill, but
of a national system of education, because I believe that the
national Government is the guardian of the liberties of all its
subjects. And having within a few days incorporated into the
body-politic a class of uneducated people, the majority of
whom, I am sorry to say, are colored, the question for solution and the problems to be solved, then, are: can these
people protect their liberties without education; and can they
be educated under the present condition of society in the States
where they were when freed?

Can this be done without the aid, assistance, and

supervision of the General Government? No, sir, it cannot.
Were it not that the prejudice of slavery is so prevalent
among the former slaveholder against the education of the
negro it would be superficial to say that the negro could not
protect his educational interests, or could not be educated
without the establishment of a national system of education.
This prejudice is attributable to the fact that they were compelled to keep the negro in ignorance in order to hold him in
slavery; and with the advantages of education and enlightenment they were enabled to keep their slaves successfully in
bondage; for we know that the advantages of education are
great.

We are told that the Persians were kept for ages in
slavery from the power of intellect alone. Education constitutes the apprenticeship of those who are afterward to take a
place in the order of our civilized and progressive nation.
Education tends to increase the dignity and self-respect of a
people, tends to increase their fitness for society and important stations of trust, tends to elevate, and consequently
carries with it a great moral responsibility. This is why the
Democratic party in the South so bitterly oppose the education
of all classes. They know that no educated people can be
enslaved. They know that no educated people can be robbed
of their labor. They well know that no educated people can
be kept in a helpless and degraded condition, but will arise
with a united voice and assert their manhood. Hence, to educate the negro in the South would be to lift him to a state of
civilization and enlightenment that would enable him not only
to maintain and defend his liberties, but to better acquit himself as an honorable and upright citizen, and prove himself
more worthy of the rights conferred upon him. This, then,
being the result of educating the negro. I cannot believe that
the Democracy of Georgia or any other State manifests this
patriotism or has taken this sudden departure. They know
the negro is loyal, and while their present educational institutions are fosterers of disloyalty and nurseries of enmity
and hatred toward the Government and loyal blacks and whites,
I cannot hope to ever see this Democratic party endowed with
sufficient patriotism and justice to lend their energies and
support in favor of the education and elevation of my people.
While the Democratic party adhere to the ideas and principles
that they have now it would be against their interests to educate the negro; not only against their interests, but entirely
inconsistent with their faith. Can we then suppose that these
firm adherents to slavery and State rights are willing to educate the negro and loyal whites, who are opposed to their

principles, and thereby enable them to wield the controlling
power of the South? No, sir, I should think not. They are
more consistent and patriotic toward the principles of the
lost cause than this. Let us not mistake ourselves, Mr.
Speaker. The Democratic party are opposed to any system
that will have the effect of making a majority of the present
or rising generation loyal to the Government. It has been
admitted by every lover of free government that popular education, or the education of the masses, is necessary to and
inseparable from a complete citizenship. Then let the nation
educate her subjects. It is to the interest of the Government, as also to the people, to do so. And educated people
possess more skill, and manifest more interest and fidelity
in the affairs of the Government, because of their chance to
obtain more general information, which tends to eradicate the
prejudices and superstitions so prevalent among an ignorant
people.

An educated people seek always to improve their condition, not only at home, but in all their surroundings. An
educated people are more social, more refined, and more
ready to impart their knowledge and experience to others;
more industrious because more ambitious to accumulate and
possess property; while the ignorant and uneducated are more
prone to idleness, more addicted to low habits and dissipa-
tion, more careless and less ambitious, being more of a
"turn" to content themselves and let things go about as they
are. The uneducated person cannot have the influence among
his fellow men that educated persons have. As knowledge is
power, in short, education is the panacea for all our social
evils, injustices, and oppressions. The general diffusion of
education among the whole people of the South would render
them less submissive to the social and political stigmas under
which they are to-day laboring.

Now that our whole people throughout this broad land
are free, it yet remains for this Government to give them
that which will not only enable them to better enjoy their
freedom, but will enable them to maintain, defend, and perpetuate their liberties. Imagine your race, Mr. Speaker, as
having been in bondage for over two hundred years, subjected
to all the horrors of slavery, deprived of every facility by
which they might have acquired an education, and in this
ignorant and helpless condition they were emancipated and
turned loose in the midst of their enemies; among those who
were opposed to not only seeing them educated, but opposed
to their freedom; among those who possessed all the wealth,

controlled all the educational facilities of the country; among
those who believed your race to be naturally inferior to themselves in every particular, and fit only to be considered as
goods and chattels.

Imagine, I say, your race to-day in this deplorable
situation. Would you be considered as comprehending their
desires and situation, were you to admit that their former
enslavers would take an impartial interest in their educational
affairs? I think not. Hence, I cannot believe that the Democratic party South would provide equal educational advantages
to all classes. The gentleman from the District of Columbia
(Mr. CHIPMAN) has correctly said that the lately enfranchised people are peculiarly the wards of the Government.
Still, we ask that equal advantages, impartial protection, and
the same educational facility may be extended to all classes,
to the whole people. Give us this, and we will further endeavor to remove the ignorance from our people, and about
which so much has been said by those who have occasioned it
and who are justly responsible for it; they who have imposed
it upon us through the operation of that once loved and cherished institution, slavery--that institution which has cost the
nations millions of dollars, and many of her best and bravest
men, and has stamped upon the negro a curse which this
generation will fail to obliterate.

In conclusion, Mr. Speaker, I might here pay a passing notice to the arguments generally used against the negro,
and against his being educated. It has been said that the
negro is an inferior race, with minds unfit for cultivation,
with no traits of science, skill, or literature; with no ambition for education and enlightenment; in short, a perfect
"booby brain. " But these arguments, Mr. Speaker, fell to
the ground many years ago, and have been rendered insignificant from the fact that notwithstanding all the laws enacted
prohibiting the negro from being educated, in spite of the
degradation of over two hundred and forty-seven years of the
most inhuman and barbarous slavery ever recorded in the
history of any people, and coupled with five years subjugation
to the reign of terror from the Ku Klux Klan, the dastardly
horrors of which those only know who have been victims, and
those who commit the deeds. Notwithstanding all these ob-
stacles and oppositions, we find in nearly every town and
village, where the whipping-posts and auction-blocks were
once visible, school-houses and freedmen's savings banks
erected in their stead, which are the growth of only five
years, and which stand to-day as living refutations to the

foul, malignant, unjust, and untrue agruments used against
the negro. We still find him, however, loyal to his Government and friendly toward his former master, to-day looking
to this Congress for the passage of a measure that will aid
in increasing the educational facilities throughout the country
for the benefit of all classes, and thereby enable him to rear
his children to truly comprehend their relations with and
duties toward their Government.

Believing, then, as I have before said, that the national Government is the guardian of all the liberties of her
subjects, I think we should lend all our aid to the establishment of a national educational fund. I think, sir, it be-
hooves us, as the guardians of the rights and liberties of the
people of this nation, to do so; for we are told that all there
is of a nation that is good, that is mighty, that exercises
influence and promotes prosperity, are the products of the
education of its citizens. Then, let us make provisions for
the education of all classes; and if the State government are
unwilling to provide equal facilities for all, then let the national Government take the matter in hand.

BIBLIOGRAPHY

1.   Biographical Directory of the American Congress 1774-
      1971. Washington, D. C. : United States Government
      Printing Office, 1971.

2.   U. S. Congress. House. Establishment of a National
      Fund. 42nd Congress, 2nd session, 1872.

BIBLIOGRAPHY

1. Aptheker, Herbert. A Documentary History of the Negro People in the United States. New York: The Citadel Press, 1951.

2. Bennett, Lerone, Jr. Before the Mayflower: A History of the Negro in America 1619-1964. Maryland: Penguin Books, 1961.

3. Bowers, Claude G. The Tragic Era: The Revolution After Lincoln. Boston: Houghton Mifflin Company, 1929.

4. DuBois, W. E. B. Black Reconstruction in America: 1860-1880. Cleveland: The World Publishing Co., 1935.

5. Dunbar, Alice. Masterpieces of Negro Eloquence. New York: Bookery Publishing Company, 1914.

6. Dunning, William A. Reconstruction, Political and Economic: 1865-1877. New York: Harper and Brothers, 1907.

7. Franklin, John Hope. From Slavery to Freedom. 3rd ed. New York: Alfred A. Knopf, 1967.

8. _____. Reconstruction After the Civil War. Chicago: The University of Chicago Press, 1967.

9. _____, ed. Reminiscences of an Active Life: The Autobiography of John Roy Lynch. Chicago: The University of Chicago Press, 1970.

10. Grant, Joanne. Black Protest. New York: Fawcett World Library, 1968.

11. Logan, Rayford W. and Cohen, Irving S. The American

Negro. Boston: Houghton Mifflin Company, 1967.

12. Lynch, John R. "More About the Historical Errors of
    James Ford Rhodes, " The Journal of Negro History,
    vol. III. (1918).

13. _____. "Some Historical Errors of James Rhodes, "
    The Journal of Negro History, vol. II, no. 4 (Octo-
    ber 1917).

14. Lynd, Staughton. Reconstruction. New York: Harper
    and Row, 1967.

15. _____. "Rethinking Slavery and Reconstruction, "
    The Journal of Negro History, vol. 50, no. 1 (Janu-
    ary, 1965).

16. Meier, August and Rudwick, Elliot M. From Plantation
    to Ghetto. New York: Hill and Wang, 1966.

17. Moseley, J. H. Sixty Years in Congress and Twenty-
    Eight Out. New York: Vantage Press, 1960.

18. Rhodes, John Ford. History of the United States 1864-
    1866, vol. V. New York: The Macmillan Co. , 1906.

19. _____. History of the United States 1866-1872, vol.
    VI. New York: The Macmillan Co. , 1906.

20. _____. History of the United States 1872-1877, vol.
    VII. New York: The Macmillan Co. , 1906.

21. Smith, Samuel Denny. The Negro in Congress 1870-
    1901. Chapel Hill: University of North Carolina
    Press, 1940.

22. Stampp, Kenneth M. The Era of Reconstruction 1865-
    1877. New York: Vintage Books, 1967.

23. Taylor, A. A. "Negro Congressmen a Generation
    Afterwards, " Journal of Negro History, vol. VII
    (April 1922), 127-171.

24. Woodson, Carter G. Negro Orators and Their Orations.
    Washington, D. C. : Associated Publishers, 1925.

25.   Work, Monroe N.   "Some Negro Members of Recon-
      struction Conventions and Legislature and of Con-
      gress, " <u>Journal of Negro History</u>, vol. V, 63-119.